THE ELDER SENECA

MNEMOSYNE

BIBLIOTHECA CLASSICA BATAVA

COLLEGERUNT

W. DEN BOER · A. D. LEEMAN · W. J. VERDENIUS

BIBLIOTHECAE FASCICULOS EDENDOS CURAVIT

W. J. VERDENIUS, HOMERUSLAAN 53, ZEIST

SUPPLEMENTUM QUINQUAGESIMUM PRIMUM

LEWIS A. SUSSMAN

THE ELDER SENECA

LUGDUNI BATAVORUM E. J. BRILL MCMLXXVIII

THE ELDER SENECA

BY

LEWIS A. SUSSMAN

LUGDUNI BATAVORUM E. J. BRILL MCMLXXVIII

ISBN 90 04 05759 5

UXORI ET PARENTIBUS CARIS

CONTENTS

PREFACE

The elder Seneca (*ca.* 55 B.C. - *ca.* A.D. 39) towards the end of his life gathered a collection of extracts from declamations; ten books from *controversiae* (practice court cases), and at least one book from *suasoriae* (practice deliberative speeches). Originally each book in the collection was introduced by a preface which dealt with various famous declaimers and contained criticism, not always Seneca's own, of the practitioners and the state of the art. Included within the text of the books themselves are criticisms of the specimens reproduced, anecdotes, and quotations from other literary works.

Although declamation originated as a schoolboy exercise, during the early years of the Principate of Octavian Augustus it became a very fashionable fad for adults of the upper class and even professional rhetoricians. These adult declamation sessions were usually public and attracted large crowds. Various speakers would present speeches on the same theme, competing for applause and approbation. After a speech concluded there would be a good deal of critical comment about the performance. The elder Seneca's collection of extracts is our major source for understanding this unusual phenomenon and the profound effect it soon had on literary style.

While certainly, by the very nature of his works, Seneca cannot be considered a writer of the first rank, nevertheless he is important not only for preserving this useful information but for the sound, perceptive literary criticism contained in the works. His career and especially those of his sons reflect a vital trend in the Empire—the growing distinction of provincials in politics and literature. To date a general work dealing with Seneca's life and writings has not appeared; the existing studies are usually treatments of specific questions such as the laws in the declamations and their relationship to actual Greek and Roman laws, the declaimers named in the works, the lost *Histories*, critical vocabulary, manuscript tradition, or textual criticism. [1] Elsewhere he is treated insofar as his works concern the growth of declama-

---

[1] The closest thing to a general study of Seneca is H. Bornecque, *Les Déclamations et les Déclamateurs d'après Sénèque le Père* (Lille 1902, repr. Hildesheim 1967) 9-135. Pp. 137-201 contain biographical sketches of the various speakers who appear in Seneca.

tion, ancient education, and Latin literary criticism. [2] Some very useful studies of the Annaei, Seneca's sources, and his critical theory exist, but are dissertations and thus not easily available. [3] Until Whitehorne's critical bibliography came out, even locating scholarly contributions on Seneca was a difficult task. [4] Thus the student interested in Seneca had to cull his information from a variety of different sources, many of which were of limited availability, out of print, or in foreign languages.

In this study I am attempting to provide the student of Latin literature or rhetoric with a convenient source of information on the elder Seneca's life, works, criticism, and influence. Since a knowledge of declamation is requisite for understanding Seneca, I have introduced the book with a brief survey of the exercise. Further, more specialized studies such as Bonner's excellent book may also be consulted with profit. Except where unavoidable, I have tried not to duplicate the existing specialized studies, but have referred the reader to them.

The *Controversiae* and *Suasoriae* are difficult works to read in Latin. Specimens from over a hundred declaimers in a wide variety of styles are presented, often out of context. The text itself has suffered in transmission with a number of substantial *lacunae*. These anthologies were intended to be reference works, and are often dull reading, despite Seneca's efforts to liven them up with anecdotes, digressions, quotations, and the charming prefaces. Luckily he made a conscious effort to use as little technical rhetorical vocabulary as possible; nevertheless some key terms (e.g., *subtilitas*) are exceedingly difficult to translate accurately. With the exception of Edward's edition and translation of the *Suasoriae* (Cambridge 1928) there is no full, modern commentary on the work. Michael Winterbottom has therefore done a great service by providing an English translation in

---

[2] E.g., S. F. Bonner, *Roman Declamation in the Late Republic and Early Empire* (Liverpool 1949, repr. 1969); E. Patrick Parks, *The Roman Rhetorical Schools as a Preparation for the Courts under the Early Empire* (Baltimore 1945); J. F. D'Alton, *Roman Literary Theory and Criticism: A Study in Tendencies* (London and New York 1931, repr. 1962).

[3] E.g., Ernest Joseph Weinrib, *The Spaniards in Rome from Marius to Domitian* (Harvard Univ. diss, Cambridge 1968); Charles W. Lockyear, Jr., *The Fiction of Memory and the Use of Written Sources: Convention and Practice in Seneca the Elder and Other Authors* (Princeton Univ. diss, Princeton 1970); Lewis A. Sussman, *The Elder Seneca as a Critic of Rhetoric* (Univ. of North Carolina diss., Chapel Hill 1969).

[4] J. E. G. Whitehorne, "The Elder Seneca: A Review of Past Work," *Prudentia* 1 (1969) 14-27.

the Loeb series (London 1974), with many helpful notes. The only other full modern translation of the work is by H. Bornecque, into French and also with notes (2nd ed., Paris 1932).

The most important Latin edition of Seneca is H. J. Müller's text (Wien 1887, repr. Hildesheim 1963) improved upon by Bornecque and Winterbottom. Bornecque is now out of print; Müller was reprinted by Olms in 1963 but is of limited availability and frightful expense. For all practical purposes Winterbottom's Loeb is the most useful text, although the format of the series precludes an *apparatus criticus*. His three indexes (names; commonplaces, colors, and rhetorical terms; and general index) add greatly to its value. Throughout this book I have generally relied upon the Winterbottom text, which is essentially an updated and improved version of Müller. On a few occasions, however, I have preferred Müller himself or Bornecque.

Since a good and widely circulated English translation is now in existence, I did not think it necessary to provide a rendering of a sample Senecan *controversia* (or *suasoria*) theme in this book, assuming that the interested reader would prefer to consult the Loeb. For the reader whose Latin is non-existent or rusty, I have provided wherever possible an English translation in the running text and the Latin in a note. At times certain Latin terms are not translated because they are either very readily understood, or to do so would cloud the issue.

In a fairly large number of cases where my own translation could conceivably be construed as flavoring or altering the interpretation of the original Latin to suit my argument, I have reproduced the Loeb version. I would therefore like to thank the Harvard University Press and the Loeb Classical Library for permission to quote from Michael Winterbottom (ed. and transl.), *The Elder Seneca: Declamations* (2 vols., London 1974), copyright © 1974 by the President and Fellows of Harvard College.

In order to minimize the confusion between the similarly named father and his more famous son, in all instances the son will be referred to as the younger Seneca, while his father will be called the elder Seneca, or just Seneca. The publishers of *Speech Monographs*, the *American Journal of Philology*, and *Rheinisches Museum* have kindly allowed the use of some material from articles of mine published in those journals. Professor George A. Kennedy of the University of North Carolina, Chapel Hill, on numerous occasions took time off from an extremely busy schedule to read and reread versions of this book, and to make many helpful suggestions. Professor Harry Caplan also

XII   PREFACE

contributed a number of corrections and clarifications for which I
am very grateful. Any infelicities or inaccuracies are, of course, totally
my responsibility. My thanks also to Mrs. Joan Herer who typed the
major portion of the manuscript with great diligence and accuracy.

Gainesville, Florida   Lewis A. Sussman
December, 1976

ABBREVIATIONS OF FREQUENTLY CITED WORKS

The following works will be referred to by the last name of the author, except as otherwise noted. Ancient works and authors are abbreviated with minor exceptions on the pattern found in the *Oxford Classical Dictionary* (2nd ed., Oxford 1972) ix-xxii.

References to the prefaces or body of the elder Seneca's *Controversiae* will be given by numbers only (e.g., 1.3.3; 2 pr. 1) except in cases where confusion might result without first inserting *Contr.* The *Suasoriae* will be referred to in the standard manner (e.g., *Suas.* 7.14).

Atkins, J. W. H., *Literary Criticism in Antiquity: A Sketch of its Development* (2 vols., Cambridge 1934; repr. New York 1952), Vol. 2: *Graeco-Roman*.

Bardon, Henry, *Le Vocabulaire de la Critique Littéraire chez Sénèque le Rhéteur* (Paris 1940).

Bonner, S. F., *Roman Declamation in the Late Republic and Early Empire* (Liverpool 1949, repr. 1969).

Bornecque, Henri (ed. and transl.), *Sénèque le Rhéteur: Controverses et Suasoires* (Paris 1932). Cited as Bornecque (ed.).

——, *Les Déclamations et les Déclamateurs d'après Sénèque le Père* (Lille 1902, repr. Hildesheim 1967).

Butler, H. E. (ed. and transl.), *The Institutio Oratoria of Quintilian* (4 vols., London 1920).

Caplan, Harry (ed. and transl.), *Ad C. Herennium Libri IV De Ratione Dicendi* (*Rhetorica Ad Herennium*) (London 1954).

Clarke, M. L., *Rhetoric at Rome: A Historical Survey* (London 1953, repr. with corr. 1962).

D'Alton, J. F., *Roman Literary Theory and Criticism* (London and New York 1931, repr. 1962).

Duff, J. Wight; Duff, A. M. (ed.), *A Literary History of Rome in the Silver Age* (2nd. ed., New York 1960).

Edward, William A. (ed. and transl.), *The Suasoriae of Seneca the Elder* (Cambridge 1928) .

Ferrill, Arther (sic) Lee, *Seneca: The Rise to Power* (Univ. of Ill. diss., Urbana 1964).

Griffin, Miriam, "The Elder Seneca and Spain," *JRS* 62 (1972) 1-19.

Grube, G. M. A., *The Greek and Roman Critics* (Toronto 1965).

Kennedy, George A., *The Art of Persuasion in Greece* (Princeton 1963). Cited as Kennedy *APG*.

——, *The Art of Rhetoric in the Roman World* (Princeton 1972). Cited as Kennedy *ARRW*.

Kiessling, A. (ed.), *Annaei Senecae: Oratorum et Rhetorum Sententiae Divisiones Colores* (Leipzig 1872).

Leeman, A. D., *Orationis Ratio: The Stylistic Theories and Practice of the Roman Orators, Historians, and Philosophers* (2 vols., Amsterdam 1963).

Müller, H. J. (ed.), *L. Annaei Senecae Patris: Scripta Quae Manserunt* (Wien 1887, repr. Hildesheim 1963).

Norden, Eduard, *Die Antike Kunstprosa* (2 vols., Leipzig and Berlin 1923). Cited as Norden *A.K.*

Parks, E. Patrick, *The Roman Rhetorical Schools as a Preparation for the Courts under the Early Empire*. Series 63, No. 2, in *The Johns Hopkins University Studies in Historical and Political Science* (Baltimore 1945).

Schanz, Martin, and Hosius, Carl, *Geschichte der Römischen Literatur bis zum Gesetzgebungs werk des Kaisers Justinian* (2 vols., 1935, repr. Munich 1959). All references to vol. 2 unless otherwise noted.

Sihler, E. G., "Θετικώτερον," *AJP* 23 (1903) 283-294.

Sochatoff, A. Fred, "Basic Rhetorical Theories of the Elder Seneca," *CJ* 34 (1938-39) 345-354. Cited as Sochatoff "Theories."

Sussman, Lewis A., "The Elder Seneca's Discussion of the Decline of Roman Eloquence," *California Studies in Classical Antiquity* 5 (1972) 195-210. Cited as Sussman "Decline of Eloquence."

Teuffel, W. S., rev. by Schwabe, Ludwig. Warr, G. C. W. (transl., from the 5th German ed.), *History of Roman Literature* (2 vols., London 1891, 1892). All references to vol. 1, unless otherwise cited.

Weinrib, Ernest Joseph, *The Spaniards in Rome from Marius to Domitian* (Harvard Univ. diss., Cambridge 1968).

Whitehorne, J. E. G., "The Elder Seneca: A Review of Past Work," *Prudentia* 1 (1969) 14-27.

Winterbottom, Michael (ed. and transl.), *The Elder Seneca: Declamations* (2 vols., London 1974).

CHAPTER ONE

DECLAMATION IN ROME

A major intellectual force in the time of the elder Seneca was declamation, a much-maligned, often baffling type of practice speech that has only recently been placed in its proper perspective. [1] Its effect on Roman education was profound and pervasive; it comprised the central core of the school curriculum until the fall of the Empire and also contributed in large measure to the educational system of the Middle Ages.

The swift development from essentially a simple schoolboy exercise to a consuming pastime enjoyed and practiced during the prime of life by the leading intellectual and political figures of the early Empire (including Augustus, Pollio, Ovid, Messalla, Agrippa, and Maecenas) occurred within the lifespan of the elder Seneca. [2] Latin literature and style were never the same again, so extensively and immediately did declamation affect the literary trends of the period. Also, the habits and artifices of rhetorical logic marked Roman thought forever afterward.

Not only did the elder Seneca live through this period of momentous intellectual and political change, but he also recorded in the *Controversiae* and *Suasoriae* much of what he heard in these declamatory sessions. Nor does he just provide us with quotes—although these are themselves an invaluable record for the study of the vast changes occurring in literary style—but also, throughout, he reproduces penetrating literary criticisms of these extracts made by others, and often provides us with his own well-informed and sensible opinions. Thus the elder Seneca's life, works, and thought are inextricably tied to the world of Roman declamation, and it is to this topic we must first turn before any judicious estimate of the elder Seneca can be formed.

Originally, declamation was the delivery by school-boys of practice speeches on invented themes, which in its final stage of development took two forms: *suasoriae* and *controversiae*. The former was a speech

---

[1] Chiefly by S. F. Bonner, *Roman Declamation in the Late Republic and Early Empire* (Liverpool 1949).

[2] As he himself noticed: ... *studium* (i.e., declamation) *ipsum nuper celebrari coepit: ideo facile est mihi ab incunabulis nosse rem post me natam* (I pr. 12).

of advice for or against a particular course of action by a historical
figure, for example, "Alexander deliberates whether he should cross
the ocean" (*Suas.* 1). Obviously a preparation for deliberative oratory,
it was considered the easier exercise of the two and practiced extensively
until the student was considered ready for the *controversia*, a practice
legal speech delivered within the confines of a particular situation as
it related to one or several laws given the student by his teacher.
A rather provocative example is furnished in *Contr.* 1.5: (Law)
"A raped woman may choose either to marry her violator or have him
executed." (Situation) "In one night a certain man rapes two women;
one demands his execution, the other wants to marry him." The
student would then be assigned to write a speech for either woman's
attorney. Thus the *controversia* prepared specifically for judicial
oratory.

1. *The Greek origins of declamation*

Since Roman rhetoric was essentially Greek in origin, it is to Greece
we must first turn in order to examine the origins of these exercises. [3]

The Greek predecessors of the *suasoria* are numerous, extending
back to the early sophists who employed debates on mythological topics
very similar in conception to the Roman *suasoria* in its final form. [4]
Later in this development it is possible to trace the *logos protreptikos*
and *logos apotreptikos*, prominently mentioned by Aristotle (*Rhet.* 1.3,
3-6; 1.4) and the more elaborate and nearly perfected forms in the
Rhetorica ad Alexandrum (1-2; 34). [5]

The roots of the *controversia* are usually traced back to Aeschines,
who, in 330 BC, founded a school of rhetoric on Rhodes and apparently
assigned his students to practice judicial (and perhaps also deliberative)
speeches. [6] Yet the origins of the exercise may extend back in time even

---

[3] The account which follows is intended only as a general outline of the nature
and growth of declamation. More detailed treatments may be found in Edward
xiii-xxii; Parks 61-107; Clarke *passim*, esp. 85-99; Bonner *passim*; Lewis A.
Sussman, *The Elder Seneca as a Critic of Rhetoric* (diss., Chapel Hill 1969) 1-48.
Bornecque 3-6 has a useful and comprehensive bibliography on the subject up to
1901, which may be supplemented by Bonner 1, note 1 and 170-174; he leaves off
at 1949. See also the study of the word *declamatio* in G. François, "Declamatio
et Disputatio." *AC* 32 (1963) 513-540, and W. Kroll, *Melete, P-W* vol. 15, cols.
496-500.

[4] Cf. Bonner 11 and note 2.

[5] Cf. *ibid.* Bonner 11-12 reasonably assumes that the topics would be based upon
familiar situations in Greek city-states, such as debates on war and peace, national
defense, and public expenditures.

[6] See *ibid.* 12.

further, to the times of Gorgias, one or more of whose speeches were mythical court cases. [7] Quintilian, however, records the commonly accepted tradition of his time that Demetrius of Phalerum (*ca.* 350-*ca.* 280 BC) or someone contemporary with him originated the use of the practice themes from court cases or questions of public policy. [8]

Also contributing to the development of the Roman *controversia* were the various Greek preliminary school exercises known collectively as *progymnasmata*. These included the composition of *chriae*, [9] fables, narratives, praise and reproach of notable men, refutation and/or confirmation of legendary stories, and *theses*.

The last named exercise is one of some importance for the history of declamation. In some respects similar to the commonplace (a conventionalized narrative on a particular topic such as the vicissitudes of fortune or the degeneracy of youth), the *thesis*, though equally conventionalized, dealt with a more debatable general topic, often philosophical in nature; for example, whether or not marriage is desirable. [10] The mounting importance of the *thesis* in the Greek rhetorical schools aroused philosophers to complain that their province was being invaded, since they felt that rhetoricians should only be concerned with *hypotheses*, a species of *thesis* which dealt with general themes only insofar as they related to particular persons and situations. [11] However, the rhetoricians believed that they had a strong case for the inclusion of *theses* in their curriculum since, as Bonner has correctly noticed, a *thesis* was frequently the fundamental issue of a case and in order to argue effectively the speaker was required to transcend the immediate circumstances and deal with this basic question. [12] Although of some importance in the origins of the *controversia*, the *thesis* was a vital stage in the development of the *suasoria*, the exercise in composing

---

[7] Cf. the *Palamedes* and (to a lesser extent) the *Helen*; also the *Ajax* and *Odysseus* of Antisthenes, and the *Odysseus* attributed to Alcidimas. See Kennedy *APG* 168-173. The *Tetralogies* of Antiphon, on the other hand, seem to be actual practice court cases on current themes and are quite early, dated by Kennedy to the period between the 440's and 430's (*ibid.* 129-131).

[8] *Nam fictas ad imitationem fori consiliorumque materias apud Graecos dicere circa Demetrium Phalerea institutum fere constat. An ab ipso id genus exercitationis sit inventum, ut alio quoque libro sum confessus, parum comperi* ... (Quint. 2.4.41-42).

[9] See Suet. *Rhet.* 1; cf. Clarke 7, 15ff. A *chria* was the most elementary exercise and consisted of declining a famous saying to illustrate the use of the different grammatical cases (on this see Clarke 16 and note 38).

[10] See on this Bonner 8-11.

[11] Cf. Clarke 9.

[12] Bonner 6ff.

a speech to a historical figure faced with a decision whose underlying basis was often philosophical. Thus for example a *thesis* might be stated *an ducenda est uxor?* (ought one to marry?), while the *hypothesis-suasoria* would read *Cato deliberat an uxor ducenda sit* (Cato deliberates whether he should marry).

2. *Origins and Development of Declamation in Rome*

Before the extensive importation of Greek rhetorical theory, we can be fairly certain that there was in Rome some practical education in the basics of rhetoric which may well have included practice exercises of some sort. [13] But the crude indigenous rhetorical theory and exercises characteristic of the elder Cato's day were quickly supplanted by the more highly refined models imported and dazzlingly displayed by the enterprising Greek professors of rhetoric. By the time of Cato's death Rome had reached a level of political, legal, and literary sophistication ripe for the acceptance and success of this new science of persuasion. Recognizing the dangers of such an effective tool and its potential for weakening their grip on the reins of government, the conservative aristocracy vigorously opposed and persecuted the newly arrived professors. On occasion, when they felt sufficiently powerful, the conservatives even banished them. [14] This cloud of disapproval on the teaching of rhetoric was reflected in the opinion commonly held for a long time in Rome that rhetoric should only be taught by Greeks; though worthwhile to learn, it was thought unseemly for a Roman to be a professor of rhetoric (2 pr. 5). The first Roman to break this barrier was L. Plotius Gallus, as late as Cicero's boyhood (2 pr. 5; Quint. 2.4.42; Suet. *Rhet.* 2). The profession finally achieved respectability under Blandus, when the elder Seneca was a boy. [15]

The types of rhetorical exercises which the Greeks introduced into Rome were essentially the *progymnasmata*, with the additional practice of translating from Greek to Latin (Suet. *Rhet.* 1). But all these exercises, including an apparent forerunner of *suasoriae*, soon fell from fashion (or were relegated to the elementary pupils of the *grammaticus*), and were supplanted by the *controversia*. According to Suetonius (*Rhet.* 1) these original *controversiae* were drawn from two types of subject matter: [16]

---

[13] See *ibid.* 17.

[14] See Edward xiii-xiv; Bonner 16, 18.

[15] See 2 pr. 5; cf. Quint. 2.4.42; Suet. *Rhet.* 2; Edward xiv.

[16] See the discussion in Bonner 18-20. An interesting and important parallel to this usage occurs in Ovid *Am.* 2.5.44.

a) *ex historiis*: here, apparently, in the sense of fantastic, mythological or romantic tales.

b) *ex veritate ac re*: based on actual occurrences, with the names of the localities also added.

The latter type of subject matter was heartily endorsed by Crassus speaking in the *De Oratore*, and, if Cicero's claim to historical accuracy for the dialogue is believable, we can assume that these *controversiae* were current in the opening half of the 1st century BC—at any rate, their latest date would be 55 BC, when *De Oratore* was written. [17]

The term "declamation" for these rhetorical exercises seems to be comparatively late. Apparently it was first applied to a type of vocal exercise, and in exactly such a context the word makes its initial appearance in the *Rhetorica ad Herennium*. [18] Similar in conception to this work (though incomplete), Cicero's very early *De Inventione* (*ca.* 91-89 BC) does not include this term, and we must wait until the speech *Pro Sexto Roscio Amerino* (80 BC) for his earliest use of *declamare*, here apparently in the sense of a rhetorical exercise stressing delivery. [19] But the term was evolving steadily, as an investigation of its progressively changing usages in Cicero plainly reveals, from the name of a voice exercise to the whole concept of practice speeches. [20] The various derivatives of *declamare* seem to have acquired a derogatory connotation in the process. Cicero himself preferred a more theoretical and philosophical subject matter (akin to *theses*) which the conventional declamations of the time obviously did not possess. [21] Cicero's remarks add an interesting fact; during the late Republic not only did boys in school deliver practice speeches, but also mature men, who performed either in private or before small groups of friends. [22] Concurrent with this development was the inception of a trend towards excessive elaboration and a preoccupation with the fantastic.

[17] Crassus, in *De Or.* 1.149, 244; examples in 1.175 and 2.100; cf .Clarke 17-18. For Cicero's claim to historical accuracy, see *De Or.* 2.8-9; the difficulties engendered by this claim are discussed in Bonner 29.

[18] 3.20; cf. Bonner 20-22 who traces the term to theatrical and non-derogatory origins. However, it seems some orators abused the exercise; e.g., *De Or.* 1.149. The date of the *Rhetorica ad Herennium* can only be located approximately to the early 80's B.C.; cf. Kennedy *ARRW* 113; the authorship is still in question; *ibid.* 112-113.

[19] 29.82; cf. Bonner 28. I have adopted Kennedy's dating of *De Inventione*, *ARRW* 106-110.

[20] Bonner 28-31.

[21] *QFr.* 3.3.4 (54 BC); cf. Sihler 283-294; Bonner 29.

[22] See Clarke 20-21.

The preferred declamation exercise was the judicial cause, usually termed in the elder Seneca a *controversia*. As with *declamare* and its derivatives, the meanings of *controversia* also grew from the particular to the inclusive, since in the Sullan age it applied to the issue, or disputed point, of a case. [23]

> However, Cicero did not declaim what we now call controversies, nor even *theses*, such as they were termed before Cicero's day. For this kind of subject matter in which we are now trained is so new that its name is new also. We call them controversies, while Cicero called them causes. There is indeed another term, the Greek noun *scholastica*, but so often transferred into Latin that it stands for the Latin *controversia*, and it is a much more recent usage. In a similar manner the very term declamation can be found in no classical author before Cicero and also Calvus who distinguished declamation from a speech. For he said he declaimed not too badly but delivered speeches well. He thought one was characteristic of practice at home, the other of a real court case. The name alone bears this out, for even this very exercise has become popular in only comparatively recent times; and since it was born after me, I can easily be well informed on it from infancy. [24]

In this crucial passage, a *locus classicus* for the subject, the elder Seneca states that declamation had undergone a transformation from the *thesis* (before the time of Cicero) to the *causa* (contemporary with Cicero), and finally to a newer exercise, the *controversia* (also called by the Greek name *scholastica*) which, according to this account, arose after Seneca's birth. [25] While the elder Seneca has overstated the importance of *thesis* in the growth of declamation, this is not a terribly

---

[23] See Bonner 22. The first appearance of *controversia* in the sense of *causa* appears in *De Or.* 3.109, there modified by *finita*.

[24] 1 pr. 12: *Declamabat autem Cicero non quales nunc controversias dicimus, ne tales quidem, quales ante Ciceronem dicebantur, quas thesis vocabant. Hoc enim genus materiae, quo nos exercemur, adeo novum est, ut nomen quoque eius novum sit. Controversias nos dicimus: Cicero causas vocabat. Hoc vero alterum nomen Graecum quidem, sed in Latinum ita translatum, ut pro Latino sit, scholastica, controversia multo recentius est, sicut ipsa "declamatio" apud nullum antiquum auctorem ante Ciceronem et Calvum inveniri potest, qui declamationem a dictione distinguit; ait enim declamare iam se non mediocriter, dicere bene; alterum putat domesticae exercitationis esse, alterum verae actionis. Modo nomen hoc prodiit; nam et studium ipsum nuper celebrari coepit: ideo facile est mihi ab incunabulis nosse rem post me natam.* J. B. Hall, "Seneca, *Controversiae* 1. praef. 12," *Proc. Afr. Class. Assoc.* 12 (1973) 11, argues that *Ciceronem et* is an interpolation and therefore, according to Seneca at least, Calvus was the first to coin the abstract noun *declamatio*.

[25] *Ca.* 55-53 B.C. (For discussion of these dates, see below, 20).

serious error. [26] More intriguing is the clear distinction made between the Ciceronian *causa* and the Augustan *controversia*, especially in the light of the existing evidence which apparently contradicts Seneca's account.

For example, a comparison of the various declamation themes employed during the Republic (as mentioned in the *Rhetorica ad Herennium* and the *De Inventione*) with those of the Empire (as presented by the elder Seneca, Pseudo-Quintilian, and Calpurnius Flaccus) reveals little apparent difference in the topics of the exercises. Obviously the older type was still being declaimed in Seneca's youth, if we follow the implications of his biological metaphor of the new *controversia*'s growth. At any rate, Seneca must have known many people familiar with the old exercise; therefore he should have been aware of exact differences between the old and the new versions. Seneca himself says that Cicero delivered a *controversia* (not a *causa*) and indeed, the very theme mentioned in this instance is similar to others in the works of the elder Seneca and Pseudo-Quintilian. [27]

Suetonius also distinguishes the older exercise on the basis of subject matter since he says the *veteres controversiae* were drawn from fantastic tales [28] or from contemporary events often accompanied by geographical names (*Rhet.* 1). Quintilian, usually reliable on such matters, records a change in the nature of the *controversia* (2.10), especially the introduction of such topics as magicians, plagues, oracles, savage step-mothers and the like. But he makes no mention of actual themes. This omission, therefore, might well be crucial when coupled with the following evidence:

(1) The *Rhetorica ad Herennium* and *De Inventione* use illustrative themes quite similar to the declamation themes of the Empire. [29]

(2) Cicero includes in his works numerous declamation topics similar to those in the elder Seneca. [30]

[26] See Bonner 1-11; Sussman (above, note 3) 2-17.

[27] *Contr.* 1.4.7: *Color pro adulescente unus ab omnibus qui declamaverunt introductus est: "non potui occidere," ex illa Ciceronis sententia tractus quam in simili controversia dixit.* ... Indeed, Seneca mentions the rhetorician Aeschines, a contemporary of Cicero's, as a declaimer of the new type of *controversia*; 1.8.11; cf. Cic. *Brut.* 325; cf. Clarke 87 and 183, note 13. On the theme, see also *Contr.* 9.1; for the many ancient parallels, see Bonner 119-122.

[28] Cf. above, 4 and note 16; Clarke 87.

[29] Some of the parallels between *Ad Her.*, the elder Seneca, Ps. Quint., and Calpurnius Flaccus have been detailed in F. Marx (ed.), *Incerti Auctoris de Ratione Dicendi ad C. Herennium Libri IV* (Leipzig 1894) 106-107.

[30] On this see Edward xiv and note 6.

(3) Suetonius (*Rhet.* 1) purports to show the difference between
the two kinds of *controversiae* by giving examples of the old themes.
His illustrations however do not confirm that a sharp dividing line
existed between the two.

The inescapable conclusion drawn from this evidence is that no
dramatic differences existed between the old and new *controversia*
in subject matter. A clue to the precise nature of the little difference
which did exist may be found in *De Oratore*, if indeed it reflects
the time in which it was written. [31] In this dialogue, Cicero complains
that school declamations were an inadequate preparation for the realities
of a court since they were too easy and lacked the particulars of a real
case; i.e., evidence, oaths, and contracts. [32] If Cicero is reacting to
current abuses, we can then presume that a characteristic of the
evolving new *controversia* was a progressively smaller emphasis on
the *particulars* of a case, and an ever freer rein to the imagination.
Cicero also tells us elsewhere that the older *controversia* was rather plain
and probably did not allow much room for ornamentation, for which
reason he preferred to declaim in Greek, which did admit this. [33]
Cicero also mentions that declamation was abused by its early practitioners who considered it merely a voice exercise, while on the other
hand he praises those who tried to make declamation similar to a court
case (*De Or.* 1.149). We can conclude, then, that the older *controversiae*
were somewhat more factual and similar to a court case, while the
newer type had a tendency to be vaguer and allow more scope for
imagination.

A more significant means for discovering the difference between old
and new exercises is Cicero's pointed criticism of rhetors whose declamations became displays of vocal virtuosity, frequently not well executed, while they strove for "nimbleness of expression, a presto of
delivery, and a great array of words." [34] This comment reveals that

---

[31] 55 BC—very close to the time of Seneca's birth.

[32] *De Or.* 2.100; cf. 1.149; 2.75.

[33] *Commentabar declamitans—sic enim nunc loquuntur—saepe cum M. Pisone
et cum Q. Pompeio aut cum aliquo cotidie, idque faciebam multum etiam Latine,
sed Graece saepius, vel quod Graeca oratio plura ornamenta suppeditans consuetudinem similiter Latine dicendi afferebat, vel quod a Graecis summis doctoribus,
nisi Graece dicerem, neque corrigi possem neque doceri (Brut. 310).*

[34] Sihler 288; cf. *De Or.* 1.149-150: ... *sed plerique in hoc vocem modo, neque
eam scienter, et vires exercent suas, et linguae celeritatem incitant, verborumque
frequentia delectantur. In quo fallit eos, quod audierunt, dicendo homines, ut
dicant, efficere solere. Vere enim etiam illud dicitur, perverse dicere, homines,*

in the time of Cicero declamation was swiftly becoming a display of the rhetor's cleverness. [35] The roots of this process, noted before, no doubt lay in the origins of Roman declamation as a vocal exercise (*Ad Her.* 3.20). In the original form, apparently, it was a passage assigned to a student first for memorization and then delivery, perhaps in front of the class, after which the teacher criticized his *pronuntiatio*. The new *controversia* seems to have emphasized this dramatic vocal aspect in both importance and exaggeration. [36]

Rooted in its original emphasis on *pronuntiatio* was another striking development in the new *controversia*, its heavy theatricality. We know from Quintilian (3.8.51) that declaimers often acted out the roles they were portraying in the simulated cases. For example, if the situation required, the declaimer would assume the character of an old man, a prodigal son, a war hero, or any of the other stock figures in the world of declamation. As delivered by an expert, such a *controversia* must have been quite remarkable and entertaining. [37] This theatrical flavor pervaded the new *controversiae* of the Empire, and though it may not have been exactly what a master of oratory desired to teach, it was expected, even demanded, by students, parents, and audiences. [38]

Associated with this theatrical element was the evolution of declamation into a public and social function whose aim was primarily to please and delight a critical audience. We have had occasion to remark on the private nature of the old declamation; for instance, mature men like Cicero declaimed only in the company of a few close friends, [39]

---

perverse dicendo, facillime consequi. Quam ob rem in istis ipsis exercitationibus, etsi utile est, etiam subito saepe dicere, tamen illud utilius, sumpto spatio ad cogitandum, paratius atque accuratius dicere.

[35] Cf. in particular Cic. *Orat.* 65.

[36] See esp. Tac. *Dial.* 35 and Gudeman's note *ad loc., sequitur ut*; cf. *Contr.* 1 pr. 16; younger Seneca *Ep.* 15.7; Quint. 1.11.12-14; 3.8.51; 11.3.22ff; Macrob. *Sat.* 3.14.12. Cf. Bonner 20; E. M. Jenkinson, "Further Studies in the Curriculum of the Roman Schools of Rhetoric in the Republican Period," *SO* 31 (1955) 123.

[37] Cf. Clarke 96-97: "The vivid delivery, combined with the melodramatic themes and the epigrammatic sparkle, was irresistible."

[38] Petr. *Sat.* 3.2. See also on the theatrical quality of declamation *Contr.* 3 pr. 3; Quint. 2.10.12-14.

[39] Even in Seneca's day the conservatives refused to declaim publicly: e.g., Cassius Severus (3 pr. 7), Pollio (4 pr. 2), Montanus (9 pr. 1), and Labienus (10 pr. 4). This was in part due to what they felt was declamation's division from reality and other factors which in their eyes made it an unsuitable preparation for the forum. Some also considered the exercise ostentatious and worthless (cf. 3 pr. and 9 pr. *passim*). Cicero in his youth declaimed privately with his friends Marcus Piso, Quintus Pompeius, or Vibius Crispus (*Brut.* 310; Cicero *apud* Quint. 6.3.73) and near the end of his life with Hirtius and Pansa (see

although there is evidence that a change may have been occurring in
this respect during his later years. But for all practical purposes declamations were at this time an exercise delivered by boys in school or
grown men in private for practice only. In the early Empire, however,
public declamation sessions were popular and attended by great throngs
(e.g., 7 pr. 8), while there is only one recorded instance of such a
spectacle during the late Republic (Suet. *Gramm.* 7). Thus, an essential
difference between declamation in the two different periods was the
emergence of the adult declaimer, often, though not always, a professor
of rhetoric who performed primarily not to sharpen his oratorical
ability for the courts and forum, but rather to please and delight a
highly sophisticated audience. And in order to impress this select
group with his wit, eloquence, and mastery of all the intricate subtleties
of the genre, the speaker was impelled to employ every artful device
at his command. In such an artificial surrounding, it mattered not so
much what he said, but how he said it. Consequently gestures, intonation,
jingling *clausulae*, and even dress assumed an exaggerated importance.

To summarize: The old *controversia* was a relatively simple and
unadorned treatment of a legal case which was itself not necessarily
very dependent on reality for theme, procedures, or applicable laws.
Intended primarily for practice, it was usually delivered privately or
in school, and was probably directed equally at voice training, rhetorical
finish, and argumentation. In themes it differed little from the new
controversiae. [40] The essential difference between the two sprang from
the introduction of audiences and the status of these sessions as a social
medium of entertainment. [41] In an effort to please an audience often
composed of men with oratorical and literary pretensions of their own,
the declaimers extensively employed the elements of display, especially
in matters of style and delivery, and it is the exaggeration of these
aspects which characterized the new *controversia* and differentiated
it from the old. [42]

---

references below, note 54). The intimate quality of friendship between such
declaimers is revealed by Cicero: ... *fuit enim mecum et cum M. Pisone cum
amicitia tum studiis exercitationibusque coniunctus* (*Brut.* 240).

[40] See Jenkinson (above, note 36) 123. If indeed there had been a trend from
a more to less particular type of *causa*, it was such a gradual evolution that it
played no major role in differentiating the two exercises.

[41] In this it is also easy to detect the lessened opportunities for and dangers of
political and judicial oratory under the Empire.

[42] Quint. (1.2.30-31) perceptively noted the influence of an audience on a
speaker's manner of expression.

3. *The Suasoria*

Because it was considered an easier declamation exercise, the *suasoria* was practiced by schoolboys before the *controversia* (Tac. *Dial.* 35.4), and was greatly influenced by the Greek *logos apo(pro)treptikos* and *thesis*. Deliberative in nature, *suasoriae* were speeches of advice to or deliberation by figures drawn from Greek or Roman history in a crisis situation. [43] As in the case of the *controversiae*, during the early Empire both schoolboys and adults declaimed *suasoriae*. The more mature speakers particularly revelled in the latitude they offered for *descriptio*, in which the declaimer poetically described picturesque geographical features, cities, and customs. [44] This aspect of the exercise would especially call for an ornate style, and, as Quintilian observes, in his day, it was customary to use an impetuous, torrential style (3.8.58-61). Cicero refers to deliberate speeches as *suasiones,* the term *suasoria* applied to deliberative exercises first occurs in the elder Seneca. [45] The themes of these exercises do not seem to have changed any more from the time of the *Rhetorica ad Herennium* to the elder Seneca than did those of the *controversiae*.

4. *The Schools of Rhetoric in Rome* [46]

After a Roman youth attained proficiency with the *grammaticus* in simple composition, reading, and explicating the major poets and historians (usually between the ages of 12-16), he went to study under the *rhetor*. Here, he may have continued to study on a more advanced level the subjects studied with the *grammaticus* until it was felt he could begin actual declamation, first with *suasoriae,* and then with *controversiae.*

As nearly as it can be reconstructed, the class procedure began with the assignment of a declamation theme for the class. Then the *rhetor,*

---

[43] It was not considered necessary to adhere closely to historical fact in the *suasoriae.* Inaccuracies ranged from the minor, e.g., the exact numbers of Greeks at Thermopylae in *Suas.* 1, to the utter absurdity of *Suas.* 7 (cf. Quint. 3.8.46) where Cicero is deliberating whether or not he could convince Antony to spare his life by offering to burn his own published works; cf. Seneca's own remarks in *Suas.* 6.14. These two *suasoriae*, incidentally, are a good indication of the range of historical topics these exercises covered.

[44] Cf. 2 pr. 3; also, below, 62.

[45] *De Or.* 2.333; *Orat.* 37; *Part. Orat.* 4.11, 13; 24.85; cf. Bonner 22 and note 4. Bardon 55 states that the term *suasoria* first appears in the elder Seneca.

[46] Cf. the accounts of Edward xx-xxii and Parks 61-67.

sitting at his elevated desk, would address the class with hints on how
to treat the theme, and in particular, how to divide the argumentation. [47]
Next, the students began work on the themes, submitting their versions
when finished to the *rhetor* for suggestions and correction. After the
student had revised the draft in accordance with the teacher's recom-
mendations, he then memorized the declamation, and finally delivered
it before the class with the appropriate gestures and intonation. Often,
on such occasions, the parents and relatives of the student might attend.
We can assume that the *rhetor* then delivered a critique of the performance and perhaps invited comments from the other students and
members of the audience, if any. After each student had delivered
his declamation on the theme, the *rhetor* would deliver his own version
as a model of how that particular theme should be handled. The teacher
apparently varied this entire procedure with occasional lectures on
various aspects of rhetorical theory, treating such topics as the principles
of argumentation, style, gesture, and the like.

At frequent intervals the schools were opened up, enabling the
general public to witness displays by gifted students or by the master
himself, perhaps in order to advertise his expertise as a teacher and
practitioner of rhetoric and so attract new students. On such occasions
many grown men attended the sessions for amusement or even to
declaim, themselves, on the topic selected. After delivering their
declamation, they too would receive critiques from both the *rhetor*
and the audience. Though sometimes abusive, more often these critical
exchanges were witty and entertaining. At other times, either in a
school or auditorium, public declamation sessions were held exclusively
for adults and attracted the most famous rhetoricians and declaimers.
Habitués of these open declamation exhibitions included most of the
prominent political and literary figures of the day, including such
eminent notables as Messalla, Pollio, Maecenas, Agrippa, Livy, and
Augustus himself. [48] What was it in these exercises, ostensibly for
schoolboys, which excited the interest of these men and caused them
to flock both as listeners and practitioners to declamatory displays?

Certainly, the changed political conditions coincident with the emergence of the Principate must be a basic cause for the popularity of
declamation. [49] Although advocates yet enjoyed great prestige and

---

[47] Preserved in the *Declamationes Minores* of Ps. Quint. under the heading
Sermones are typical examples of such comments by a rhetor.

[48] See Edward xx and Bornecque 42-43, 46.

[49] Cf. Edward xvi-xx; Parks *passim*; Clarke 100-108; Bonner 42ff.

political oratory retained some measure of its former importance, [50] nevertheless there can be no doubt that the new government had a stultifying effect on eloquence. Declining freedom of speech narrowed the range of subject matter and an orator always had to be watchful lest he offend the *princeps* or one of his favorites. The reform of the court system begun by Pompey during his sole consulship was continued, and during the Empire the new regulations made all but impossible judicial speeches of the sort on which Cicero based his reputation. [51]

At the risk of simplification, the decline of oratory concurrent with the introduction of the Principate, and in large measure caused by it, gave rise to factors which greatly encouraged the adult practice of display declamation. A large number of talented men, the product of an educational system whose overriding concern was with rhetoric, were now set adrift in a period when their oratorical training could no longer be employed for gaining wealth and political power. It occasions little surprise that they redirected their energies and talents to the safer, yet more sterile arena of declamation.

In one sense, declamation was also an escape to an exciting, often violent and unreal world populated by wicked stepmothers, pirates, tyrants, prodigal sons, rapists, or historical figures from the dim past. This escapist value first becomes visible during the civil wars of the late Republic, when the leading actors of that drama turned to declaiming in the darkest moments of turmoil. Such exercises may have recalled to mind carefree student days, as it did for the elder Seneca writing during his old age (1 pr. 1; 10 pr. 1), or provided these active men with a period of repose enabling them to regain their perspective during perilous days, much as Winston Churchill in the darkest hours of World War II turned to painting pastoral landscapes.

In this regard Cicero reports a fairly revolutionary concept in the *Brutus* when the addressee of the dialogue praises the pursuit of

---

[50] The main thesis of Parks (p. 19) as he states it is: "(1) the courts continued to function under the emperors with little established evidence of restriction, and were even overworked; (2) the advocates found ample opportunity for eloquence; (3) the rhetorical schools, rather than redoubling their effort when they had allegedly lost their aim, continued to offer a practical preparation for these advocates, and to offer capable administrators for the complex machinery of the empire and men sufficiently educated and cultured to take their place in a refined literary age." Though the general direction of Parks' thesis is correct, he tends to overstate the case; cf. the even-handed appraisal of Parks in Bonner 43-49.

[51] There are, of course, other factors in the concurrent declines of oratory and eloquence. See Sussman "Decline of Eloquence" *passim*.

eloquence not just for the obvious practical advantages, but because, he says, the very study of rhetoric and the exercises themselves are a source of pleasure and respite. [52] Not surprisingly, then, at a critical juncture of his life, Cicero himself turned to declaiming *theses* for and against themes applicable to the current political situation in order to distract his mind from its worries. [53] In the turbulent period following Caesar's assassination, Cicero also found time to declaim with the consuls of the next year, Hirtius and Pansa. [54] Not even the critical events at Mutina prevented Antony or Octavian from declaiming (Suet. *Rhet.* 1; *Aug.* 84); in fact, throughout this period Antony declaimed frequently and had in his retinue a teacher of rhetoric (Cic. *Phil.* 2.17).

After the fall of the Republic, the men who by experience, background, talent, wealth, and ambition would have been drawn to active political careers were discouraged from participation because of their distaste for the new regime, or the dangers and uncertainties inherent in close association with court politics. Most chose the realistic path of accepting and cooperating with the Principate, if doing so grudgingly. Others lost the all-consuming preoccupation with politics which so typified the Republic, while some retired altogether from public life. The end result was the creation of a class of capable and intelligent men who found themselves with considerable leisure time. In a city where there was relatively little intellectual activity (beyond a few literary circles), this new leisured class sought an outlet for its wit, intelligence, and oratorical skill. Perhaps these men also felt the need to display safely on occasion their Republican feelings or inveigh against thinly disguised tyrants (a practice which became dangerous

---

[52] ... *dicendi autem me non tam fructus et gloria quam studium ipsum exercitatioque delectat, quod mihi nulla res eripiet te praesertim tam studiosum et ...* [lacuna]. *Dicere enim bene nemo potest nisi qui prudenter intellegit; qua re qui eloquentiae verae dat operam, dat prudentiae, qua ne maximis quidem in bellis aequo animo carere quisquam potest* (Cic. *Brut.* 23).

[53] (1) *Ego etsi tam diu requiesco quam diu aut ad te scribo aut tuas litteras lego, tamen et ipse egeo argumento epistularum et tibi idem accidere certo scio. Quae enim soluto animo familiariter scribi solent ea temporibus his excludentur, quae autem sunt horum temporum ea iam contrivimus. Sed tamen, ne me totum aegritudini dedam, sumpsi mihi quasdam tamquam* θέσεις, *quae et* πολιτικαὶ *sunt et temporum horum, ut et abducam a querelis et in eo ipso de quo agitur exercear. Eae sunt huius modi:...* (3) *In his ego me consultationibus exercens et disserens in utramque partem tum Graece tum Latine et abduco parumper animum a molestiis et* τῶν προὔργου τι *delibero* (Cic. *Ad Att.* 9.4.1,3). Cf. the practice of Pompey at another crucial time of the civil wars, Suet. *Rhet.* 1.

[54] *Contr.* 1 pr. 11; Suet. *Rhet.* 1. Additional references in Bonner 31, note 1.

in later years). Declamation was therefore a popular recreational activity among the ruling class for which we have no modern parallels. Those with a Machiavellian cast of mind might well consider the very careful support of declamation by Augustus and succeeding emperors as a device to keep this talented group busily and happily diverted. [55]

The growing status of the declamatory sessions as an entertaining and stimulating social activity in their own right also contributed greatly to the popularity of these exercises. The process is relatively simple to trace. In the late Republic adults declaimed primarily in private gatherings of close friends, as in the case of Cicero. [56] From this beginning, Bonner envisions the following developments: [57]

(1) Professors declaim in schools for the benefit of pupils (3 pr. 16; 7 pr. 1); and orators at home among friends (4 pr. 2; 10 pr. 3, 4).

(2) Professors invite the public to their schools on special occasions (3 pr. 1); some kept an open school (3 pr. 16). But the conservative orators viewed this with contempt (10 pr. 4), though some admitted the public (4 pr. 7). The professors invited parents to hear their sons (Persius 3.45; Quint. 2.7.1; 10.5.21).

(3) The presence of other professors encouraged the introduction of meetings for friendly competition which became popular social occasions, often elsewhere than in the schools. Even those who did not declaim publicly came to listen and joined in the critical discussion, many of whom were famous people.

The meetings of adult declaimers must have been very competitive, since it seems that the speakers declaimed on the same subjects, sometimes over a period of several days (*Contr.* 1.7.13; 2.1.25). Each man tried to outshine his predecessor in "brilliance of epigram, originality of comment, vividness of description, ingenuity of argument, subtlety

---

[55] Among the close associates of Augustus (including Maecenas, Agrippa, Messalla, and Tiberius) declamation was especially popular, and there are frequent notices of their attendance and sometimes performance at recitals. See *Contr.* 2.4.12-13; 4 pr. 7; 10.5.21; *Suas.* 3.6-7; Suet. *Aug.* 89. Augustus himself was a keen critic of declamation and eloquence; e.g., 4 pr. 7; 10 pr. 14; Suet. *Aug.* 86.

[56] Cic. *Brut.* 310; *Fam.* 9.16.7; *Contr.* 1 pr. 11; Suet. *Rhet.* 1. Seneca reports the term *domestica exercitatio*, 1 pr. 12; 3 pr. 1; cf. 3 pr. 13; 10 pr. 4. See also the mention of Pollio in 4 pr. 2, and the discussion with numerous references in Bornecque 44. Seneca also notes that even of those who habitually spoke before a small circle (*secretae exercitationis*), some spoke occasionally before larger groups on invitation; e.g., Haterius (4 pr. 7) and Albucius (7 pr. 1).

[57] Bonner 39-42.

of misrepresentation." [58] As each one spoke, the difficulty increased, and outdoing those before became a game that was "a means of sharpening their wits, elaborating and exhibiting their legal knowledge, and spending their leisure hours in a friendly, amusing, and by no means futile intellectual exercise." [59] Criticism must have been an integral part of these proceedings, no doubt clever and witty. The crowds they drew, according to Albucius, were even larger than those in the forum (7 pr. 8).

Another factor in the great popularity of declamation, touched upon before, was its value as an entertainment medium. Public diversions in Rome centered otherwise on second-rate theatrical performances such as mimes, or on the gory spectaculars of the arena. [60] The romantic and unreal world of the declamation also provided pleasant diversion and satisfied a desire for escape. The attractiveness of the themes, especially to the younger generation, as well as the older, was readily evident to Cicero (*QFr.* 3.3.4). Sometime later Quintilian (1.1.20) suggested that the themes employed should be fun for the students; the topics should be more interesting than contract suits and the like. [61] Bornecque finds that seven out of eight times the themes in Seneca resemble a *"roman"* or at least *"a la nouvelle."* [62] Pursuing this line of development, the declamation took on a definite literary cast, "carefully formed on the best literary models, and content to be judged by literary standards." [63] We should remember, too, that the audiences to which these exercises appealed were highly sophisticated and cultured, and whose critical taste is revealed by the excellent reception accorded to Vergil, Horace, Tibullus, and others of this golden age. [64]

Finally, we must not overlook the primary factor in the popularity of declamation: it was the basis of acquiring literary style, and was

---

[58] *Ibid.* 49.

[59] *Ibid.* 40.

[60] One serious intellectual activity of sorts should be mentioned briefly though—the public recitation of literary works. This practice seems also to have become very popular in the early Empire, and perhaps for the same reasons as declamation. On this see A. C. Dalzell, "Asinius Pollio and the Early History of Public Recitation at Rome," *Hermathena* 86 (1955) 20-28.

[61] See Quint. 10.5.14-16; also 2.10.5-6. Cicero enumerates the more mundane kinds of cases in *De Or.* 1 1.173.

[62] See Bornecque 88-89.

[63] Aubrey O. Gwynn, *Roman Education from Cicero to Quintilian* (Oxford 1926, repr. New York 1964) 248.

[64] Cf. Bornecque 128-129.

considered indispensable to the education of the orator. [65] Even the elder Seneca who could be very critical of declamation recognized it as the keystone of all education (2 pr. 3). Although oratory and its importance were declining, training in this skill still had its rewards and comprised the central core of Roman education until the very last. Besides such obvious skills as delivery and literary style, the declaimer received practice in clear thinking, manufacture of argument, and legal interpretation. A thorough knowledge of rhetoric and a modicum of eloquence were considered requisite for any political or professional career; [66] even formally technical writers (such as Vitruvius and Celsus, and nearly everyone else for that matter) display a comprehensive knowledge of rhetoric in their writings. After extensive discussion, Parks concludes,

> I can in no way accept the theory that the practical Roman mind could suffer an educational machine to continue, for purely aesthetic reasons, when it could no longer be justified from the standpoint of pragmatism. [67]

Perceptive Romans recognized the defects and excesses of declamation, but never questioned the primacy of the educational system of which it formed the core.

---

[65] Provided, as Quintilian points out, that the exercises were not totally removed from reality (10.5.14; cf. Bornecque 88).

[66] Tac. *Dial.* 36; cf. Parks 15ff.

[67] *Ibid.* 95.

CHAPTER TWO

THE LIFE OF THE ELDER SENECA

1. *Sources*

Few facts concerning the life of the elder Seneca have survived. Although his son preserves some information in the *Consolatio ad Helviam* and *Epistle* 108, the single work of his which would have proven most useful, the biographical *De Vita Patris*, has perished except for a tantalizingly brief fragment from its beginning. [1] The other writers of the Silver Age are exceedingly vague on the elder Seneca and one early observer detected only a "deep silence" in the ancient sources. [2] Tacitus mentions only the sons of Seneca and his grandson Lucan. This is not unexpected since the *Annales* begin with the death of Augustus when Seneca was advanced in age. He was also inactive in politics and so, when Tacitus describes the parentage of the sons, he refers only to their provincial and equestrian origin (*Ann.* 14.53,

---

[1] On the *De Vita Patris* see below, 137 and note 1.

[2] N. Faber in the preface to the Elzevir edition of the elder Seneca (Amsterdam 1672) remarked on the *altum silentium* in the sources. He was referring to unequivocal references to the man. Two passages in Martial (1.61.7-8; 4.40.1-2) may refer to the elder Seneca; cf. below, 145 and notes 25, 26; 148 and notes 35, 36. Tacitus alludes to the elder Seneca when mentioning the equestrian background of the sons (*Ann.* 14.53; 16.17). Quintilian may have reproduced two *sententiae* of the elder's; but they are ascribed only to a Seneca, unqualified (Quint. 9.2.42, 98). Winterbottom (I, xxi) thinks that in 9.2.42 by referring to Seneca Quintilian might loosely mean one of the declaimers quoted by him, while in 9.2.98 he probably refers to the younger Seneca. Müller 584, however, lists these as genuine fragments of the elder, as does Kiessling 526 who also includes a third (Quint. 8.3.31). Kennedy *ARRW* 324 suspects that Quintilian is reproducing Seneca in 9.2.91, 95 also. Both Suetonius (*Tib.* 73) and Lactantius (*Div. Inst.* 7.15.14ff) quote material from a Seneca which may have originated in the elder's lost *Histories*; cf. below, 137-142. Suetonius may have been familiar with the *Contr.*; cf. the resemblances in the anecdotes about Albucius (7 pr. 7; *Rhet.* 6). A. Grisart, "Suétone et les deux Sénèque," *Helikon* 1 (1961) 302-308 calls attention to some other possibilities where a Seneca (unqualified again) might well be the elder in Suet. *Verg.* 28 and *Gaius* 53. (See also below, 139 and note 6; 143-144). However, none of the above possible references are certain, and strong arguments exist for assigning most of them to the younger. The crux of the problem lies in the lack of qualifiers to the name Seneca (e.g., *pater, filius*). Two possibilities exist: (1) the father and son were confused at a very early date because of the identical names, or (2) both were so well known, at least for a while, that Roman readers would easily be able to distinguish between them. See also Grisart *op. cit. passim*; Griffin 10, 19.

16.17). Nevertheless we might have expected a brief notice in the *Dialogus de Oratoribus.* The most glaring omission exists in Quintilian's exhaustive and thorough *Institutio Oratoria*, where he does not directly refer to works of the elder Seneca. [3]

Therefore our last remaining source of information on the elder Seneca must remain his own body of extant works, titled collectively *Oratorum et Rhetorum, Sententiae, Divisiones, Colores.* [4] These were addressed to his sons who were familiar with his life; thus any biographical information which he imparts is incidental. Although tattered, the works are large and some facts slip through as does the informal portrait of "one of the most charming and loveable characters in Roman history." [5]

Seneca's full name in our best manuscript tradition is Lucius Annaeus Seneca, and nearly all modern authorities now agree with this, although there was some confusion dating from the Renaissance. [6] He was born to a wealthy equestrian family in Cordova, a deeply Romanized and cultured city in southern Spain. [7] Founded by the Romans in 152 BC (Strabo 3.2.1), the city soon became the most important in the province of Hispania Ulterior. [8] The inhabitants were predominantly of native, Italian, and Illyrian stock. The Annaei themselves were not native Spaniards—the name itself is either

---

[3] See below, 161-166.

[4] The elder Seneca's anthologies are divided into the *Controversiae*, originally ten books of excerpts from this popular type of declamation exercise, with each book introduced by a preface, and the *Suasoriae*, in their original state one or more books of excerpts from the declamation exercise of the same name, each book also presumably introduced by a preface. On the present state of the texts, see below, 34-35.

[5] Edward xxiii.

[6] See Müller VII-VIII; Teuffel-Schwabe 568; Eduard Wölfflin, "Der Vorname des Rhetors Seneca," *RhM* 50 (1895) 320; Bornecque 9; Schanz-Hosius 340; Edward xxiii; Griffin 4, note 42. In the Renaissance both the persons and the works of both Senecas were hopelessly confused. Finally Raphael Volaterranus and later Justus Lipsius saw that there must be two different men. Since the Romans customarily named sons after the grandfather, and since two of the elder Seneca's grandsons bore the *praenomen* Marcus, Raphael assumed that the elder Seneca's *praenomen* was also Marcus and most editors until this century followed his lead. However, as Müller VIII note 1 and Edward xxiii note 1 both point out, this naming custom was not rigid, and identical *praenomina* would help explain how the Senecas were confused.

[7] *Suas.* 6.27; Martial 1.61.7-8. On equestrian rank see 2 pr. 3; Tac. *Ann.* 14.53; 16.17; younger Seneca *Helv.* 14.3.

[8] On Cordova see below, note 53.

Etruscan or Illyrian. 9 The origin of the Seneca *cognomen* is more doubtful. 10

The date of Seneca's birth probably fell between the dates of 58-53 BC. He tells us that he could have heard Cicero declaiming with Hirtius and Pansa (i.e., in 44 BC), if the civil war then raging had not forced him to stay home (1 pr. 11). This suggests that his family had planned to send him to Rome for training in rhetoric, and the customary age for beginning these studies was between twelve and sixteen. 11 A talented student like Seneca might begin earlier; thus an approximate birth date in the mid-50's BC. 12

When the wars subsided, Seneca, still a boy, 13 arrived in Rome to continue his education, apparently in the company of his life-long fellow Spaniard, Marcus Porcius Latro. 14 Both were students together at the school of another Spaniard, Marullus (1 pr. 22). Seneca does not locate the school in either Rome or Cordova, a city noted as a center of literary activity (Cicero *Arch.* 10.26), but a chance comment places it at Rome. He tells us that more than 200 students attended, therefore probably too many for a provincial town. 15 Since he has

9 William Schulze, *Zur Geschichte lateinischer Eigennamen* (Berlin 1904) 345 supports Etruscan origin; Hans Krahe, *Lexikon altillyrischer Personennamen* (Heidelberg 1929) 6 favors Illyrian origin, while Ronald Syme, *Tacitus* (2 vols., Oxford 1958) II, App. 80, 784-785 concurs. Cf. Ferrill 8 and note 10; Griffin 4.

10 It and the variant Senecio are found widely in inscriptions throughout the Empire so that acquisition in Spain, Italy, or elsewhere is possible. Cf. Griffin 4 and note 40.

11 Teuffel-Schwabe 568; Bornecque 9-10; Schanz-Hosius 340; Edward xx; Parks 61 and note 2; Duff 38. On the flexibility of the ages in accordance with the individual's ability see Quint. 2.1.7.

12 Edward xxiii-xxiv first challenged the long-held assumption that Seneca's birthdate must be directly related to the age at which a boy usually went to the *rhetor*. As a precocious student Seneca could well have been brought to Rome for study, perhaps with a *grammaticus*, or else with a *rhetor* at an earlier age than normal. He therefore concludes that the birthdate need not be placed any earlier than 50 BC; cf. Griffin 5. But it seems excessively premature for a child of seven or so to be an avid devotee of declamation, and I also believe that in this instance we must take Seneca at his word (1 pr. 11) that if he were at Rome in 44 BC he would have been able to sit in on a private declamation session of Cicero's.

13 A *puer*, as he himself says (1 pr. 3; cf. 1 pr. 2).

14 1 pr. 13; cf. 1 pr. 22, 24; 2.2.7 (see Winterbottom note 1 *ad loc.*); 7.2.11.

15 1 pr. 2. Indeed, there is no record of Latin rhetorical schools in the provinces until the reign of Augustus; cf. Griffin 6. Seneca was almost certainly talking of a rhetorical school and not the school of a *grammaticus* (as Griffin 6 implies). In the text he uses the term *praeceptor* when referring to the school's master and this is the title he applies only to professors of rhetoric, especially his teacher Marullus (*Contr.* 2.2.7; 7.2.11; cf. 1.8.15; 2.3.23). Quintilian also, in effect, differentiates between the *praeceptor-rhetor* and the *grammaticus* (1.2.13-14; cf. 2.1.1; 2.2.3).

also told us that he was a *puer* when he came to Rome, it follows that he attended rhetorical school there. [16] Marullus was also from Cordova; an identical provincial background could be the only recommendation for a teacher who was otherwise decidedly inferior. [17] Seneca also attended the school of the more renowned Arellius Fuscus (*Suas. 2.10*).

Seneca must have spent a long period of time in Rome. As he himself says, he heard every famous speaker of the age except Cicero (1 pr. 11). The number, variety, and extent of the quotations preserved certainly confirm this boast. Seneca made numerous friends and acquaintances among the leading literary and political men of the period, while acquiring an extensive repertoire of anecdotes about them. Surely this required a long time to accomplish.

On the other hand, because the home and major financial interests of the Annaei remained in Spain, Seneca returned there for visits, some quite long. Lengthy periods of residence in Spain are necessary to account for Seneca's acquaintance with Gavius Silo and his close friendship with Clodius Turrinus, both of whom never went to Rome (10 pr. 13-16). Relatively short trips home are also possible since the passage from Rome to Cordova was not exceptionally long or difficult; a trip of twenty days is attested (*Helv.* 2.5; cf. 15.2).

A reason often proposed for one journey home was to marry Helvia, who is usually assumed to be of Spanish birth. [18] But Weinrib has challenged this assumption and marshalled evidence which suggests that hers was an old, wealthy Italian or Latin family. [19] Lending support to his argument is the picture that emerges of Helvia in her son's writings. Although brought up by a stern stepmother, she was an unusually cultured and intellectual lady for her times and also a keen businesswoman and administrator: one might not expect to find such qualities in a provincial woman. [20] Therefore Seneca need not have gone to Spain to marry Helvia, and even Edward (who believes that she is Spanish) admits the possibility that the marriage took place

[16] As a *iuvenis*; 1 pr. 24; cf. 2.2.7; 4 pr. 3; Schanz-Hosius II, 340; A. Gwynn, *Roman Education from Cicero to Quintilian* (New York 1964) 158.

[17] Cf. Bornecque 10, 179; Griffin 6 and note 71. For Seneca's own judgments of Marullus see 1 pr. 22; 2.2.7; 2.4.7.

[18] On the marriage see *Helv.* 16.3; cf. 2.4. On her supposed Spanish birth see Bornecque 11; Edward xxv. More substantial evidence for Spanish birth is presented in Griffin 8 and note 83, based on name reconstruction and an inscription in Baetica (*CIL* II, 999), attesting to the presence of Helvii Novati in the area. This would account for the cognomen given Seneca's eldest son.

[19] See Weinrib 153-158.

[20] *Helv.* 2.4; 15.1; 16.3; 17.3, 4.

in Rome. 21 Since their three sons were born at about the turn of the century, it is tempting to date the marriage just before this date.

Seneca says that he heard Asinius Pollio (76 BC—AD 5) declaim when the orator was in his prime and also much later as an old man; this has caused needless confusion and speculation concerning the whereabouts of Seneca during the long intervening period. 22 It is totally unnecessary to assume that he was absent from Rome during this entire time. The statement only means that Seneca did not hear Pollio declaim often, and this is easily understandable since he declaimed only in private (4 pr. 2).

As a boy Seneca went to Rome, after the end of the civil wars, perhaps in 38 BC. 23 Shortly afterward he heard Pollio declaim (4 pr. 3), completed his rhetorical education, and began making the rounds of the various declamation performances, perhaps in the company of Pollio himself at times, since he was apparently a close friend of the Annaei. During this period of youth and young manhood in Rome, to which he later looked back in fond nostalgia (1 pr. 1), Seneca heard many of the notable declaimers whose words he records. 24 Among these was the young Ovid, then a student of Arellius Fuscus (*Contr.* 2.2.8). Born in 43 BC, the poet would have been a student in such a school between 29 and 24 BC. Nearly a decade later in 17 BC Seneca was in the audience which included Augustus, Agrippa, and Maecenas when Latro made some very embarassing remarks about adoptions (*Contr.* 2.4.12-13). Additional evidence suggests residence in Rome until shortly before 9 BC. 25

We can assume that in approximately 8 BC Seneca returned to Spain since that is the probable year in which Novatus, the eldest of his three sons, was born there. Several years later, between 4 BC and AD 1, he was still in Spain for the birth of the younger Seneca, also

---

21 Edward xxv.

22 *Audivi autem illum et viridem et postea iam senem, cum Marcello Aesernino nepoti suo quasi praeciperet* (4 pr. 3). The first date might be shortly after Pollio's consulship, or about 39 or 38 BC, when Seneca first came to Rome. The last date might be a year or two before Pollio's death in AD 5. Cf. Griffin 5. The relatively frequent mentions of Pollio indicate that Seneca heard him a good number of times in between these terminal dates.

23 Griffin 7 points out that this date could conceivably be 36 BC.

24 The many citations of Marullus, Latro, Fuscus, Albucius, and Rubellius Blandus probably belong to this period. Cf. Griffin 7.

25 Griffin 7 and notes 75, 76. She dates Seneca's conversation with Cassius Severus (3 pr.) shortly before 9 BC, as well as a visit to Messalla with his friend Gallio reported in *Suas.* 3.6.

in Cordova. [26] Seneca was present in Spain when Latro committed suicide in 4 BC. [27] Some time before he had witnessed Latro's running debate with Clodius Turrinus over the use of *colores* (10 pr. 15) and Latro's solecism in a Spanish court (9 pr. 3). This evidence indicates a fairly lengthy residence in Spain, or until about 4 BC.

Next, a journey back to Rome where he could oversee the education of his sons; but the infirm younger Seneca remained behind until he was strong enough for the trip. [28] The latest possible date for the elder Seneca's return is AD 5, the year in which Pollio died, since Seneca heard him declaim in advanced old age. During this next protracted residence in Rome, Seneca attended numerous public declamation sessions, often in the company of his sons (10 pr. 2). A series of events and many quotations attest to his presence in Rome around AD 16 and thereafter into the mid-30's. [29] Seneca therefore must have spent the greater part of his later years in Rome but occasional trips back to Spain are a distinct possibility. At least one is fairly certain, since he died in Spain. [30] Whether Seneca made any other journeys throughout the Empire is uncertain, although there is a hint that he may have been in Crete or Asia, possibly in an official capacity. [31]

The available evidence allows for a relatively precise dating of Seneca's death. He mentions the extinction of the Scaurus family, an event no later than AD 34. [32] In the *De Vita Patris* the younger Seneca describes a historical work which his father assiduously worked on until nearly the day of his death. A possible fragment of that work appears in the Suetonius life of Tiberius (73) which describes the manner of that Emperor's death. Moreover, Seneca was able to read and quote the historian Cremutius Cordus in a work he intended to publish. This man's writings had been banned by Tiberius in AD 25 as were those of Cassius Severus, whose works were burned in

---

[26] Cf. Edward xxv; Griffin 7 and notes 77, 78.

[27] If we can trust the dating of St. Jerome; cf. Bornecque 12, 188-189. See also 1 pr. 13 and the discussion in Griffin 7.

[28] *Helv.* 19.2; cf. Bornecque 12.

[29] The citations are conveniently collected in Griffin 8.

[30] See *ibid.* for convincing argumentation locating his death in Spain; he may have returned there for the birth of Mela's son, Lucan, in November, AD 39, and then died shortly thereafter.

[31] Cf. the vivid recollections in an anecdote about Asilius Sabinus in Crete (9.4.19ff); also on Cicero's son as governor of Asia (*Suas.* 7.13-14).

[32] *Suas.* 2.22; cf. Dio 58.24; Tac. *Ann.* 6.29; Suet. *Tib.* 61; cf. Duff 38-39.

AD 12: both were republished in the reign of Gaius. [33] Seneca denounces the book burnings under Augustus in very harsh terms (10 pr.
5-7); under Tiberius this would have been too dangerous. Therefore
he must have written the preface after the Emperor's death in AD
37. [34] Seneca refers to the death of his father in the *Consolatio ad
Helviam*, written in AD 41, two years after he began his exile.
The tone indicates that Helvia's grief has had ample time to settle and
that his father was not alive when he left for exile (*Helv.* 2.4-5).
A reasonable date for the death would then be about AD 39, but at any
rate somewhere between AD 37 and 41. [35]

The eldest of Seneca's sons, Novatus, was later adopted by the close
family friend Junius Gallio and therefore more commonly known
by the adoptive name of Junius Gallio Annaeanus. A successful
politician (cos. AD 55), [36] he is best known for his role as governor
of Achaea during the visit of St. Paul (*Acts* xviii.12). The middle
son was the younger Seneca—the politician, writer, and philosopher
who was the minister of Nero and a dominant figure in the early
years of his reign. Unlike his two older brothers, Mela had no taste
for an active political career (2 pr. 3; *Helv.* 18.2), although his father
thought him to be the most talented of his three sons (2 pr. 4). Mela
filled his time and the family purse by holding lucrative equestrian
procuratorships in the emperor's service. [37] His son was Lucan, the epic
poet and ill-fated companion of Nero.

---

[33] Cf. 1 pr. 10 (on the intended publication); *Suas.* 6.19, 23 (quotations of
Cremutius Cordus); Tac. *Ann.* 4.35; Suet. *Gaius* 16 (on re-publication; cf. *Aug.*
35); also Griffin 4, notes 44, 45. She points out that Seneca might have consulted
the works in a private edition (cf. younger Seneca *Ad Marciam* 1.3-4); "... but
he could hardly have hoped to publish excerpts while the works were under an
imperial ban. While Tiberius lived there was little hope that the ban would be
lifted and Seneca was too old to count on outliving Tiberius" (Griffin 4, note 44).
That Seneca speaks of Tiberius (*Suas.* 3.7; cf. *Contr.* 7.1.27; 7.5.12) and Cassius
Severus (3 pr.) for whom a death date of AD 37 is conjectured (cf. Griffin 4,
note 43) does not necessarily prove in the instances cited that they were dead
when he was writing, but it is strong presumptive evidence.

[34] See Weinrib 151-152.

[35] See Teuffel-Schwabe 568; Bornecque 12; Edward xxiv-xxv; Duff 38-39;
Griffin 8.

[36] *PIR²* I, 757. There is some question on the exact date; cf. Weinrib 79,
note 2. On the order of the sons' birth see Griffin 7.

[37] Cf. 2 pr. 3-4; younger Seneca *Helv.* 18.2; Tac. *Ann.* 16.17. See also A.
Vassileiou, "A propos d'un passage de Sénèque le Père (*Controv.*, 2, *Praef.* 4):
La psychologie d'un père ambitieux pour ses enfants au Ier siècle ap. J.-C."
Latomus 32 (1973) 162-165.

2. Career of Seneca

Seneca's extant works deal only with declamation and so it is understandable how through the centuries librarians and scholars have
differentiated him by the title *"rhetor"* from his more famous son of
the same name. This in turn has caused the identification of him as a
practicing rhetorician when, in fact, all the evidence in his works
proves that he most assuredly was not. The collections of rhetorical
specimens were a labor of his advanced old age [38] and he most em-
phatically demonstrates a long lapse of time between their compilation
and his own participation in declamation. His days of declamation
go back to his youth—they were *antiqua studia* (1 pr. 1; cf. 10 pr. 1).
Further, there is not one single passage in all his works which indicates
that Seneca ever declaimed as an adult, though he may well have
done so on occasion. [39] The sobriquet "rhetor" should therefore be
laid to rest permanently. [40]

From his vantage point in old age and retirement, Seneca refers to
his days in school as the best of his life. [41] Such a view naturally
invites speculation that he had spent his mature years in the active
pursuits of either finance or politics and looked back nostalgically
on the declamation halls as isolated refuges from the harsh realities
and pressures of the world outside. [42] No direct evidence supports
this contention, but his circle of influential friends and the family's
wealth do not contradict either or both careers. A succession of minor
though lucrative posts—not unlike Mela's—is easily possible. In all
Seneca's critical comments, moreover, he maintains his distance from
the more frenzied followers of the fad and is also able to appreciate the

---

[38] See Italo Lana, *Lucio Anneo Seneca* (Torino 1955) 85-86; cf. Ferrill 9.
Also on the composition date see below, 91-93.

[39] Cf. the *sententiae* which may be his, cited in Quintilian (above, note 2).

[40] It is puzzling that the term has been used for such a long time and even still
persists. Cf. Bornecque 13; Edward ix-x; Ferrill 9-10; Griffin 6, 9. He should
properly be called Seneca the elder, the elder Seneca, or Lucius Annaeus Seneca
pater.

[41] *Exigitis rem magis iucundam mihi quam facilem; iubetis enim quid de his
declamatoribus sentiam qui in aetatem meam inciderunt indicare .... Est, fateor,
iucundum mihi redire in antiqua studia melioresque ad annos respicere, et vobis
querentibus quod tantae opinionis viros audire non potueritis detrahere temporum
iniuriam* (1 pr. 1). Cf. 10 pr. 1. *Primo libenter adsilui velut optimam vitae meae
partem reducturus ....* See also on the implications of these statements A. Fred
Sochatoff, "The 'Meliores Annos' of the Elder Seneca," *CW* 39 (1945-46) 70-71,
and Lewis A. Sussman, "The Artistic Unity of the Elder Seneca's First Preface
and the *Controversiae* as a Whole," *AJP* 92 (1971) 285-291.

[42] See Bornecque 13.

advantages and disadvantages of the exercise. [43] Any career as a teacher of rhetoric is inconceivable in these circumstances.

The Annaei were very wealthy, and the source of the family fortunes was almost without question in land holding and agriculture. [44] The Annaei had not only riches, but political stature in Rome. They could afford to send Seneca to school in Rome and support him for a protracted period of residence. Not long after his arrival he appears as a member of the leading political and literary sets. Seneca numbered among his friends and acquaintances Messalla, Passienus, Augustus, Maecenas, Ovid, Cassius Severus, Tiberius, Pollio, Labienus, and Haterius. His best friends, however, were the noted declaimers Latro (1 pr. 13), Gallio (who adopted his son), and Clodius Turrinus (10 pr. 14). [45]

3. Character, Philosophy, and Politics

Seneca was a provincial equestrian, and like so many of this class during the early Empire, he exemplified the conservative ideals of Roman manhood. His model was the elder Cato, whom he speaks of reverently (1 pr. 9). The younger Seneca greatly admired his father's old-fashioned sternness and dedication to the ancient moral code (*antiquus rigor*; *Helv.* 17.3); in all, he says, his father was the best of men: *virorum optimus ... maiorum consuetudini deditus* (*Helv.* 17.4). Not surprisingly, the old man was a patriot. [46] He also believed in the eventual triumph of divine justice and therefore evidently held

---

[43] A professional rhetor would certainly not have included material such as that in the third, seventh, and ninth prefaces which are so derogatory towards declamation and some of its most famous practitioners. Seneca displays a sensible perspective on the exercise, its role in education, usefulness as a preparation for the forum, and relationship to literature. See below, 71-75, 86-89; also Chapter IV *passim*.

[44] The evidence is collected in Griffin 6: the three sons of Seneca inherited their wealth from their father and Helvia managed their *patrimonia* (*Helv.* 14.3). Griffin *ibid.* finds it difficult to believe that she could manage an export business or mines, but there is a parallel to a woman supervising vineyards and olive groves (Tac. *Agr.* 7). The younger Seneca was highly interested in agriculture, took a personal hand in the management of his Italian estates and vineyards, and, in his old age, desired to learn about the techniques of transplanting trees and transferring vines. Cf. Griffin 6, note 67.

[45] See Bornecque 14. Also on Seneca's circle see Ferrill 13, 16-21, 34-37; Weinrib 109ff; also Bornecque's index of names mentioned in Seneca (143-201). The index in the Kiessling edition provides a convenient form of reference for this purpose since it records not only the place where a particular name occurs, but also Seneca's remarks about him.

[46] 1 pr. 6, 11; 10.5.28; *Suas.* 2.12; 7.10.

the proper Roman regard for religion (10 pr. 6). The obscenity and
vulgarity then rampant in the declamation schools offended his sense
of decency (1.2.21), as did the luxurious living and effeminacy of the
younger generation (1 pr. 7-10). Seneca admired the resilience and
inner strength of Pollio, who was able to attend a banquet and declaim
resolutely shortly after the death of his son. [47] And there is no mis-
taking the impression throughout the works of a *paterfamilias* deeply
concerned about the moral enlightenment of his sons, their education,
and their future careers. [48] He was a model of industry for his sons;
in advanced old age he began the arduous task of compiling the
collections of rhetorical specimens and the more ambitious project
of writing an historical account of Rome. Nor did he flag in his
efforts until shortly before the day of his death.

Several remarks by his son indicate that Seneca displayed the
typically Roman dislike of philosophy. [49] Examination of the crucial
passages forces us to temper this conventional assessment. In one
of the letters to Lucilius (*Ep.* 108.22), the younger Seneca relates
how his father dissuaded him from vegetarianism. Various new cults
had then come into vogue—and official disfavor. [50] Abstinence from
certain kinds of meats could be construed as evidence of participation
in the forbidden cults. At his father's request the younger Seneca
gave up his vegetarianism, and he attributes his father's efforts to his
dislike of philosophy. As a young man he may well have misread
his father's motives; prosecution for such an offense would not

---

[47] With this example he unfavorably contrasts the overly sentimental and weak
Haterius who wept uncontrollably during the course of a declamation which
reminded him of his dead son (4 pr. 6, 11; cf. *Suas.* 2.15).

[48] See 2 pr. 4; younger Seneca *Ep.* 108.22; also the good descriptions of Seneca
in Bornecque 16 and Griffin 13.

[49] *In primum Tiberii Caesaris principatum iuventae tempus inciderat. Alienigena
tum sacra movebantur, sed inter argumenta superstitionis ponebatur quorundam
animalium abstinentia. Patre itaque meo rogante, qui non calumniam timebat,
sed philosophiam oderat, ad pristinam consuetudinem redii* (younger Seneca *Ep.*
108.22). Cf. *Helv.* 17.3-4: *... quantum tibi patris mei antiquus rigor permisit,
omnes bonas artes non quidem comprehendisti, attigisti tamen. Utinam quidem
virorum optimus pater meus, minus maiorum consuetudini deditus, voluisset te
praeceptis sapientiae erudiri potius quam imbui! Non parandum tibi nunc esset
auxilium contra fortunam, sed proferendum. Propter istas quae litteris non ad
sapientiam utuntur, sed ad luxuriam instruuntur, minus te indulgere studiis passus
est. Beneficio tamen rapacis ingenii plus quam pro tempore hausisti: iacta sunt
disciplinarum omnium fundamenta.* See also 7 pr. 1.

[50] *Actum est de sacris Aegyptiis Iudiacisque pellendis ...* (Tac. *Ann.* 2.85; cf.
H. Furneaux (ed.), *The Annals of Tacitus* (2nd ed.; 2 vols., Oxford 1896) I,
note *ad loc.*

recommend itself for one planning a career in politics. [51] In another passage (*Helv.* 17.3-4) the younger Seneca reports that his father dissuaded his mother Helvia from deep study in philosophy. But the grounds here are interesting; he thought such studies unbecoming for a Roman matron.

More instructive is the elder Seneca's very favorable attitutde towards two Stoic philosophers and his compliment to Stoicism in general which he terms "such lofty and manly teachings." [52] Of course the elder Seneca was not a Stoic or even much interested at all in philosophy, although his wife and son obviously were. But he certainly did not hate philosophy and may well have absorbed some Stoic doctrine through their influence.

For a man of Seneca's sentiments and character, his politics are not as easy to reconstruct as it might first seem. His provincial background may help to clear up some of the complexities.

Cordova was a deeply Romanized city founded about 152 BC and inhabited largely by distinguished settlers who possessed the *ius Latii*. [53] The city was noted for its poets, prosperity, and literary atmosphere. During the civil wars it passed through the hands of Pompey, Caesar, and perhaps Sextus Pompey. [54] Although Pompeian *clientela* was very powerful in this part of Spain, there was also a strong and distinguished Caesarian party. The political position of Cordova throughout the wars was characteristically ambiguous. [55]

---

[51] See Ferrill 26-27. Philosophers were expelled from Rome in AD 16 and AD 19.

[52] ... *tam sanctis fortibusque praeceptis* (2 pr. 1). Here he is speaking of the Stoic philosopher Papirius Fabianus then studying declamation as a preparation for philosophy. Throughout the second preface Seneca is complimentary to the man. His remarks on the philosopher Attalus Stoicus are also favorable: ... *magnae vir eloquentiae, ex his philosophis, quos vestra aetas vidit longe et subtilissimus et facundissimus* (*Suas.* 2.12; cf. Weinrib 95-96).

[53] Strabo 3.2.15. It is referred to in the early Empire as a *colonia patricia* (Pliny *HN* 3.1.10; cf. *CIL* II Suppl. 1143), and was composed of an elite group (Strabo 3.2.1). Cf. Hübner, "Corduba," *P-W* vol. 4, cols. 1221-1224. The inhabitants of the city vigorously asserted their devotion to Roman ways (Cic. *Arch.* 10.26). Strabo is in error when he suggests that the city was established as a *colonia*; the title *colonia patricia* dates to the reign of Augustus; cf. Griffin 2, 4, 17-19.

[54] Sextus Pompey is not definitely known to have molested Cordova, although he was in the general vicinity (Broughton *MRR* II, 329; Cic. *Att.* 16.4.2). Some trouble may have occurred fairly close to the city (*Anth. Lat.* 409). But he was harbored at least for a time in the city (Dio 45.10.1; cf. 43.39.1).

[55] During the civil wars Caesar summoned an assembly in Cordova and at one time the city refused entrance to the Pompeian general Varro (Caes. *BCiv.* 2.19). In 48 BC Cordova begged not to be forced to move against Caesar

But because the Pompeians were so strong in the region and because of the Republican tone evident in all their writings, the loyalties of the Annaei are conventionally termed Pompeian. Seneca himself speaks of the arch-Pompeian historian Labienus in favorable terms and ringingly denounces the burning of his writings. This is the same Labienus "... who had not yet laid aside his Pompeian loyalties in this time of such an extensive peace." [56] Quite possibly the Annaei did have Pompeian leanings, for a while. But they emerged from the civil wars with their fortunes flourishing, and soon, imperial favor. The combination suggests Caesarian connections and perhaps an early alliance with Octavian. [57]

Strong evidence attests to friendship and a political alliance between the Annaei and Asinius Pollio. By implication we may be able to deduce a shared allegiance to the Caesarian cause. Pollio declaimed only in private (4 pr. 2), yet he allowed Seneca, a young Spanish provincial of equestrian family, to enter these secluded declamatory sessions shortly after his consulship (40 BC), and then much later, shortly before his death. [58] The inception of this relationship must date back to 43 BC when Pollio was living in Cordova. [59] In such

---

(BAlex. 58.4), but later it became a stronghold for Pompeians (BHisp. 33; Cic. Fam. 9.13.1; Dio 43.29.3). There were still Caesarian stalwarts, however, ready to betray the city (BHisp. 2, 34; Dio 43.32.3), one of whom apparently was the father of Clodius Turrinus, the friend of Seneca; cf. 10 pr. 16; Weinrib 32-33, 37, 54-55. On the divided loyalties of the region see Griffin 14-15.

[56] ... qui Pompeianos spiritus nondum in tanta pace posuisset (10 pr. 5). Cf. Griffin 5, 13-15. Apparently pro-Pompeian sentiments appear also in the works of the younger Seneca and Lucan, but a more balanced opinion of Caesar exists in these writers than previously supposed; cf. R. E. Wolverton, "Speculum Caesaris," in Mary Francis Gyles and Eugene Wood Davis (eds.), Laudatores Temporis Acti: Studies in Memory of Wallace Everett Caldwell (Chapel Hill 1964) 82-88.

[57] As does the close relationship with Clodius Turrinus and his family (10 pr. 14-16); cf. Weinrib 54, 104-105; Griffin 15. The elder Seneca was sent by his family to school at Rome fairly soon after the events of 43 BC, therefore the basis of their wealth must have been essentially intact at the close of the fighting.

[58] We know from Seneca's own statement that Pollio did not declaim in public (4 pr. 2). Yet Seneca was a member of that select group which was admitted into Pollio's private declamatory sessions throughout his lifetime: Audivi autem illum [Pollio] et viridem et postea iam senem, cum Marcello Aesernino nepoti suo quasi praeciperet (4 pr. 3). The adjective viridem would suggest a relatively young age for Pollio; cf. Verg. Aen. 5.295; Ovid Tr. 4.10.17; Quint. Curt. 10.5.10. Griffin 5 places the event early in Pollio's retirement after his triumph, or 39-38 BC. This, the detailed description which follows (4 pr. 3-6) of Pollio's declamatory and oratorical styles, and the vivid portrayal of his personal qualities (4 pr. 3-6) testify to much more than a casual relationship between the men.

[59] Cic. Fam. 10.31, 32, 33; cf. Broughton MRR II, 327, 343.

a cultured city known for its literary aspirations, Pollio would not have failed to make the acquaintance of the leading families and especially the writers of the area in whom he exhibited a lasting critical interest. [60]

At the time of Pollio's residence in Cordova, Seneca was a schoolboy aged perhaps ten or twelve who was impatiently awaiting the day when the war would subside and he could continue his rhetorical study in Rome (1 pr. 11). When the civil war finally did end, Seneca went to the imperial capital and was admitted into Pollio's house. Soon the young provincial became acquainted with the leading literary and political luminaries of the day. His acceptance in these circles attests to wealth, leisure, ability, and ambition. Especially notable is Seneca's high regard for Augustus and certain acquaintance with him: the Annaei may have cast their lot with him early and so reaped the rewards. [61]

Through Helvia's sister, also named Helvia, Seneca became the brother-in-law of C. Galerius, the equestrian prefect of Egypt under Tiberius for an unprecedented sixteen years, and undoubtedly "the most important equestrian official in the imperial administration of the Emperor Tiberius." [62] This useful political connection did not go unused; the younger Seneca lavishly thanked his aunt for her assistance in furthering his political career (*Helv.* 19.2). Some evidence suggests that through Galerius the Annaei may have become adherents of

---

[60] Griffin cites the Cordovan poet Sextilius Ena and Seneca's friend Latro (Griffin 5, note 54; cf. *Contr.* 2.3.13; *Excerpta* 4.6 *extra*; *Suas.* 6.27).

[61] *Tanta autem sub divo Augusto libertas fuit* (2.4.13); ... *divus Augustus, ut erat mos clementissimo viro* (4 pr. 5); cf. 2.4.12; 2.5.20; 10 pr. 14; 10.5.21-22. The younger Seneca's opinions reflect those of his father (*De Ira* 3.23.7-8; *Ben.* 3.27.1-4; cf. Ferrill 122, note 85 and the works there cited). One may compare the remarks of Velleius, who saw and similarly appreciated the Principate as the reestablishment of a stable order (2.131.1); cf. Richard L. Anderson, *The Rise and Fall of Middle Class Loyalty to the Roman Empire: A Social Study of Velleius Paterculus and Ammianus Marcellinus* (diss., Berkeley 1962) 53-54 (with much citation), 56ff, 65-66.

[62] Ferrill 12; cf. Weinrib 88, 130; Griffin 7-8 and note 82. Shrewd marriages of the Annaei are attested: Mela and the daughter of a prominent Cordovan orator (Weinrib 90); the younger Seneca and Pompeia Paulina, whose father was a *praefectus annonae* and whose brother was a consul (Weinrib 89); Lucan and Argentaria Polla, a wealthy and cultured lady (Weinrib 90-91). The geographic origin of the wives was diverse: "What mattered was not geographical origin but wealth, social standing, and education, and these were elements which all the women of the Annaei shared in various degrees" (Weinrib 91-92).

Sejanus. [63] Such a connection could help to explain the younger Seneca's vitriolic hatred of Tiberius. Seneca also knew the Vinicii well. One member of this influential political family was briefly a candidate for emperor. [64]

4. *Views of the Republic and the Principate*

The intense and bitter civil discord in Spain during his childhood left its mark on Seneca; he characterizes the time with the term *furor* (1 pr. 11). Three *Controversiae* deal with the period of the proscriptions (4.8; 7.2; 10.3) as do *Suasoriae* 6 and 7. Seneca also describes in sympathetic terms the varying fortunes of his friends the Clodii Turrini, caused by the ebb and flow of civil war in Spain (10 pr. 16). The Annaei unquestionably welcomed the stability of the Principate and the opportunities afforded to the provincial *equites* by Augustus for new prospects of enrichment, participation in the government, and eventual advancement to the senatorial order. [65]

Seneca lived through the worst years of the Republic and the best of the Principate. Nevertheless in the extant works there appears disillusionment with the Principate and the uncovering of some Republican sentiments. He recognized the system for what it was; not a "Republic restored" (*res publica restituta*) as the Augustan slogan went, but rather an autocracy which could be benevolent at times— or despotic. The actions of Tiberius in the 20's and 30's AD may have

---

[63] See Zeph Stewart, "Sejanus, Gaetulicus and Seneca," *AJP* 74 (1953) 70-85 *passim*; Ferrill 29-30; but Weinrib 153.

[64] The elder Seneca quotes or mentions two of the Vinicii, at some length and usually in a complimentary way: L. Vinicius (son of the cos. of 33 BC; perhaps cos. suff. of 5 BC; cf. Winterbottom II, 634) 2.5.19-20; also P. Vinicius (perhaps cos. AD 2; cf. Winterbottom II, 364) 1.2.3; 1.4.11; 7.5.11-12; 7.6.11; 10.4.25. Velleius dedicated his historical work to a member of this family, M. Vinicius, cos. AD 30 and 45, a man briefly mentioned as a candidate for emperor after the death of Gaius (Joseph. *AJ* 19.251). There is a connection between this Vinicius and the Annaei: the younger Seneca was apparently a member of his circle of friends and a political ally of his wife, Julia Livilla, with whom he was accused of adultery and therefore exiled by Claudius at Messalina's behest in AD 41. She was a daughter of Germanicus and a granddaughter of Tiberius (cf. Tac. *Ann.* 6.15; *PIR*² 4.1674). The Vinicii have not received the attention they deserve, but a good beginning has been made by G. V. Sumner, "The Truth about Velleius Paterculus," *HSCP* 74 (1970) 28ff. See also Ronald Syme, "M. Vinicius (cos. 19 BC)," *CQ* 27 (1933) 142-148.

[65] See 2 pr. 3-4, where he dwells on the political ambitions of the younger Seneca and Novatus as opposed to their absence in Mela, who is content to remain an equestrian. Cf. the remarks of the younger Seneca on his rank; *Helv.* 18.1-3; echoed in a different context, Tac. *Ann.* 14.53.

prompted this incipient anti-imperialism, or perhaps the behavior of Augustus near the end of his reign when *libertas* was curtailed, histories burned, and Seneca's friend Ovid exiled. The roots may even extend further, but the evidence is clear:

(1) Although he was aware of the man's faults, Seneca genuinely admired Cicero in a period when that orator, his works, and his career were in low esteem. [66] He surely did not forget the young Octavian's implication in the death of his cherished hero. The idealization of men such as Cicero and the elder Cato of course is not *prima facie* evidence of staunch Republicanism. [67] Nevertheless, it is suggestive in the larger context.

(2) Seneca isolates three possible causes for the decline of eloquence (1 pr. 6-7), two of which implicate the Principate. [68] For one he suggests that the immorality of the age may have inhibited eloquence. Obviously, then, he regards the Augustan program for moral rejuvenation as a sham. His lengthy discussion of contemporary moral corruption is particularly damning (1 pr. 8-10). Another reason which he submits for the decline is the lack of rewards for eloquence, and the consequent transferral of ambition to baser but more lucrative pursuits. Perhaps he means here sycophancy and delation, both perversions of true eloquence. Seneca has astutely recognized the basic

[66] On the faults see Seneca's quotation of and praise for Livy's impartial assessment of Cicero (*Suas.* 6.21-22). Seneca frequently mentions (and indirectly censures) the *obtrectatores Ciceronis,* so prominent when he was writing; e.g., Cestius (3 pr. 15-17; *Suas.* 7.13-14) and even Pollio (*Suas.* 6.14-15, 27; cf. Edward 140 note *ad loc., Asinio Pollione*). Cicero was little read and Seneca says that it was possible to deliver a Verrine oration as one's own without detection (*Suas.* 2.19). Also on the detractors of Cicero see Quint. 9.4.1; 11.1.17ff; 12.1.14, 16ff; 12.10.12-15; Tac. *Dial. 18.* Seneca thinks Cicero the equal of the best Greek orators (1 pr. 11; cf. 1 pr. 6-7; 7.4.6; *Suas.* 6.14-27 *passim*; 7.10; also see Quint. 10.1.105). He thought Cicero's career marked the high point of Roman eloquence (1 pr. 6-7; 7.4.6; 10 pr. 6-7). Seneca was himself deeply indebted to Cicero's style and critical vocabulary (Bardon 65-67). Seneca's interest in Cicero is reflected also by the three declamations in the collection which concern the last days of the orator's life (*Contr.* 7.2; *Suas.* 6, 7).

[67] A point made well by C. Wirszubski, *Libertas as a Political Idea at Rome during the Late Republic and Early Principate* (Cambridge 1950, repr. 1960) 127-128. For example, the younger Seneca is able to admire Brutus, Cato, and the other heroes of the Republic, yet he could criticize their inability to recognize the political realities of their day (*Ep.* 14.13; *Ben.* 2.20.2). Literary Republicanism was conventional; cf. Griffin 13-14.

[68] The third cause of decline, a natural cycle of growth and decay in all matters, is apparently without political significance. See Sussman "Decline of Eloquence" 195-210 (and citations there) for further discussion of the issue.

change of the system. Freedom was lost and political distinction could no longer be assured through eloquence in the forum.

(3) Seneca directly warns his sons that politics in the Empire is a very dangerous game (2 pr. 3-4).

(4) He violently opposes imperial interference with freedom of speech, in particular the policy of burning books. [69]

(5) Several of the elder Seneca's closest acquaintances were critical of the regime; e.g., Cassius Severus, Labienus, Pollio, and perhaps Gallio. [70]

(6) Augustus or Tiberius had persecuted several friends; e.g., Ovid, Labienus, Gallio (Tac. *Ann.* 6.3), and Attalus Stoicus (*Suas.* 2.12). [71]

But Seneca was a realist who recognized that the Republic was dead. Though sometimes repressive, the Principate was necessary to maintain order. So these critical attitudes in no way dissuaded the Annaei from enjoying the perquistes of influence, prosperity, and public office:

> The Annaei provide the best-attested and most spectucular example of the advancement of provincials under the regime of the Julio-Claudians. [72]

They rightly concluded that the best way to deal with the system was to accept it, work within it, and manipulate it to one's own advantage. And in just this fashion the family achieved its notable success. Seneca's sons became reigning figures in literature and politics through the influence of shrewd political friendships, beneficial marriage connections, and, of course, their own native abilities. The father himself must have been a well-known figure in the various influential Roman circles: the ambitious, wealthy, and witty provincial, busily laying the foundations of an ill-starred dynasty which enjoyed a brilliant if brief period of political and literary ascendancy. His political views then were neither wholly Republican nor Augustan, but were characterized by cold realism mingled with regret—and opportunism. A comparison with the politics of Tacitus is instructive.

---

[69] See below, 87 and notes 181, 182.

[70] See Weinrib 109-114.

[71] If the Lactantius fragment of the lost *Histories* (on which see below, 139-141) is genuine, then there is a sixth indication of anti-imperial sentiments: *Amissa enim libertate, quam Bruto duce et auctore defenderat, ita consenuit, tamquam sustentare se ipsa non valeret, nisi adminiculo regentium uteretur* (*Div. Inst.* 7.15.16). Cf. Jacqueline Brisset, *Les Idées Politiques de Lucain* (Paris 1964) 6.

[72] Weinrib 164. It is apparent that the elder Seneca saw himself as the patriarch of a growing political dynasty; cf. 2 pr. 3-4; also see René Waltz, *Vie de Sénèque* (Paris 1909) 22-23.

CHAPTER THREE

THE *CONTROVERSIAE* AND *SUASORIAE*

1. *Title and Text*

In their original state the rhetorical works of the elder Seneca formed two separate entities. The larger work consisted of ten books of extracts from *controversiae* grouped within the respective books according to the declamation themes from which they were taken. A prefatory letter to his sons introduced every book. Two or more books of *suasoriae* extracts, each also divided according to theme and presumably introduced by a preface, formed the smaller work. [1] The inclusive title generally given to the entire collection of specimens is *Oratorum et Rhetorum Sententiae, Divisiones, Colores* (*The Sententiae, Divisions, and Colors of the Orators and Rhetoricians*), but they are usually referred to separately as the *Controversiae* and the *Suasoriae*.

Unfortunately, in the best MSS only five books of *controversiae* (Books 1, 2, 7, 9, 10) and one book of *suasoriae* remain. The prefaces to *Controversiae* 1 and 2 and also to the *Suasoriae* are lacking in this tradition. In the fourth or fifth century an excerptor prepared a summary of all ten books of the *Controversiae*, to which he added six of the prefaces (to Books 1, 2, 3, 4, 7, 10). This abridgement has survived intact and attests to the popularity of Seneca in that period. [2]

Thus there are two main groups of MSS: (1) those containing the full surviving text of the *Controversiae* and *Suasoriae* with the exception of the prefaces to *Controversiae* 1 and 2, and (2) those containing the *excerpta* and the prefaces to *Controversiae* 1, 2, 3, 4, 7, 10. The three primary MSS of the first group, all of the ninth and tenth

---

[1] In the manuscripts B, V, and D after *Suas.* 7 there is a note explaining that the first book of *Suasoriae* ends there, and a second one will now begin. Cf. Bornecque 32; Edward xxx. In *Contr.* 2.4.8 Seneca promises to report a quotation from Latro in the *suasoria* about Theodotus; the *suasoria* itself (and thus the quotation) does not survive. His statement also proves that the *Contr.* were assembled first and this is the order in which they should appear: *Contr.*, then *Suas.* However, the contemporary educational practice had students composing *suasoriae* first, and therefore many older editions ordered the works in reverse of their composition.

[2] The preface to Book 9 breaks off in the middle, while the declamations ending Books 2 and 10 of the *Contr.* are incomplete.

centuries, are the Codex Antverpiensis (A), the Codex Bruxellensis (B), and the Codex Vaticanus (V). Because of their basic similarities Müller concludes that all three are from the same archetype (C), now lost. [3]

2. Sententiae, *Divisions, Colors*

As the inclusive title of the work suggests, the extracts from the various declaimers were grouped under the three headings of *sententiae*, divisions, and colors. The adoption of this arrangement is in itself highly significant and sheds light on the state of declamation in the early Empire. A better understanding of Seneca's work and the changes then occurring in rhetorical style requires some inquiry into the nature of *sententiae*, divisions, and colors as they were known in that period.

Sententiae

An integral and extremely popular ornament of rhetoric in Seneca's day was the *sententia*: a brief, pointed, clever or profound expression whose use especially delighted Roman audiences when it occurred at the end of a periodic sentence (Quint. 8.5.2-3) or long paragraph. *Sententiae* could be gnomic, proverbial, and universal in application or pertain expressly to the specifics of the individual speech. [4] No single English word adequately describes this device and it is therefore convenient to retain the Latin term.

Analogous in some ways to the Greek γνώμη, the *sententia* developed independently in Rome, but undoubtedly felt some Greek influence. The anonymous author of the *Rhetorica ad Herennium* confines the *sententia* to a universal usage, and does not allow it to apply to particular instances:

> A *sententia* is an utterance taken from life which shows briefly what either is or ought to be in life. For instance, "Each beginning is difficult" (*Ad Her.* 4.24).

---

[3] Pp. XII-XIII. Müller gives an additional conjectural stemma which describes the relationship between these MSS and the major later ones. On the textual tradition cf. the articles cited in Whitehorne 15-16 and Winterbottom's "Note on Text and Translations," I, xxvi-xxix.

[4] See Bonner 54-55 (with numerous examples of both types and citations). A typical example of the universal type is: *omnis instabilis et incerta felicitas est*, "All happiness is unstable and uncertain" (1.1.3; Winterbottom transl.). An example of the more specific type is in the words of Alexander's advisor as the king deliberates whether or not to sail across the ocean: *Non quaerimus orbem, sed amittimus*, "We are not in search of a world—we are losing one" (*Suas.* 1.2; Winterbottom transl.).

This older conception of the device was therefore nearly identical to
the Greek γνώμη, and the *sententia* did not acquire its more limited
applications until much later (Quint. 8.5.3). The early versions fell
in two categories: (1) the short *sententia* which expressed a generally
held truth, and (2) the extended *sententia* which added an explanation
to the short gnomic statement:

> They who think that the sins of youth deserve indulgence are
> deceived, because that time of life does not constitute a hindrance
> to sound studious activities. But they act wisely who chastise the
> young with especial severity in order to inculcate at the age most
> opportune for it the desire to attain those virtues by which they
> can order their whole lives. [5]

In this same section the anonymous author tells us that the charm of
a *sententia* lies in brevity and infrequent usage. As Aristotle did
centuries before (*Rhet.* 1395 b), he correctly emphasizes the persuasive
effect of introducing a universally held principle into an individual case.

However, the exclusively gnomic *sententia* was soon supplemented
by those with more limited applications (Quint. 8.5.4, 7, 10-13, 15-25)
and both kinds appear in the speeches of Cicero. As with so many
other aspects of rhetoric, numerous sub-classifications were added
(Quint. 8.5.5-25).

Seneca presents *sententiae* in the first portion of each theme. They
also occur in the colors section, since these were frequently expressed
through *sententiae*. But an examination of the sections assigned to
sententiae does not reveal just a succession of individual, unrelated
aphoristic sentences. On the contrary, in the opening *sententiae*
sections there are often longer portions of a declamation presented
in connected form, as for example the opening three sections of
Contr. 1.1, devoted to the remarks of Latro. Although most of these
and similar texts are sententious in nature, it would not be accurate
to classify each and every one as a *sententia* in the sense we have
so far discussed. Therefore either Seneca is using a broader definition
of *sententia* which includes any type of uttered expression, or, more
likely, he finds it more congenial and less numbing to present relatively
continuous sections of a declamation. However, in the sections devoted
to colors we find many short *sententiae* placed out of context. These
are closer to the conventional notion of the device.

The following *sententiae* are typical of this terse form of expression:

---

[5] *Ad Her.* 4.25; Caplan transl. Cf. Quint. 8.5.3-4.

nulla satis pudica est de qua quaeritur ("no woman is sufficiently chaste about whom an investigation is made," *Contr.* 1.2.10); *nunc illi militent quibus necesse est*; *tu militabis si erit necesse* ("now let those go to war for whom it is a necessity; you will go to war if it becomes necessary," 1.8.12); *facilius in amore finem inpetres quam modum* ("in love you may obtain an end more easily than a limit," 2.2.10); *in scholastica quid non supervacuum est, cum ipsa supervacua sit* ("in declamation what is not superfluous when declamation itself is superfluous?" 3 pr. 12); *misero si flere non licet, magis flendum est* ("If we are not allowed to weep for a pitiable person, then we must weep all the more," *Excerpta* 3.8); *miserrima soror, sub tyranno patrem desiderabas, sub patre tyrannum desideras* ("most pitiable sister, under a tyrant you were longing for your father, under your father you are longing for a tyrant," 7.6.7).

We should not look at *sententiae* as purely rhetorical in origin or usage. Undoubtedly their appearance in such diverse poetical genres as tragedy, comedy, epigram, mime, and Atellan farce influenced their use in prose. [6] But Roman poets in the early Empire often looked to *sententiae* in declamation for inspiration. The well known discussion of this trend occurs in Seneca's reminiscences of Ovid, who adapted many of the *sententiae* authored by M. Porcius Latro into his own poetry. [7] Declamatory *sententiae* abound in Ovid's works, most notably in the *Heroides* which in many ways resemble poetic *suasoriae*. [8] Although it is fashionable now to criticize the Roman preoccupation with *sententiae*, when intelligently and sparingly applied they could be quite effective and attractive, as Quintilian observes:

> ... who can deny their usefulness, provided they are relevant to the case, are not too diffuse and contribute to our success? For they strike the mind and often produce a decisive effect by one single blow, while their brevity makes them cling to the memory, and the pleasure they produce has the force of persuasion. [9]

Quintilian rightly emphasizes the utility of *sententiae*, a factor which contributed greatly to their popularity. Seneca records an occasion on which one *sententia* served also as an elegant transition and an

---

[6] Cf. Kennedy *ARRW* 325 and note 34.

[7] *Contr.* 2.2.8; cf. Winterbottom's notes *ad loc.*

[8] Concerning the influence of declamatory *sententiae* upon the literature of the early Empire, see Bonner 149-167 *passim*.

[9] Quint. 12.10.48; Butler transl. On the excessive use of *sententiae* see Norden *AK* I, 280ff.

effective figure (1.1.25). This use of a *sententia* for a transition
from one part of the speech to another became widespread, and finally,
overdone. [10] The rhetoricians liked the versatility of *sententiae*: they
could be used for a multiplicity of functions within a speech. [11]

Seneca and his generation enjoyed *sententiae* and employed them
extensively, but it was the younger generation, as exemplified by his
sons, who became really enamored of them. One of Seneca's main
motivations in assembling his collection of rhetorical reminiscences
was to satisfy the intense desire of his sons to inspect outstanding
sententiae authored by the great declaimers of the past. [12] Famous men
and important politicians frequently used *sententiae* and would often
critically discuss the merits and failures of various examples. [13] An
exceptionally good one passed swiftly among the declaimers and could
confer an instant reputation upon its author. [14]

Originally speakers saved *sententiae* for the end of a periodic sentence, but so popular did they become that eventually the period itself
gave way to a more choppy arrangement of numerous *sententiae*
strung loosely together. We should not assume that the *sententiae*
sections reflect the predominant style of composition in all declamations. Seneca is obviously providing his readers with extraordinary
examples, and it would be inaccurate to conclude that the periodic
style had died by the time Seneca was writing. [15] The style of his
own prefaces amply demonstrates otherwise. But the obvious pleasure
of Seneca in reproducing especially good *sententiae* and the great
interest they held for his sons are indicative of the transition then
occurring towards the shorter, terse sentences characteristic of the
emerging Silver Age style.

Division

Division was the manner in which a declaimer planned and outlined
the argumentation of his case, and is not related to the similar term

---

10 *Contr.* 1.1.25; 1.8.1; 7.1.26; cf. Bonner 54 and notes 3, 4. In a similar function
it was applied to poetry, most notably Ovid in the *Met.* (cf. Quint. 4.1.77-78).

11 As commonplaces (e.g., 1 pr. 23), proverbs (e.g., 7.3.8-9; cf. younger Seneca
Ep. 8.8-10), *exempla* (e.g., 2.1.17), colors, stylistic ornaments, comparisons (e.g.,
9.4.5), in the narration portion of a speech (e.g., 2.5.1-2), and in the argumentation.

12 1 pr. 22; cf. 2 pr. 5; 4 pr. 1. On the high regard for *sententiae* see Bornecque
106-107 and Clarke 95; also Quint. 8.5.14; cf. Quint. 1.8.9; 2.11.3; 2.12.7; 4.1.77;
5.13.31, 42; 8.4.29; 8.5.1ff.

13 Cf. Clarke 96-97; also *Contr.* 2.2.8; 10.1.14; Petr. *Sat.* 6; Tac. *Dial.* 20.

14 See Bornecque 28-29; D'Alton 212; cf. *Contr.* 2.4.9; 7.6.15; 9.2.23; 10.1.14;
10.2.10; Tac. *Dial.* 20.

15 Cf. Norden *AK* I, 283.

meaning the disposition of the various parts of a speech (*prooemium, narratio, argumentum, epilogus*). From his own comments, Seneca appears to have considered division the least important of the three topics he planned to treat in the *Controversiae* (I pr. 22), yet practice in division would undoubtedly form the most useful preparation for a future advocate. [16] Perhaps this lower regard for division is due to the regular practice of advocates to employ consultants on these fairly complex and technical matters. [17] At any rate, Seneca was sure that extended discussion of this highly technical subject would bore his sons, who were not genuinely interested in this aspect of rhetoric (I pr. 22).

The argument, of which division was the outline, occurred after the narration. The most skillful declaimers often made the division very elaborate. Consequently the argumentation sometimes became very confusing to the audiences. Latro habitually delivered a short clarification before beginning a *controversia* in order to avoid such confusion (I pr. 21).

Since the number of *controversiae* themes was limited, the manner in which the declaimers argued them probably became fairly stereotyped. [18] Therefore after he set forth the various points of contention in the speech, a good declaimer would try to find a new point to argue, or would attempt to follow some freer, more clever line of argumentative reasoning. This display of mental dexterity must have been one of the more worthy elements of declamation.

In the *controversiae* which have survived, the arguments are usually divided under the two headings of the law (*ius*) and equity (*aequitas*). [19] As the Latin name implies, *ius* refers to a strict, legalistic definition applied to the defendant's action. Thus the declaimer would ask the *quaestiones iuris*: was the defendant allowed to act or could he act as he did under the terms of the law (*An liceat? An possit?*). When appealing to *aequitas*, the declaimer asked philosophical questions on the equity of the defendant's action. Often he employed commonplaces for support. The declaimer's management (*tractatio*) of this aspect of argument thus rested on asking whether the defendant should have

---

[16] Exercise in division was certainly "most valuable practice in logical thinking, legal interpretation, and clear coordination of argument" (Bonner 39). Cf. *Decl. Min.* 270.

[17] See Kennedy *ARRW* 14, 332.

[18] Cf. Edward xxxv.

[19] See Bornecque 51-52; 103-104; Bardon 71-76; Bonner 56-57.

done the act or whether it was necessary (*An debeat? An opor-tuerit?*).[20] An appeal to equity was especially effective when there was no conflict on the commission of an illegal act, or when the act was covered under two contrary laws. For example, in the situation of *Contr.* 1.1 the law says that a son can be disinherited for disobedience, but on the other hand he is also legally compelled to provide support for his father. The declaimers had ample material for appealing to an abstract sense of justice in showing that the latter law must take precedence over the former. Such an appeal would also be useful in a court system where the jury was often free to dismiss evidence and even the applicable law in arriving at its decision.

The division of argument according to *ius/aequitas* generally fol-lowed the *stasis* theory of Hermagoras, and was usually simple, straightforward, and suitable to most of the declamatory cases.[21] Such a division of argument probably resembled very closely the practice in the courts; Seneca himself assigns this plan of argument to the ancient practitioners.[22] But the younger generation of declaimers became dissatisfied with the older, simpler arrangement, and desired

---

[20] Seneca does not always use the correct terminology, nor do all declaimers employ this conventional system which has been described (e.g., 1.1.13). Seneca recognizes a gray area between *tractatio* and *quaestio*, and also appreciates the imperfections of the nomenclature system (1.1.14). The development of equity is usually termed *quaestio,* sometimes *pars* (7.8.9), and such a *quaestio,* modified slightly can become a *tractatio.* For discussion of this, see the citations above, note 19.

[21] Kennedy *ARRW* 325-326. For a more detailed exposition of this theory see esp. his remarks on Hermogenes (*ibid.* 620-625, with much citation) and on Hermagoras *APG* 306-313. Kennedy's observations on *stasis* in *controversiae* are helpful (*ARRW* 325-326):

"Division" does not refer to arrangement of the speech, but to the logical divisions of the subject into its principal issues, usually along the lines of the theory of *stasis* originally developed by Hermagoras. Hermagoras made an overall division into questions of law and questions of fact or justice. This commonly appears in Seneca as a division between law and equity. The divisions of Porcius Latro almost always involved the question *an liceat,* "Is it permitted?" and *an debeat,* "Is it right?" (cf., e.g., *Contr.* 1.1.13; 7.1.16-17). If there is no doubt about the law, the question then becomes one of fact, definition, or quality (cf., e.g., *Contr.* 2.5.10). Seneca occasionally uses the technical term for *stasis* of fact, *coniecturalis* ... but he is not very rigid in his classification. Sometimes rather considerable subdivision of the question or involved argumentation is found ... though declaimers often neglected argumentation ... and relied on ethos, pathos, and general hyperbole for proof. They were much given to arguing along *a fortiori* lines from an unwarranted assumption to a foregone conclusion ....

[22] 1.1.13. Cicero himself used it; cf. Bonner 46.

more intricate treatments of division. 23 Since a declaimer did not regularly face an opponent, he had to anticipate each possible point on which the opposition might base his case. This practice, a necessary one owing to the conditions of declaiming a *controversia,* also contributed greatly to the extent and complexity of the division. 24 On the other hand, the division of argument in the deliberative *suasoriae,* given the simpler nature of the issues, was quite straightforward, often employing philosophical commonplaces and historical examples while resorting to the standard questions, "is it honorable?" "is it expedient?" and the like.

Colors

Colors are subtle, unusual, and clever twists of circumstance and argumentation by which the declaimers tried to alter the interpretation of the facts in a case. Since they involved judicial questions of guilt or innocence, colors were not used in *suasoriae.* Depending upon the side he represented, the declaimer would use colors which tended either to intensify or mitigate the blame of the accused. Colors were important adjuncts to formal argumentation. An effective color occurs in the first *controversia* of Book 1 (1.1.16ff), where the son defends himself for breaking his adoptive father's order not to support his poverty-stricken natural father. The son heavily emphasizes the strong bonds of emotion and filial devotion which compelled him to aid his natural father. More specifically, in this declamation Albucius has the natural father confront his son, read out the statute requiring sons to support their fathers, and then demand obedience to the law. Next he adds a damaging blow to the other side: says the son in his own defence, "I offered him not as much as I ought to offer a father, but as much as I could take secretly from one who forbade it" (1.1.17). Another declaimer in the same case vividly describes an unknown, disheveled old man falling at the feet of the youth, who was at the time known for his generosity. "I lifted him up when I did not know who he was. Do you want me to reject him because he is my father?" (1.1.19).

---

23 E.g., 1.1.13. Parks 78-79 notices that within the treatment of *aequitas* is one of the most important contributions of Roman law : the development of a concept of equity in which the object of the legal process becomes justice and completeness. Cf. *Cambridge Ancient History* II, 907; also Quint. 3.6.73. Complete devotion to the letter of the law was beginning to give way to the spirit of the law. Cf. *Contr.* 9.4.9; Quint. 3.6.87.

24 Cf. above, 15. For a case of extreme complexity, cf. 7 pr. 1-2. On the employment of proofs in a declamation see 1.5.9; on witnesses, 7 pr. 1. See Bornecque 51-52.

Some colors could also be far-fetched and ridiculous, as one in the declamation (1.7) concerning a father who hated his son since he had killed his two own brothers, although legally. When captured by pirates, the son wrote to his father begging for ransom. The father replied directly to the pirates that he would pay double the ransom price if they cut his son's hands off. In court the father pleaded in excuse that his secretary had made a mistake in copying. According to him, the sentence in question should have read, "I will give you double ransom if you do *not* cut off both his hands" (1.7.18).

Success in contriving successful colors depended on vivid imagination and skillful juggling of facts. Here, too, the schools were a useful preparation for the legal system of the day:

> Cases, especially in the literary age of the empire, were not won on legal knowledge exclusively, but on the advocate's ability to color his facts, to appeal to the emotions of the judge, and to set forth persuasive arguments, couched frequently in the rhetorical conceits of the day. [25]

In a *controversia* the declaimer had to marshal all his resourcefulness and imagination to fill out the explanation of the character and motives of the defendant, and, with the fairly limited number of declamatory themes, he tended to reject the simple and obvious for the fantastic and unusual. [26]

Originally the term color signified the general tone of style, and this usage appears in Cicero and even Seneca on occasion. [27] So employed, it parallels the Greek χρῶμα and was apparently, for a time, the Roman equivalent. [28] In a manner yet to be explained fully it was also applied to describe the device of argumentation under discussion. [29]

---

[25] Parks 93-94. Ancient souces there cited include Quint. 4.1.15; 6.2.4; cf. Arist. *Rhet.* 1408a; Cic. *De Or.* 2.49. For the validity of Parks's statement in the days of Cicero see Kennedy *ARRW* 170-171. On colors in general see Quint. 4.2.88 (Butler's note *ad loc.* is helpful); cf. Schanz-Hosius 339; Bornecque 34, 52; Edward xxxv-xxxvi; Bardon 19; Parks 79-80; Bonner 55-56; Clarke 93-94; Kennedy *ARRW* 326.

[26] Cf. Clarke 93-94; Duff 29.

[27] Cic. *Brut.* 162, 171; *De Or.* 3.96; *Contr.* 10 pr. 5; cf. Quint. 6.3.110; also Bardon 19-20, 96.

[28] Cf. Bonner 55 and notes 3, 4. See the entry on color in I. Chr. Ernesti *Lexicon Technologiae Latinorum Rhetoricae* (Leipzig 1797; repr. Hildesheim 1962) 63-66.

[29] Apparently the word is related to the concept of the covering of a body, and thence the body's color. A frequent gloss given is the Greek χρώς; cf. *The-*

The declaimers preferred to express colors in the form of *sen-tentiae*, [30] usually placed in the section of the speech devoted to argument. Nevertheless, colors occur sometimes in the narration (e.g., 7.1.20) or even in both places (7.1.21). Pollio suggested that a color should be displayed in the narration and pursued fully in the argumentation. [31] A competent declaimer would not confuse a color with a *quaestio* (1.5.9), with argumentation itself (7.1.21; 7.5.8), or with the *defensio* (7.6.17).

3. *Format*

So far we have discussed three major aspects of declamation which formed the skeleton of Seneca's work. Why did he choose such an unusual format? He could have divided it into the conventional parts of rhetoric (invention, arrangement, style, memory, and delivery), into the parts of a speech (*prooemium, narratio, argumentum, epilogus*), or even into a conflation of the two as in the *Rhetorica ad Herennium*. Since Seneca was not a professional schoolmaster, we would not, of course, expect an arrangement similar to Quintilian's, based essentially on the education and career of an orateor from infancy until retirement but which also discussed the five parts of rhetoric. However, we might have expected Seneca to reproduce full declamations, or portions of them introduced by helpful hints as in the two collections ascribed to Quintilian. But in particular we must ask why he singled out *sententiae*, divisions and colors: why not commonplaces or descriptions, both of which were also important parts of declamation? [32]

If we consider the audience Seneca was addressing, the answers become readily apparent. His sons, to whom he dedicated the works, were at the time of composition busily engaged in their adult careers, perhaps in their late thirties and early forties. Although the work was intended for wider distribution, he probably had an audience of similar age in mind. Such people would have long finished their schooling and would not require instruction in the basic rudiments of declamation and rhetoric. In any event such works, written by

---

saurus Linguae Latinae vol. 3, fasc. 8 (Leipzig 1911) col. 1713. Perhaps its equivalent in meaning is the English colloquialism, "cover story." The earliest use of the word in its rhetorical sense is in *Ad Her.* 4.16; cf. *TLL* vol. 3, fasc. 8, cols. 1721-22.

[30] Cf. *Contr.* 1.1.20; Bornecque 53; Bonner 55.

[31] *Contr. Excerpta* 4.3 *extra.* Cf. Bardon 96; also *Contr.* 2.6.7; 7.1.21; 10.2. 13-15, 17.

[32] Cf. Bonner 58ff.

professionals, already existed in profusion and it is hardly likely that
an amateur like Seneca believed that he could have improved on the
existing texts. Thus we can eliminate an arrangement according to
the five parts of rhetoric.

As for the inclusion of full declamations rather than excerpts,
we must keep in mind that Seneca's sons and the rest of his intended
audience were interested in learning about the famous declaimers of
the past whom they were unable to hear and the manner in which they
expressed themselves. [33] If Seneca had wished to present quotations
from several different speakers in the same declamation, he would
have been forced to give each man's entire declamation, a boring
prospect. Then, too, it is doubtful whether Seneca could have remem-
bered declamations in their entirety from half a century before, or
whether he had complete notes on which to rely. Undoubtedly his
pen, his brain, or his other sources recorded chiefly the extraordinary.
For his purposes this was sufficient, since he could pass over the
ordinary, and compare the relative successes of different men in the
same declamation (cf. 1 pr. 4; 3 pr. 18).

More important is the question of why Seneca decided to present
samples of *sententiae*, divisions, and colors. We have mentioned two
other possible topics for inclusion: commonplaces and descriptions.
But it is clear from the various references to them in his works—and
there are a goodly number of both preserved—that these aspects of
declamation were rather standardized and did not allow room for great
originality. [34] Thus Seneca considered *sententiae*, divisions, and colors
to be the crucial mechanical features of declamation as he understood
it, and for this reason he adopted them as the headings under which
he presented the specimens. Indeed, one observer has suggested that
declamation and rhetorical theory were so hackneyed and familiar
in the early Empire that the chief attraction of a declamation centered
on the originality with which a declaimer expressed himself—the novelty
of his *sententiae*, unexpected lines of argument, and unusual colors. [35]
A jaded audience after hearing a succession of speakers on a given
theme could only be roused from their lethargy by the unusual, to

---

[33] 1 pr. 1, 4; but cf. the exception made in the case of Scaurus whom the sons
had seen declaiming (10 pr. 2).

[34] Bonner 58ff. Some descriptions, for example, were so standardized that
Seneca refrains from quoting them, merely indicating their presence with a brief
statement; e.g., *descriptio pugnantis viri fortis* (1.4.2; cf. 1.4.12; *Suas.* 2.8). On
the commonplaces cf. 1 pr. 23; Bonner 61; Winterbottom II, 635-637.

[35] Edward xxxv-xxxvi.

which *sententiae* especially lent themselves by amusing and impressing
them while eliciting their enthusiastic applause:

> ... the themes were so empty in themselves that only adventitious
> sparkle could enliven them, and so hackneyed that only novelties
> could amuse. Roman ears were no longer hungry, as they had
> been in Cicero's youth, for the rhythmical period; they required a
> new stimulant and got it in the ingenuities of the *sententia*. The
> manner became a habit; the rhetorician 'could not ope (sic) his
> mouth, but out there flew'—not a trope but a *sententia*. [36]

In a declamation one received the applicable law or laws and a brief
description of the situation. But to fill the bare outlines of a case one
needed to visualize and then invent the character, motives, and possible
exculpatory pleas of the individuals involved. For instance, how does
one portray and excuse the conduct of a man who finds exposed
children, deforms them, sends them out to beg, and takes a portion
of the receipts (*Contr.* 10.4)? The declaimer Pompeius Silo approached
the problem this way: he said that the man was merciful; he wished
to preserve their lives, but was unable to support them. Therefore each
child forfeited a part of his body in behalf of the whole (10.4.17).

Students in the declamation schools were also studying to be advocates
in the courts, and the conditions there obviously had an effect on the
form of the *controversiae*. When a case required detailed knowledge
of the law and legal precedent, the advocate regularly turned to a
specialist. The jury was not bound by strict rules of evidence or in-
structions from a presiding judge and was free to decide a case
according to its own feelings, thus allowing the advocate an extremely
wide latitude of operation. His major task was to convince a jury,
also of non-experts, by "clever and advantageous interpretation of the
facts." [37] Through such manipulation, and also emotional appeals,
stylistic perfection, and resourceful argumentation, the lawyer won
his case. For all this he relied on *sententiae*, divisions, and colors.
There were other factors of course, and we shall see that success in
declamation did not insure success in the courts. Nevertheless, these
elements of declamation were the three which one of our best critics
of the age singled out, and not without good reason.

4. *Structure and Unity*

The elder Seneca's rhetorical works are an aparently haphazard
collection of rhetorical specimens divided into the categories of *senten-*

---

[36] Clarke 95 (valid, if somewhat exaggerated).
[37] Parks 93.

tiae, divisions, and colors, arranged according to declamation theme. In the extant works and the *Excerpta* there are 74 *controversiae* and seven *suasoriae* themes. In the former case, Seneca probably preserves the bulk of the themes that would ever be declaimed. The utility of this collection is self-evident. A prospective declaimer could look up the particular theme on which he was going to speak and there see examples of how others had handled the topic. He would also take note of Seneca's various criticisms and those presented by other critics whom Seneca often quotes. For this reason the works survived and were later excerpted for the use of schoolboys. But if Seneca's only goal were to provide this sort of material, there would have been little necessity for a general preface to the work, and virtually none at all for the prefaces to each individual book—witness the two collections attributed to Quintilian. Seneca had other, more serious goals; the anthologies were not to be a strictly utilitarian compendium. Ample evidence for this assumption exists in the prefaces to the individual books of the *Controversiae*. In them Seneca provides a theoretical and critical background for the material in the book that follows each. He also attempts to unite the prefaces to the following material both structurally and thematically. In this fashion he attains some literary merit while promoting his more basic motives in assembling the collection.

The Prefaces: Content and Form

The prefaces to *Contr.* 5, 6, 8; also to *Suas.* Book 1 and probably to *Suas.* Book 2 are lacking, while the preface to *Contr.* 9 is incomplete. The length of the prefaces varies from the approximately two and one-half Müller pages of the truncated ninth preface to the nearly fifteen pages of the important first preface. In two of the prefaces the bulk of the discussion is not Seneca's but extended quotations from Cassius Severus (3 pr. 8-18) and Votienus Montanus (9 pr. 1-5).

The prefaces contain valuable, though often neglected, information on rhetoric in the early Empire. In them Seneca not only provides incidental material on his own life, the family's political ambitions, and the education of his sons, but he also identifies his immediate motives for compiling the work and provides historical background on the growth of declamation. Scattered throughout are charming personal touches, such as his emotional outburst against the declining state of morality and its pernicious effects upon oratory (1 pr. 7-10), his concern for his son Mela's education and future career (2 pr. 3-4), and, most notably, his eloquent denunciation of book burning (10 pr.

5-7). Of more interest are the anecdotal critical analyses of the era's leading speakers. Employing a non-technical terminology, Seneca succeeds eminently not only in describing and evaluating their oratorical styles but also in penetrating the peculiarities of their psychological endowment which he linked closely to their speaking abilities. Thus Seneca, who subscribed wholeheartedly to the elder Cato's *vir bonus* dictum (1 pr. 8-10), pursued the implications of this theory by analyzing both character and performance as inseparable elements in critical evaluation. He was unquestionably following and perfecting the methods which Cicero employed in the pioneering *Brutus*.

A significant and recurring topic in the prefaces is the decline of eloquence after the death of Cicero and two related subjects, the relationship of declamation to the oratory of the forum and the proper role of declamation in education. With the exception of a few vague references in Cicero on the decline of eloquence, this is the first extended discussion of the most pressing intellectual debate of the first century AD. [38] In passing, Seneca also provides us with a priceless picture of the world of declamation and the unusual people who inhabited it, both proponents and critics of the new exercise.

The style of the prefaces is relaxed and informal. Each one is addressed to Seneca's sons who have been asking their father to tell them about the declamation and the declaimers of the past. Adding to the charm of the prefaces is Seneca's habit of supporting his critical judgments with colorful and entertaining anecdotes.

The preface to Book 1 serves also as the general preface to the work and is therefore the most important and longest. In the first half (1 pr. 1-12) Seneca discusses his motives for writing, provides us with some biographical information, and also comments on the decline of eloquence and the growth of declamation in the early Empire. The remainder of the preface (1 pr. 13-24) is a brilliant sketch of Seneca's best friend and fellow Spaniard, M. Porcius Latro, whose habits, mind, and peculiarities are related to his manner of speech. [39]

---

[38] See the discussion below, 85-89.

[39] He was Seneca's best friend (1 pr. 13; cf. 1 pr. 20, 22, 24) and was born in Spain (1 pr. 16), perhaps within a year or two of Seneca, since both were schoolmates (1 pr. 13, 22); thus a birthdate *ca.* 53 BC. According to Jerome, Latro died in AD 14. He conducted a well known school of rhetoric in Rome, numbering among his admiring listeners (if not pupils) Ovid (2.2.8). As an attorney he encountered difficulties (9 pr. 3), although Seneca considered him the best of the declaimers (10 pr. 13; cf. Pliny *HN* 20.160; Quint. 10.5.18; Bornecque 188-192).

The preface to Book 2 concerns Papirius Fabianus, a declaimer
later known as a Stoic philosopher and the teacher of the younger
Seneca. 40 In his portrait of this man, Seneca emphasizes that declamation is a good preparation for any career. Here he pointedly refers
to his son Mela who, unlike his two other brothers, is reluctant to
enter politics and may have been considering a career as a *rhetor.*
While explaining that the teaching of rhetoric had only recently
become respectable for a member of the equestrian class, Seneca
urges Mela to continue with his rhetorical studies in the hope that he
would eventually change his mind and go into government service
where such training would be useful to him.

The pervasive theme of the preface to Book 3 is the deep gulf
which separates declamation from oratory. In his youth Seneca was
puzzled that some excellent orators were poor declaimers. Therefore
he asked Cassius Severus, a most notable example of such a case,
why this was so. 41 After describing this orator's manner of speech
and his personality (3 pr. 1-7), Seneca presents Severus' reply at
length (3 pr. 8-18). Through him Seneca is warning his audience
that there is indeed a great deal of difference between declamation
and the oratory of the forum. Declamation is highly artificial and
lacks the real tests of a court case. Therefore, as Severus says,
it is an unsuitable exercise for forensic speech since it is so much
easier. As a case in point, Severus relates an anecdote about the
famed declaimer Cestius who, when confronted by an unexpected
prosecution, became hopelessly muddled and unable to function. 42
A contributing factor to the unsuitability of declamation as a preparation for forensic pleading was the decline in the critical standards of

---

40 Born *ca.* 35 BC (Bornecque 185). His teachers were the rhetoricians Arellius
Fuscus (2 pr. 1) and Blandus (2 pr. 5); he studied philosophy under Sextius
(2 pr. 4). Fabianus abandoned rhetoric as his major study for philosophy, although
he still retained some interest in declamation (2 pr. 5). His style was greatly
influenced by Fuscus, even the faults, and these Fabianus struggled to escape
(2 pr. 1-2). Befitting his philosophical temperament he especially liked to expound
upon the evil influence of wealth and the instability of fortune in his declamations
(2.1.10-13, 25; 2.4.3; 2.5.6-7; 2.6.2; *Suas.* 1.9). Cf. Bornecque 185-186.
41 Severus (*ca.* 40 BC—*ca.* AD 37) died on Seriphos after twenty-five years
of exile. He was a rather bitter and outspoken orator and his works were burned
by order of the Senate (Tac. *Ann.* 1.72; 4.21; Suet. *Gaius* 16). Cf. Bornecque
157-159.
42 Cf. Latro's experience, 9 pr. 3. L. Cestius Pius (born *ca.* 65-60 BC) was a
Greek from Smyrna who founded a fashionable rhetorical school in Rome. His
sarcastic wit (e.g., 7 pr. 8-9), excessive conceit, and hatred of Cicero were well
known. Cf. Bornecque 160-163.

the school audiences. This prompted the declaimers to act foolishly. The products of these schools were bizarre and impractical individuals, and this to Severus demonstrated the great division between declamation and oratory. For this reason he did not find it incongruous that a highly regarded orator like himself was unable to declaim well. Nevertheless Severus did declaim, although infrequently and privately, and this is important: declamation as he saw it was a helpful exercise, but no more.

Seneca contrasts two opposite personalities and speakers in the preface to Book 4: Asinius Pollio and Q. Haterius.[43] Pollio only declaimed in private, but thought enough of the exercise to instruct his grandson in it personally. Seneca praises Pollio's sternness in the face of adversity and his ability to speak vigorously when he declaimed shortly after his son's death. He then contrasts Pollio with the overly emotional and voluble Haterius, who broke down in tears while delivering a declamation which reminded him of his son who had died a long time before. In this preface Seneca concentrates upon the character of the two declaimers and the effect of real emotion on performance. In both cases the emotion, though manifested differently, resulted in a memorable speech (cf. *Suas.* 2.15). Seneca seems to be more interested in Haterius and isolates his lack of self-control as the underlying cause of his numerous deficiencies as a declaimer.

Seneca devotes the entire seventh preface to C. Albucius Silus at the earnest request of his sons who desired more information about the man.[44] Along with many other declaimers, Albucius was unable to argue effectively and developed an overly sensitive personality in the sheltered world of the schools. Excessive feelings of anxiety detrimentally affected his style and argumentation. Seneca uses Al-

---

[43] C. Asinius Pollio (76 BC—AD 5) was a noted Caesarean general, consul, orator, and man of letters. Also hostile to Cicero, he was an able critic and maintained Republican sentiments even during the reign of Augustus. His historical works on the period of 60—42 BC were a source for Plutarch and Appian. There was some close connection between him and the Annaei; cf. above, 22, 26, 29-30. Q. Haterius (63 or 62 BC—AD 26) was a senator and consul. Both an orator and declaimer, his swift delivery and ease of improvisation were legendary. Cf. Bornecque 170-171.

[44] Seneca ranked Albucius (*ca.* 60-55 BC—*ca.* AD 10) among the four greatest declaimers (10 pr. 13). He came from Novaria in Cisalpine Gaul to Rome where he opened a school of rhetoric and also pleaded cases, the latter with considerably less success. Cf. Bornecque 145-148.

bucius to demonstrate the gulf separating court oratory from declamation. During a trial this declaimer employed an oath figure which,
though effective in the schools where there was no opposing attorney,
was nevertheless utterly foolish in court. The opposing side accepted
the condition of settling the case in their favor by swearing an
embarrassing oath while Albucius vainly claimed that he was only using
a figure of speech. After this fiasco Albucius never again appeared
in court and retired to the artificial world of declamation.

While the seventh preface touches upon the differences between
courtroom oratory and declamation, what remains of the preface to the
ninth book dwells on them dramatically and harshly through the words
of Votienus Montanus. [45] Although even a speaker like Severus, who
disdained declamation, still practiced these exercises privately, Montanus refused to have anything to do with declamation at all. He
maintained that declaimers acquired bad habits in the schools, which
led to disaster in real court cases. Montanus indicted the entire
declamatory educational system because the preparatory exercise was
too easy and frivolous. According to him, practical experience was
the only way in which to prepare for the courts. The preface then
breaks off, and we do not have Seneca's reaction to the radical views
of Montanus; nevertheless, he probably agreed with them in substance,
if not altogether.

In the beginning of the preface to the tenth book, Seneca tells
his sons that he is tiring of this extensive concentration on declamation, in his eyes a trivial subject. Nevertheless, he says that he will
fulfill the promise made in the first preface to tell about the old days
of declamation. In contrast to his previous practice of concentrating
on one or two declaimers, Seneca talks about some eleven declaimers
in this preface. Among the more important are Scaurus and Labienus,
both of whose writings were burned, and Seneca's fellow Spaniards
and close friends, the Clodii Turrini, father and son. Seneca also
establishes a critical canon of the four best declaimers: Latro, Fuscus,
Albucius, and Gallio (10 pr. 13). By far the most unusual portrait in
the preface is of the arch-Republican Labienus, a man of great talent

---

[45] Born in Narbo at an unknown date, he was exiled to the Balearic islands
for insults against Tiberius under terms of the *maiestas* law (Tac. *Ann.* 4.42).
He died several years later. Although he was a man of great oratorical talent
(9.5.15; cf. Tac. *Ann.* 4.42), Montanus liked to repeat the same idea in a variety
of ways. For this fault and lack of judgment he was called the "Ovid of the
orators" (9.5.15-17). Cf. Bornecque 200-201.

and bitterness who made numerous enemies and committed suicide when his books were burned. [46]

The preface to the first book of *Suasoriae* is lacking, but it is quite possible that the declaimer discussed there was Arellius Fuscus, and that Seneca treated in detail the gulf between declamation and true literature. [47]

The Prefaces: *Relationship to Other Latin Prose Prefaces*

In Latin prose a conventional manner developed of introducing a work to its readers through a preface which performed certain traditional tasks in a fairly rigid mode of expression. [48] Nevertheless there was room for some variation in accordance with the type of work introduced, and the author's own preference for a conventional prose or epistolary presentation. In general, the prefaces of the elder Seneca conform to the practices of the genre as defined by Janson, but there are some rather unusual departures and innovations. [49]

In determining the place of Seneca in the literary tradition of prose prefaces, most of the discussion must center on the preface to Book 1 which serves as the introduction to the entire work. In it are contained the dedication and the presentation of the work to follow. The prefaces to the subsequent books, while they reflect the themes of the first, are mechanically more concerned with introducing the major declaimers of the book to follow. [50]

From the standpoint of a literary historian, the most striking aspect of Seneca's prefaces is its epistolary form: he addresses each book to his three sons. While this was not the first appearance in antiquity of an epistolary preface, it is one of the first Latin rhetorical works ever so introduced. [51]

---

[46] On the orators and declaimers mentioned in Seneca see also the entries in Bornecque's biographical index (143-201).

[47] On this, cf. below, 69ff.

[48] The following discussion is based largely upon the standard work on the subject by Tore Janson, *Latin Prose Prefaces: Studies in Literary Conventions*, in the series *Acta Universitatis Stockholmiensis—Studia Latina Stockholmiensia* 13 (Stockholm 1964).

[49] Unfortunately Janson does not consider Seneca's prefaces sufficiently important for a thorough analysis. He devotes only about a page to them (49-50).

[50] Cf. Janson (above, note 48) 33, 49. The overriding importance of the first preface and the comparatively smaller import of the rest are both conventional practices in Latin works with more than one preface.

[51] Apparently the first instance of an epistolary preface in Greek literature was in certain works of Archimedes (287 BC—212 BC); see *ibid.* 19ff, 49. The elder Cato undoubtedly addressed his work on rhetoric to his son, while

4

Janson demonstrates that works dealing with rhetoric possess so many common features in their prefaces that they form a separate sub-species. [52] These common attributes include (1) what Janson terms a themes dedication, (2) a request from the dedicatee, (3) a statement of the author's reluctance to write because of a lack of time or self-confidence, and (4) the final submission to the dedicatee's requests. He recognizes that other material may appear, such as the background of the author himself, an invocation, and praise for the nature of the subject. Seneca presents the four major attributes of prefaces to rhetorical works in the very first section of the preface to Book 1:

SENECA TO HIS SONS NOVATUS, SENECA AND MELA. GREETINGS.

What you ask is something I find agreeable rather than easy. You tell me to give you my opinion of the declaimers who have been my contemporaries, and to put together such of their sayings as I haven't yet forgotten, so that, even though you were not acquainted with them, you may still form your own judgement on them without trusting merely to hearsay. Yes, it *is* agreeable for me to return to my old studies, to look back on better years, and simultaneously to remove the sting of your complaint against Time—that you were unable to listen to men of such reputation. [53]

In the sections that follow Seneca begs indulgence for the vagaries of his memory upon which he says he is relying for meeting the requests of his sons (1 pr. 2-5). He then compliments them for their interest in the declaimers of the past, because since that time eloquence has greatly declined (1 pr. 6). There follows a speculation on the causes of this degeneration, centering upon the decline of morality

---

Cicero's *Partitiones Oratoriae* is a dialogue between himself and his son. Asconius's historical commentaries on the speeches of Cicero were also addressed to his son, but they were written at least fifteen years after Seneca's death. On the entire subject of the dedication of Seneca's work to his sons, see Charles W. Lockyear, Jr., *The Fiction of Memory and the Use of Written Sources: Convention and Practice in Seneca the Elder and Other Authors* (diss., Princeton 1970) 195-205.

[52] Janson (above, note 48) 64.

[53] 1 pr. 1; Winterbottom transl.:

SENECA NOVATO, SENECAE, MELAE FILIIS SALUTEM.

Exigitis rem magis iucundam mihi quam facilem: iubetis enim quid de his declamatoribus sentiam qui in aetatem meam inciderunt indicare, et si qua memoriae meae nondum elapsa sunt ab illis dicta colligere, ut, quamvis notitiae vestrae subducti sint, tamen non credatis tantum de illis sed et iudicetis. Est, fateor, iucundum mihi redire in antiqua studia melioresque ad annos respicere, et vobis querentibus quod tantae opinionis viros audire non potueritis detrahere temporum iniuriam.

(1 pr. 10). He indicates the utility of his undertaking in preserving works that would otherwise be lost or in attributing works to their proper authors; each man, he promises, will receive his due with the greatest possible accuracy (1 pr. 11). Seneca's lifespan was so long that he heard all the great speakers of the past with the exception of Cicero, whom he could have heard if the civil wars had not forced a delay in his departure from Cordova to Rome (1 pr. 11). Seneca provides some information on the growth of declamation (1 pr. 12), and devotes the rest of the preface (1 pr. 13-24) to a discussion of Latro, with a short digression on the ease of cultivating a good memory (1 pr. 19).

The dedication is spread through the first paragraph: there is the formal epistolary opening which immediately indicates to whom the work is addressed; then in the second sentence, speaking directly to his sons, he reveals what they have requested: i.e., his judgments on the declaimers of the past and samples of their very words. [54] In this part of a preface the author can couple the dedication of the work with its content. The dedication itself is commonly a response to a request from the addressee in which the author reveals his motivation for dedicating the work to the person instrumental in causing it to be written. This frees the author from some of the responsibility for authorship. [55] In turn, the person to whom the work is dedicated receives the compliment, not an insignificant one, of having the work written especially for him. [56] This became an increasingly convention-alized pose until in the time of Pliny the dedication was so *pro forma* that it became absurd. [57] Thus in the reference to the request the author can reveal to the general audience how he came to write the work, honor the dedicatee, and provide the logic for the dedication.

In the inception of Seneca's first preface he addresses the work to his three sons, who have requested that their father provide them with an account of the old declaimers and samples of their declamations. Generally in antiquity, authors who dedicate works to their sons do not suggest that the sons asked for it, but here Seneca violates this

---

[54] A themes dedication (as Janson terms it) is conventional in Latin rhetorical works; cf. Janson (above, note 48) 24-64 *passim*; also *Ad Her.* 1.1; Cic. *De Or.* 1.1; *Or.* 3; Quint. 1 pr. 6; Tac. *Dial.* 1.

[55] For the reasons, see Janson (above, note 48) 28-30, 124-127.

[56] *Ibid.* 28.

[57] Cf. Pliny *Ep.* 6.15.1-3: *Passenus Paulus ... scribit elegos .... Is cum recitaret, ita coepit dicere: "Prisce, iubes." Ad hoc Iavolenus Priscus (aderat enim ut Paulo amicissimus): "Ego vero non iubeo." Cogita qui risus hominum, qui ioci. Est omnino Priscus dubiae sanitatis.* See also Janson (above, note 48) 60-61.

practice. 58 Surprising also is the vehemence of the sons' request as portrayed by Seneca. Instead of the milder words commonly used such as *rogare* and *hortari* we find such strong verbs as *exigitis* and *iubetis* in I pr. I. 59 The use of such words frequently indicates that the demand emanated from someone so influential that the author had no choice but to comply. 60 In the development of prose prefaces it became common to find increasingly stronger language expressing the request, until well into the Christian era when such strong requests were regularly addressed to social superiors. In the case of sons making a request of their father, and in the early first century AD, the vehement wording we find in Seneca is highly unusual. 61 These factors indicate that the request was probably genuine and strongly expressed, and, although Seneca obviously had a wider audience in mind, he was writing at the initial behest of his sons. 62

Another conventional aspect of Latin prose prefaces which appears in Seneca is his expressed unwillingness to shoulder the task ahead. He stresses his own humility in the face of the difficulty of his subject. 63 Both attitudes are symptomatic of the general self-deprecatory and modest air of prefaces in general, 64 and we may trace the origin of this attitude, often mock or exaggerated, to the conventions of rhetoric which stressed a humble approach in the *exordium* of a speech. The point of such an introduction is to magnify the writer's achievement, flatter the addressee, but, most of all, to gain the reader's attention and sympathy. The author would want the reader to come away with a heightened appreciation of the task after reading the work. A frequently used tactic to achieve this effect in a multi-book

---

58 *Ibid.* 117.

59 Cf. *desiderastis* (I pr. 20); *exigitis* (I pr. 10); various forms of *interrogo* (I pr. 4; 10 pr. I, 2, 4, 9); *instatis* (7 pr. I); *quaeritis* (10 pr. 13). The depiction of the request by his sons in I pr. I and 10 pr. I is rather vehement. The less forceful and more polite forms of *volo* in the second person plural occur in I pr. 6, 22; 7 pr. 9; 10 pr. I. On the common terminology see Janson (above, note 48) 117-120.

60 *Ibid.* 120.

61 Cf. *ibid.* 116-120. Janson does not remark upon the strong language of the request as related by Seneca.

62 We may compare the requests found in *Ad Her.* 1.1; Cic. *Or.* 1-3; *De Or.* 1.4. In the first two, the request is relayed in moderate terms, as in Tac. *Dial.* 1. Quintilian (*Ep. ad Tryph.*) uses fairly strong terms in relating the request of his publisher for the *Instit. Or.* However, in the preface where Quintilian dedicates the work to Marcellus Victorius, he implies that the dedicatee did not request it at all, and that this is just a straight dedication (I pr. 6).

63 Cf. Janson (above, note 48) 120.

64 Cf. *ibid.* 124ff (with examples) and 159.

work was to return to the difficulty theme in the preface of the last
book, thereby fixing it firmly in the reader's mind. [65]

Seneca therefore refers to the difficulty of his task in the opening
sentence of the first preface—it is more pleasant than easy he says. [66]
Even more, after the opening paragraph, he dwells on this subject in
greater detail. Seneca maintains the fiction that all the information
which he will impart must come from his memory, and then expatiates
on the infirmities of old age, especially as they relate to memory. For
this reason Seneca begs indulgence for certain irregularities which will
occur in the work (1 pr. 4-5). In the tenth preface Seneca again refers
to the difficulty of the task, here in a slightly different context: the
entire subject has become tedious because of the excessive time and
effort spent on a trivial exercise (10 pr. 1). Although there was
undoubtedly some truth to this statement, he nevertheless went on to
write the *Suasoriae* and his words must be considered rhetorical
exaggeration. [67]

Despite all the difficulties expressed, a Roman author would submit
on the basis of friendship or familial ties to the will of the dedicatees,
submerge his own doubts, and proceed with the work.[68] In the face of
the task all he can do is make assurances that he will be diligent.[69]

Seneca characterizes the request of his sons as "necessary and useful"
(1 pr. 6) because they will benefit from the work to follow through
the ability to inspect and imitate a greater variety of models. This is
the most important practical use of the anthology. In addition, through
comparison and contrast, the audience will be able to appreciate the
decline of eloquence since Seneca was in his prime. We might therefore
have reasonably expected more discussion of imitation theory—how
one employs models for achieving eloquence. Seneca merely states that
the more examples one inspects, the more progress towards eloquence,
and that one person should not be imitated exclusively. [70] However,

---

[65] Cf. 10 pr. 1; also e.g., Cic. *De Or.* 3.1; Quint. 12 pr. 1-4.

[66] Cf. *Ad Her.* 1.1; Cic. *De Or.* 1.2; Quint. *Ep. ad Tryph.* 1; *Instit. Or.* 1 pr. 1,
3; Tac. *Dial.* 1.

[67] There is a germ of truth to assuming some fatigue with the subject. In the
Suasoriae Seneca unfavorably compares declamation with the more substantial
genres of poetry, history, and oratory. Cf. below, 71ff.

[68] Cic. *Or.* 1; cf. Janson (above, note 48) 41-42, 159-160.

[69] E.g., 1 pr. 3: ... *nunc quia iubetis quid possit experiar et illam* [i.e., his
memory] *omni cura scrutabor.* Cf. 1 pr. 11: ... *summa cum fide suum cuique
reddam.* Janson (above, note 48) 159-160 identifies in this entire process a
renunciation of originality.

[70] 1 pr. 6; cf. Cic. *De Or.* 3.93; Quint. 10.2 *passim.*

he does treat the whole matter of a decline of eloquence since the
age of Cicero at great length (1 pr. 6-10), and we must assume that
Seneca felt this sincerely and strongly. Thus Seneca devotes a sizeable
portion of the first preface to emphasizing the importance of his
work and its difficulty, a rhetorically helpful tactic in a preface (or
exordium) which impresses upon the reader the significance of the
work to follow and the pains taken by the author in its preparation. [71]

Occasionally a prose preface may contain an invocation, although
it occurs more commonly in poetry. [72] Two outbursts with religious
overtones occur in Seneca's prefaces: one concerns the elder Cato
whose *vir bonus* definition of an orator, Seneca thinks, was actually
delivered by a divinity speaking through Cato as a medium (1 pr. 9).
The other is a denunciation of book burnings in which he refers to
the inevitability of divine retribution for such a monstrous act (10 pr.
6-7). While not strictly invocations, both passages are in a sense appeals
to a divine providence watching over the sphere of eloquence.

The preface to any work is a personal declaration of aims, motives,
methods and dedication. Rhetorically formal since it resembles the
exordium of a speech, the preface nevertheless is usually the most
personal part of a work. In it an author tends to relate himself to the
work at hand and reveal some glimpses of his own character. There
may be references to the author's busy life and career, his friendship
with the dedicatee, or extremely personal touches, as in the case of
Quintilian's remarks on the deaths of his wife and son. [73] Seneca,
too, allows us a few insights into his personality in the prefaces. He
looks back nostalgically to his youthful student days (1 pr. 1) and
describes the inroads of old age upon his physical and mental capacities
(1 pr. 2-5). Vividly portrayed is his boyhood impatience to study
rhetoric in Rome, and his bitter disappointment at having to remain
in Spain until the civil wars subsided (1 pr. 11). More touching is
the fond way in which he reminisces about his best friend, M. Porcius
Latro (1 pr. 13ff; cf. 1 pr. 20), and especially his recollections of
their days together in the school of Marullus (1 pr. 22; cf. 1 pr. 24).
There is a personal address to Mela (2 pr. 3-4) which movingly
portrays Seneca's paternal concern over the future career of his son.
The other prefaces lack any real personal touch, with the exception

---

[71] Cf. *Ad Her.* 1.1; Cic. *Or.* 1-2; Quint. 1 pr. 6, 9ff; Tac. *Dial.* 1.
[72] Cf. Quint. 4 pr. 4-6.
[73] Quint. 6 pr. 1-16. Cf. *Ad Her.* 1.1; Cic. *Or.* 1; *De Or.* 1.1-5; also Quint. 1
pr. 1, 6; 4 pr. 2-3.

of the tenth. There Seneca hearkens back to the theme of the "better years" (10 pr. 1). Later on he discusses the family's close friends, the Clodii Turrini, in fairly sympathetic terms (10 pr. 14-16). In all, his tone and occasional outbursts mentioned above provide an interesting cameo of the man, and some insights into his character.

So far we have been treating Seneca's prefaces in relation to others in the tradition of Latin rhetorical works. Janson describes in some detail the usual themes of Latin prefaces to historical works and how they differ from those to rhetorical works. [74] Under analysis by these criteria Seneca's first preface equally fits the mold of a preface to a historical work. This should not be too surprising, since he has revealed an historical perspective in compiling the work in this very same preface. [75] A commonplace of Latin historical prefaces is a praise of the subject or a demonstration of the importance of the theme. This we have already seen was an important constituent of the preface to Book 1. Secondly, it is conventional in such works to convey the reason for the choice of the subject. For example, Livy desires to demonstrate the past greatness of Rome and the necessity for glorifying it; in both the *Annales* and *Historiae* Tacitus asserts that the period he is dealing with had not yet been treated satisfactorily. [76] So, also, Seneca adds his motive: he will preserve the works and memory of the great speakers of his day, ensure that their works are properly attributed, and see to it that their reputations are accurately judged (1 pr. 10-11; 1 pr. 20-21). The historian conventionally reveals his attitude towards his work, often a declaration of impartiality. [77] Thus in Seneca we find a precursor to Tacitus' *sine ira et studio*:

> ... in general, either no lecture notes of the greatest declaimers remain, or, what is even worse, those that exist are spurious. Therefore lest they remain either unknown, or be known otherwise than they should, I will give each man his due with the greatest accuracy possible (1 pr. 11).

It is surely no accident that Seneca, who was writing a work on rhetoric viewed from a historical perspective, used the conventions of both historical and rhetorical prefaces. As this brief survey has shown, Seneca was assuredly writing in accordance with a long established

---

[74] Janson (above, note 48) 66-67.
[75] 1 pr. 1, 4, 6, 7, 11, 12, 13.
[76] Cf. Janson (above, note 48) 67.
[77] *Ibid.*

tradition, but nevertheless, he found it both advisable and necessary to depart from the practices of his predecessors in the ways described.

The Body of the Controversiae *and* Suasoriae: *Arrangement, relative size and length of parts, use of examples*

We have already discussed the obvious and external arrangement of Seneca's rhetorical works. Briefly, there were originally ten books of *controversia* selections, each introduced by a preface. The books themselves contain from six to nine separate declamation themes selected at random. Each theme was introduced by a law (or laws) and a hypothetical situation to which they applied, or merely the description of such a situation and the statement of the obvious charge emanating from it. Afterwards followed specimens gathered from various declaimers who treated that theme, arranged in order under the categories of *sententiae, divisiones,* and *colores.*

First came the *sententiae,* presented rather simply and not introduced by any explanatory title or phrasing. Without comment or literary discussion Seneca presents the words of several declaimers in a row on one side of the case, and a little more than two-thirds of the time, he adds *sententiae* from those who spoke on the other side under the title *pars altera* or some variant. [78] Since Seneca's sons are especially interested in *sententiae* (1 pr. 22), he devotes the most space to them, or about 45% of the sections. [79] The examples quoted from the 39 declaimers extracted in the *sententiae* portion may occupy anywhere from a short sentence to nine sections, but average out to nearly two-thirds of a section per declaimer. [80] Thus Seneca not only provides glittering sayings but also seeks to give some idea of the running continuity of a declamation, though admittedly selecting the more striking purple patches, both good and bad.

---

[78] In the *Contr.* there are thirty-five themes preserved in the text (i.e., not in excerpted form), of which two (2.7, 10.6) break off in the middle of the *sententiae* portion. Of the thirty-three remaining, twenty-three themes (or twenty-four, if we reconstruct the likewise fragmentary 10.6 from the *Excerpta*) give *sententiae* from the opposing side, usually at less length. In one instance the opposing side consists of a single sentence (10.4.10).

[79] Of the 590 total sections of the *Contr.* (excluding the fragmentary *Contr.* 2.7, 7.4, 10.6), 266 are in the initial *sententiae* portions, or an average per theme of about 8.3 sections.

[80] For an example of a very short utterance see 10.4.10. The longest quotation is from Latro (2.7.1-9; cf. 1.1.1-3; 1.7.1-2; 7.7.7-8; 10.1.6-8). Other long excerpts are from Fuscus (2.1.4-8; 7.6.7-8); Fabianus (2.1.10-13), Gallio (2.3.6-7; 7.1.12-13; 7.7.3-5; 9.3.2-3; 10.2.1-3), Albucius (7.1.1-3; 9.2.6-8), Cestius (7.1.8-11), Capito (9.2.9-10), Clodius Turrinus (10.2.5-6), and Fulvius Sparsus (10.4.8-10; 10.5.8-10).

The next portion of a Senecan theme was an analysis of the division of the arguments, usually in Seneca's paraphrasing. Unlike the *sententiae*, either the title *divisio* or a technical phrase with a verb or noun form of that word or of *quaestio* introduces this portion and indicates the transition from the *sententiae*. [81] There is no explicit title to a part devoted to the opposing side in the divisions. Seneca realized that analysis of argument would bore his readers and he therefore allots the least amount of space to division. [82] The relative length of the individual citations in the division is the largest of the three categories. Seneca prefers to give a fairly comprehensive treatment of one declaimer's arguments, and then note additional *quaestiones* posed by others (e.g., *Contr.* 1.1.13). In an average division treatment Seneca names only three or four declaimers as opposed to nearly thirteen in an average *sententia* portion, or about eighteen in an average color portion. [83] The declaimer most frequently cited in the divisions is Latro, followed far behind by Gallio and Fuscus.

In the division portion of two-thirds of the *controversia* themes Seneca pauses to give his own comments on the declaimers quoted, present similar comments by others (e.g., 9.6.10), or discuss various aspects of division. For instance, he explains the growing complexity of declamatory division (1.1.13) and the differences between declamatory and forensic division. This marks a departure from the *sententia* portions, in which Seneca presents quotations only. These additional comments in the division section are nevertheless quite small in extent.

The transition to the portion of the theme dealing with colors is usually clear and marked by the use of the Latin term *color* in the opening sentence. [84] Seneca devotes a little less space to colors than

---

[81] Only the division portion of *Contr.* 7.2.8 lacks this. (While various matters of argumentation are treated in 7.2.8-9, it is not in the usual format where various *quaestiones* are posed.) The title *Divisio* has been conjectured and added in 2.5.10; 9.4.9; 10.2.8. Fourteen of the division portions lack the initial title; those using a form (noun or verb) of *divisio* in the introductory phrase are: 2.2.5; 2.3.11; 2.4.7; 2.6.5; 7.3.6; 7.6.13; 10.1.9; 10.4.11; 10.5.12. A form of *quaestio* is used in 7.4.3; 7.7.10; 7.8.7; 9.2.13.

[82] 1 pr. 22; cf. 2.1.19. If we exclude the fragmentary *Contr.* 2.7, 7.4, 10.6, and the difficult to analyze 9.6, Seneca devotes in all 93.5 sections to division out of 570 total, or 16.4%. The average length per theme of a division portion is about three sections.

[83] Again excluding *Contr.* 2.7, 7.4, 9.6, and 10.6, there are 109 mentions of declaimers in the 93.5 division sections.

[84] Except 2.3.17 and 2.4.7 where we find *omnes infamaverunt*—and here the import is clear. The transition is much less direct in 2.6.6; 7.5.8-9; and 9.6 (but here probably occurring in 9.6.20).

to *sententiae*, but rather more than to division; in all, colors occupy over one-third of the work. [85] Ranging from somewhat less than one Müller section (1.5.9) to some sixteen (2.1.24-39), the color portions average about seven sections in length. Because colors can often be briefly expressed in a short *sententia*, Seneca regularly refers to or quotes many more declaimers here than in the other two portions, both in absolute terms and on a per-section basis. [86] Colors from the opposite side of a case do not regularly occur under a formal heading, although Seneca does frequently present them. In many of the declamations where it is not necessarily clear, Seneca will therefore tell his readers which side the particular color supports. [87]

Aside from colors of considerable ingenuity and verbal dexterity, this portion of the Senecan themes is easily the most attractive to modern readers because of the many anecdotes involving famous literary and political figures of the era and the terse pen sketches of some famous speakers. Seneca also pauses to give more literary analysis and criticism than in either of the two other portions. These comments, though brief, are often penetrating and perceptive. Frequently Seneca inserts or appends to a literary analysis several anecdotes which either substantiate or illustrate a point he wished to make.

By far the most well known anecdotal analysis is Seneca's long discussion of Ovid (2.2.8-12), whom he had heard declaiming at the school of Arellius Fuscus. Seneca analyzes his prose style as unversified verse, thus agreeing with the poet's own opinion of himself. [88] Supporting his contention with examples, Seneca demonstrates the influence of Latro's *sententiae* on Ovid's poetry. Considered a good declaimer (2.2.9), Ovid tended to run through commonplaces in no logical order. Seneca provides us with a valuable quotation from one of Ovid's schoolboy declamations which supports Seneca's literary judgments (2.2.9-11). After this we learn that Ovid rarely declaimed *controversiae* unless they were ones which stressed character portrayal; he

---

[85] Excluding 2.7, 7.4, 9.6, and 10.6, colors occupy 220.5 of 570 total sections, or 38.7%, as opposed to 256 for *sententiae* (44.9%), and 93.5 sections for division (16.4%).

[86] There are nearly 600 references to declaimers in the color portions as opposed to about 400 in the *sententiae*, and over 100 in the divisions. On the average, the number of declaimers found in each section is: *sententiae*, 1.5; divisions, 1.2; colors, 2.6 (excluding from analysis *Contr.* 2.7, 7.4, 9.6, 10.6).

[87] He inserts such phrases as *colorem contra patrem* (7.7.11), *pro patre* (7.7.13), *pro educatore* (9.3.10), or *a parte patris* (9.3.14)—and then in the same section, for clarity, *a parte educatoris*.

[88] 2.2.8; cf. Ovid *Tr.* 4.10.23-26.

did not care for argumentation, and therefore concentrated on *suasoriae* (2.2.12). Ovid was aware of his stylistic faults, but loved them. Then follows the famous anecdote relating how Ovid's friends persuaded him to agree to delete three verses from his works which most offended them. The poet agreed on the condition that he could select three which would be immune. Each side wrote down in secret the three verses to be excluded and the three to be made immune. On comparison, both Ovid and his friends selected the same three verses. [89] From this example Seneca concludes, quite rightly, that Ovid lacked the heart for restraining the boldness of his poetical speech, not the critical judgment. Seneca adds Ovid's apt comment that a face becomes more beautiful with the addition of a mole.

Another revealing aside (9.1.13-14) is a discussion of brevity in the works of Thucydides, Sallust, and Livy. Unfortunately the quotation ascribed to Thucydides is not genuine, but nevertheless the passage probably reflects the conventional Roman view on the relative merits of Thucydides and Sallust (cf. Quint. 10.1.101-102). To those interested in literary history and the theory of imitation, there is a rather witty and revealing account of how Cestius, Varro, and Ovid adapted Vergil's famous description of night (7.1.27; *Aen.* 8.26-27). [90]

So far we have discussed exclusively the body of the *Controversiae.* The *Suasoriae* require separate treatment because of several important differences between the two exercises and therefore the manner in which these excerpts are preserved. Since *suasoriae* are deliberative speeches there is no separate portion for colors. However, *sententiae* and divisions do occur and are treated in about the same manner and order as in the *Controversiae.*

The *sententia* portions of the *Suasoriae* are analogous to their counterparts in the *Controversiae* in average length, appearance, and

---

[89] The lines are: *semibovemque virum semivirumque bovem* (*Ars Am.* 2.24), and *et gelidum Borean egelidumque Notum* (*Am.* 2.11.10). Winterbottom translates the two lines "half-bull man and half-man bull," and "freezing north wind and de-freezing south." The third line does not survive in the MSS.

[90] Other such literary anecdotes occur concerning Vibius Gallus (2.1.25-26), L. Vinicius and Augustus's criticism of him (2.5.20), Calvus (7.4.6-8), and Votienus Montanus (9.5.15-17); cf. the anecdotes and criticisms concerning Messalla and Latro (2.4.8), Latro's ill-considered remarks before Maecenas, Augustus, and Agrippa (2.4.12-13), the imitators of Publilius Syrus and a discussion of Laberius (7.3.8-9), Cestius's remarks on the use of a rhetorical device called *echo* (7.7.19), Vallius Syriacus and Sabinus (9.4.18-21), the witty interchange between Craton and the Emperor (10.5.21), and the defiant historian Timagenes (10.5.22).

purpose. There is no literary criticism in these portions, sometimes there is an opposing side (2.9, 5.8), and somewhat fewer declaimers are mentioned on the average. The division portions are less involved than those in the *Controversiae*, but are of the same average length. Since the individual *Suasoriae* have relatively fewer sections on the average than the *Controversiae*, the divisions form a larger percentage of the material. They also contain relatively more anecdotes and literary discussion than their counterparts in the *Controversiae*.

After the division there is a portion roughly analogous to the colors of the *Controversiae*, though not introduced by any transition statement or title. In it we find samples of descriptions (*descriptiones*)—semipoetic digressions on geography, strange races of men, and the like. [91] This part allowed the freest rein to the declaimer's imagination and literary talent. Seneca quotes from the descriptions of various declaimers in both the *sententia* portions and those following the division; the latter, for want of a better term, we may call the conclusions. [92] In the *sententia* portion Seneca is concerned with the unfolding (*explicatio*) of a description, [93] which he tends to present at some length. But in the conclusion he tends to insert just short selections, usually a sentence or so, and then to comment critically upon each. [94]

Description selections occupy only a fraction of the conclusions, for as in the colors, he is equally likely to insert some lengthy critical discussions, digressions, quotations from other literary sources bearing on the subject at hand, and biographical anecdotes. [95]

---

[91] There are grounds for relating descriptions to colors, since a description itself, in the proper circumstances, could serve as a color, especially a description of a person's physical or mental state; cf. Bonner 60.

[92] The most elaborate treatment of descriptive material occurs in the first *Suasoria* (1.1-4, 11-13, 15; cf. 2.1, 3.1, 4.1). A description usually formed part of the narration or was loosely associated with a literary excursus; cf. *Contr.* 1.4.8; 7.1.27; 9.2.21. The style would naturally differ considerably from the norm for the narration; e.g., 2 pr. 1.

[93] Cf. *Suas.* 2.10, 23; 3.1; 4.5; 5.1.

[94] E.g., *Suas.* 1.12-14; 2.14; 3.4-5. There are some longer selections, but these usually come from poetry or historical works (e.g., *Suas.* 1.15; 6.17ff; 6.26).

[95] Among the more notable insertions are: the critical discussion of a Vergilian line (*Suas.* 1.12), a long quotation from an epic poem by Albinovanus Pedo describing a storm at sea (1.15), a sensible attack on a quibbling grammarian (2.12-13), a comparison of the differing emotional states of Lesbocles and Potamon (2.15), the sketch of a man obsessed by largeness (2.17), the long analysis of a Vergilian imitation (3.5-7), a digression on the treatment of Cicero's death and his *epitaphia* by various historians, an orator, and an epic poet or two (6.14-27), and also some anecdotes about the son of Cicero (7.13-14).

Overall Principles and Unity

The declamation anthologies are curiously rambling and apparently haphazardly arranged. Seneca himself does little to dispel this impression, and in fact apologizes for it at the beginning of the first preface, blaming his own failing memory; he says he is unable to follow chronological order of authorship or delivery. [96] There is also a considerable amount of extraneous material in the form of anecdotes, some quite long, biographical accounts, and extensive quotations from poetic or historical works. The individual *Controversiae* themes occur in no discernible order. *Suasoriae* themes 1-5 deal with Greek historical and mythical situations, again in no apparent pattern, while themes six and seven concern the last days of Cicero.

On the other hand there can be no question that Seneca had certain guiding overall principles in mind. His main interest is in handing down the words of men whom his sons were unable to hear (1 pr. 1, 6; 10 pr. 2). The work as a whole is presented in the light of imitation theory as it was then currently understood. Seneca was thus providing his audience with examples for imitation or avoidance. The prominent mention of imitation in the opening of the first preface is purposeful in this regard (1 pr. 1, 6), although there is less theoretical discussion than we might expect, given its importance. He also will try to vary what would otherwise be a tedious procession of quotations with background discussion and anecdotes; in fact, he clearly enunciates his intention to sprinkle the works with novel features and interesting examples to hold the attention of his audience and to avoid tedium. [97] Displaying some selectivity in the *Controversiae* themes presented, Seneca mentions several that he chose not to include, two undoubtedly because of their obscenity, and at least one that may have been too familiar. [98] Seneca is also unwilling to quote more than is necessary to make his point. [99] He will concentrate on *sententiae* and limit the discussion of division (1 pr. 22; 2.1.19). Throughout the works Seneca is careful to control his expansive tendencies when relating anecdotes; after a digression he will pointedly return to the subject at hand. [100]

---

[96] 1 pr. 4, 5; cf. Bornecque 22ff.

[97] 4 pr. 1; cf. 1 pr. 24; 2 pr. 5.

[98] Obscene themes are referred to in 1.2.23; 10.1.13. For one too well known cf. *Suas.* 4.4. Other themes mentioned, but not included as headings, are found in 1.2.22; 2.4.8; 7.4.9; *Suas.* 2.21.

[99] 2.1.27; cf. Bornecque 24.

[100] 2.1.37; 7.3.8-10; 9.2.23-24; 10.5.21-22; *Suas.* 1.5-7; 2.12-13; 2.19-20; 3.4-7; 4.4-5. In other instances the digressions or anecdotes are worked into the flow

Thus his overall approach to the work was marked by a coherent method.

The evidence so far collected indicates that Seneca, while cultivating a façade of casualness in composition, actually obeyed some unifying system in presentation. The extent of his efforts, however, has not been fully appreciated. Certain definite patterns and themes link the prefaces together, the prefaces to the body of each book following, and all of the *Suasoriae* themes to one another.

The Controversiae

The obvious and primary unifying theme throughout the prefaces and the *Controversiae* as a whole is Seneca's avowed purpose of fulfilling his sons' request to relate specimens for emulation or avoidance according to the contemporary theory of imitation. Thus each surviving preface has at least one reference to this motive, usually in the opening section. [101] The interchange between father and sons is further emphasized by the form each preface takes, namely a letter addressed to his sons in the second person, while Seneca speaks in the first person. The cumulative effect is a thread of continuity linking the whole work loosely together in both style and overall purpose.

Other relations exist between the prefaces and books of the *Controversiae*. A readily apparent one is the form of transition from preface to book. [102] Seneca uses two kinds, which may be characterized as direct transition and indirect transition. An example of a direct transition occurs at the end of the first preface (1 pr. 24). Here Seneca says that he will begin Book 1 with the first declamation which he remembers that Latro delivered. The initial *controversia* of the book then starts with an extended quotation from Latro. [103] Similarly, the seventh preface ends with the discussion of a poor figure used by

in such a manner that there is only a perfunctory statement of return to the subject, or none at all: cf. 2.2.8-12; 2.4.8, 13; 9.1.13-14; 9.3.12-14; 9.4.18-21; 9.5.15-17; *Suas.* 2.15, 17; 6.14-27; 7.13-14.

[101] 1 pr. 1, 4, 6; 2 pr. 1; 3 pr. 3; 4 pr. 1; 7 pr. 1; 9 pr. 1; 10 pr. 1; cf. 2.4.12; 9.2.27; *Suas.* 6.16; Duff 40. The following discussion of the unity of the *Contr.* and *Suas.* first appeared in substantially the same form in Lewis A. Sussman, "The Artistic Unity of the Elder Seneca's First Preface and the *Controversiae* as a Whole," *AJP* 92 (1971) 285-291, and here in shortened form, *idem,* "Arellius Fuscus and the Unity of the Elder Seneca's *Suasoriae*," *RhM* 120 (1977) 303ff.

[102] Because of the tattered state of the text we can only fully trace the transitions for Books 1, 2, 7, 10. The *Excerpta*, however, are helpful in the case of Book 4.

[103] Several MSS lack the initial ascription *Porci Latronis*. Nevertheless it is clear from the end of the preface who the speaker is.

Albucius in the *controversia* about a man charged with attempted parricide (7 pr. 9). Seneca tells his sons that he will relate *sententiae* used in this declamation. The seventh book then opens with that very declamation theme and a quotation from Albucius. Although we only have the *Excerpta* for the body of Book 4, obviously Seneca employed a similar linkage. For, earlier in the fourth preface (4 pr. 6), Seneca tells us about Haterius, who was so emotional that, in the *controversia* about the man dragged from the tomb of his three sons, the declaimer himself wept because it brought to mind his own long dead son. Seneca then concludes the preface (4 pr. 11) with a reference to the declamation in which Haterius wept, and the first *controversia* of Book 4 is that same one.

The indirect transitions take the form of an assertion by Seneca (with an apology for his poor memory) that he will recall in the following book the works of the man who is the major figure of the preface. Thus at the end of the second preface dealing with Fabianus, he says: "I shall therefore collect into this little book whatever he [Fabianus] said that I remember" (2 pr. 5). Seneca keeps his promise, since Fabianus, who is only mentioned several times outside this book, figures in some eighteen sections of the second book. [104] Although again we have only the *Excerpta* for Book 3, it is undoubtedly a similar case since Seneca closes the extant preface in the same fashion: "Nevertheless it would be unfair to form an estimate of him [Cassius Severus] from what I shall introduce next. For these are not the things he said best, but what I remember best" (3 pr. 18). The transition between the preface and body of Book 10 is less marked than the previous example and this may in part be due to the unusual nature of this preface. In it Seneca discusses eleven declaimers and establishes a critical ranking of the top four (10 pr. 13). In contrast, the other prefaces usually concentrate on one man, or once on two. [105] Thus Seneca leads into the tenth book in a slightly different manner. After mentioning the elder and younger Clodius Turrinus, he says: "You will know that I have ranked the names of these men not through excess favor but through careful consideration when I repeat their *sententiae* as either equal to, or better than, those of the most renowned authors." [106]

---

[104] Other mentions occur in 7 pr. 4; *Suas.* 1.4, 9-10.

[105] 1 pr., Latro; 2 pr., Fabianus; 3 pr., Cassius Severus; 4 pr., Pollio and Haterius; 7 pr., Albucius; 9 pr., Montanus.

[106] *Horum nomina non me a nimio favore, sed a certo posuisse iudicio scietis,*

A study of Book 10 also reveals that four declaimers critically discussed in the preface have their *sententiae, divisiones,* and *colores* reproduced and analyzed only in the body of that book, [107] and most of the remainder have their rhetorical efforts more extensively reviewed here than anywhere else in the work. [108] Carrying this analysis where the state of the text allows to the other books and prefaces of the *Controversiae,* it is evident that the major figure of each preface is treated in more detail in the following book than in any other. [109] By so doing, no matter which method of transition he employs, Seneca relates the content of each preface to the following book, and carries out the implied promise he makes in the transitional ending of each preface to analyze this or that declaimer in detail. Thus by both content and transition Seneca tries to relate each preface to the subsequent book and achieve unity.

While establishing such a unity, let us see in what other way Seneca may also be attempting to bond the whole of his work thematically. An appropriate place to begin this search is in the first preface, for it sets the tone of the entire work to follow and introduces what seems to be its unifying motif. As Sochatoff has correctly pointed out, a major topic in the first preface is the deterioration of Roman politics, literature, and social conditions in the eyes of Seneca. [110] From his vantage point Seneca is looking back to the golden period under Augustus when he himself was a young man. His sons have asked about the declaimers he knew in those old days, and Seneca confesses his pleasure in recalling the past and providing specimens from the great declaimers who flourished before his sons were born (1 pr. 1).

Before beginning his discussion of the decline of eloquence (1 pr. 6-7), Seneca apparently digresses on the subject of his own phenomenal

---

cum sententias eorum rettulero aut pares notissimorum auctorum sententiis aut praeferendas (10 pr. 16).

[107] I.e., Labienus, Gavius Silo, and the Clodii Turrini. Pacatus is mentioned only in the tenth preface.

[108] Gallio, Sparsus, Moschus, Scaurus. Exceptions are Bassus, Capito, and Musa.

[109] Duff sensed this (41); cf. Winterbottom I, xvi. To check this impression, one can employ the convenient index to Kiessling's edition and count the entries under the individual declaimer's *sententiae,* divisions, and colors, and it does substantiate Duff. For example, Montanus, the major figure of 9 pr. has twenty-six such entries for Book 9 and is otherwise there mentioned four additional times for a total of thirty. In the other books combined (excluding prefaces) he has only five entries. The case of Fabianus (discussed above) is equally striking, while the cases of Albucius and Latro are somewhat less so.

[110] A. F. Sochatoff, "The *Meliores Annos* of the Elder Seneca," *CW* 39 (1945-46) 70-71.

memory (1 pr. 2-5). But on closer examination he is subtly anticipating the causes of oratorical decline by applying these very same factors to the deterioration of memory.

There are three factors which Seneca proposes as possible causes for the decline in eloquence from the days of Cicero (1 pr. 7): (1) the licentiousness and moral laxity of the day (*luxus temporum*), (2) the loss of the rewards for political and judicial eloquence, with the consequent redirection of ambition into base pursuits flourishing with greater prospects of profit and public office, and (3) that oratory had already reached the height of its natural growth peak and was now in an inevitable state of decline.

After his introductory comments, Seneca tells his sons that old age has weakened his physical faculties, but even more, it has impaired his memory, which in his prime was of miraculous proportions (1 pr. 2). He proceeds to document his claim by relating some truly impressive feats of memory performed during his youth. But now his memory is severely impaired with age, although it retains some vestiges of its former power (1 pr. 3-4). Thus Seneca's memory had passed through a natural cycle of growth and decline roughly parallel to, and contemporaneous with, the ebbing fortunes of eloquence. Both were at their height in his school days shortly before and after the death of Cicero, [111] and had steadily deteriorated since.

In addition to aging, Seneca's memory had also been troubled by long inactivity. "Now it has been undermined by age, and a long period of idleness—which can play havoc with young minds too: to such an extent that although it may be able to come up with something, it cannot make any promises. It is a long time since I asked anything of it." [112] This corresponds to the second proposed cause for oratorical decline which states that application to the development of rhetorical skill decreased since the rewards of eloquence had diminished. Thus both oratory and memory suffered from a lack of application and use.

The first mentioned cause of the decline of eloquence, the fallen standards of morality, was apparently uppermost in Seneca's mind: "... there is nothing so fatal to genius as luxury." [113] For obvious

---

[111] 1 pr. 11; 10 pr. 6; cf. 1 pr. 2-3.

[112] 1 pr. 3; Winterbottom transl.: *Nunc et aetate quassata et longa desidia quae iuvenilem quoque animum dissolvit, eo perducta est, ut, etiamsi potest aliquid praestare, non possit promittere: diu ab illa nihil repetivi* (1 pr. 3).

[113] ... *nihil enim tam mortiferum ingeniis quam luxuria est* (1 pr. 7). This is the natural outgrowth of the elder Cato's *vir bonus* definition of an orator, one which Seneca himself accepts and repeats (1 pr. 9; cf. 1 pr. 8, 10). On the

reasons Seneca does not postulate this as a cause for his own deteriorating memory. [114] But shortly afterwards, when he describes the
immorality of the younger generation, he closely links the contemporary
low regard for memory to the current low state of morals:

> Go now and look for orators among those who are plucked and
> smooth, but are never men except in their lust. Deservedly they
> take models suited to their nature. Who is there who strives to
> attain a good memory? [115]

Considering the evidence, it is difficult not to see some conscious
effort on Seneca's part to emphasize the relationship between the
deterioration of both memory and eloquence to create a motif of decline
which occupies the first half of the preface (1 pr. 1-12). The second
half is occupied by a fond remembrance of Seneca's dear friend,
Porcius Latro (1 pr. 13-24). Thus the entirety of the first preface is
thematically and artistically unified by the concept of the "better
years" (*meliores ... annos*; 1 pr. 1), encompassing Seneca's youth
when his faculties, memory especially, and eloquence were flourishing;
and when he enjoyed his old school days, *antiqua studia*, and the
companionship of his long-departed school friend Latro.

Seneca completes the cycle in the tenth preface. Here he tells his
sons that he wishes to leave behind these studies of his youth (i.e.,
declamation), at first so enticing but now distasteful to him (10 pr.
1). [116] Really, he says guiltily, the topic of declamation is a frivolous

---

possible Stoic origin of this concept see Kennedy *APG* 293 and note 49. The
idea is aired in Cic. *De Inv.* 1, and is central to understanding Quintilian (e.g.,
12.1; cf. 1.2.3). Cf. younger Seneca *Ep.* 114 *passim*; "Long." *Subl.* 44. The
younger Pliny (a student of Quintilian's) amusingly parodies the phrase when he
describes the notorius Regulus as a *vir malus dicendi imperitus* (*Ep.* 4.7). For
further discussion see R. G. Austin (ed.), *Quintiliani Institutionis Oratoriae Liber
XII* (Oxford 1948, repr. 1965) introd. note to 12.1 and *ad loc.*, *vir bonus* ... ;
also Edward xxvii-xxviii; D'Alton 161 note 4; Atkins 168, 233; Sochatoff
"Theories" 346ff; W. S. Anderson, "Juvenal and Quintilian," *Yale Classical
Studies* 17 (1961) 23-25, 87-91; Michael Winterbottom, "Quintilian and the
vir bonus," *JRS* 54 (1964) 90-97; Kennedy *ARRW* 509 and note 23.
[114] The austere, conservative, and Republican cast of his character is well
attested; see above, 26-28.
[115] *Ite nunc et in istis vulsis atque expolitis et nusquam nisi in libidine viris
quaerite oratores. Merito talia habent exempla qualia ingenia. Quis est, qui
memoriae studeat?* (1 pr. 10).
[116] *Quod ultra mihi molesti sitis, non est: interrogate, si qua vultis, et sinite
me ab istis iuvenilibus studiis ad senectutem meam reverti. Fatebor vobis, iam
res taedio est. Primo libenter adsilui velut optimam vitae meae partem mihi
reducturus: deinde iam me pudet, tamquam diu non seriam rem agam. Hoc habent
scholasticorum studia: leviter tacta delectant, contrectata et propius admota*

pursuit for a man of his years. Seneca pleads with his sons to allow him finally to finish his recollections regarding declamation and fulfill the promises which he made at the inception of the *Controversiae* (1 pr. 1, 3).

Thus, while carrying through his avowed purpose and method of introducing his sons to the declaimers of the past and their works, Seneca at last in the tenth preface returns to the theme of the *meliores annos* and memory from the first preface in order to complete the artistic cycle and impose thematic as well as structural unity on the whole work.

The Suasoriae

The search for a unifying thread in the *Suasoriae* is hampered by the incomplete state of the work. Nevertheless from what remains it is fairly obvious that Seneca attempted to organize at least the first book around a coherent theme which probably appeared prominently in the lost preface. [117]

The key to discovering this unifying principle is the declaimer Arellius Fuscus, who nearly without question was the major declaimer treated in the lost preface. [118] Seneca includes more material on him (including nearly all of *Suas.* 4) than on any other declaimer in the *Suasoriae*, and tends to place quotations from him near the beginning of the portions devoted to *sententiae*, divisions, and conclusions. [119]

---

fastidio sunt. Sinite ergo me semel exhaurire memoriam meam et dimittite vel adactum iureiurando quo adfirmem dixisse me quae scivi quaeque audivi quaeque ad hanc rem pertinere iudicavi.

[117] I have assumed, as Edward (xxx) has, that there was a preface to the first Book of *Suasoriae*. Seneca introduced each book extant of the *Controversiae* with a preface, and it is reasonable to assume that he would introduce the first book of a new division of the anthologies with a preface also. The state of the text supports the belief that the preface to the *Suasoriae* was lost. The beginning of the first theme has been lost, including the theme statement itself, the attribution of the first section of *sententiae*, and part of the opening sentence.

[118] Arellius Fuscus was born in Greece or a Greek city in Asia Minor *ca.* 60-55 BC. The date of his death is uncertain; cf. Bornecque 150. Although he declaimed in both Greek and Latin, he performed more often in the latter language and is therefore treated by Seneca with the Latin declaimers. Seneca ranked him among the four best declaimers (10 pr. 13) and quotes him extensively; he appears in virtually every extant theme of the *Contr.* and *Suas.* His emotive and brilliant style won a large following and attracted to his school in Rome such students as Fabianus and Ovid. See also Bornecque 150-152; Edward xli.

[119] Fuscus appears in each *Suas.* theme for a total of 208 Müller lines out of a grand total 1178.5, or a proportion of 17.7%. Indeed, virtually all of *Suas.* 4 consists of quotations from Fuscus. From the pattern seen in the opening of *Suas.* 2, 3, 4, and 5, it is tempting also to ascribe the fragmentary and unattributed

This is precisely the pattern which Seneca follows in the *Controversiae* for the major figure of a preface in the book immediately following.

Seneca ranked Fuscus among the four best declaimers (10 pr. 13) and it would be reasonable to expect that he would be the subject of one preface. Since he declaimed *suasoriae* far more effectively than *controversiae*, treatment in the preface to a book of *suasoriae* would be more appropriate. [120] Remarks about Fuscus form the transition between *Suas.* 2 and 3, 3 and 4, and 4 and 5—the core of the book. Seneca also mentions several times his sons' insistence on hearing more about Fuscus. [121] This language strongly suggests that Seneca also referred in the lost preface to his sons' urgent request for information about Fuscus, gave some biographical and critical comments about him, and then promised, in a manner similar to that in the prefaces of the *Controversiae*, to give examples from his declamations in the book to follow. Thus the figure of Arellius Fuscus probably formed the unifying basis of *Suasoriae*, Book 1.

A possible objection to this conclusion exists: The role of Fuscus in *Suas.* 6 and 7 is relatively small, only 32 Müller lines. However, both themes deal with the last days of Cicero, and such a subject might not have appealed to Fuscus, a native Greek. We have also mentioned that *Suas.* 2, 3, 4, and 5 are connected to one another by direct references to Fuscus at the end of 2, 3, and 4, and quotations from him at the beginning of each. [122] Why then no mention in the transitions from *Suas.* 1 to 2, 5 to 6, and 6 to 7? An examination of these transitions reveals some important critical themes to which Seneca has related Fuscus, and it is this totality which forms the real unifying principle of the *Suasoriae*. Seneca possibly enunciated this principle more directly in the lost preface; nevertheless, it can easily be reconstructed.

The last section of *Suas.* 1 refers to the stylistic taste and critical ability of Seneca's sons; plainly he suspects that they are not yet sufficiently discriminating:

---

beginning of *Suas.* 1 to Fuscus; the style of these fourteen lines is no obstacle. For fuller statistical information see Sussman (above, note 101).

[120] *Suas.* 4.5. His two most renowned pupils, Fabianus and Ovid, likewise preferred *suasoriae* (2 pr. 3; 2.2.12). The poetic cast of his style, especially evident in his descriptions, was more congenial to *suasoriae*.

[121] *Suas.* 2.23; 3.7; 4.5; cf. 2.10; 4.4.

[122] *Suas.* 2-5 are connected by promises to provide additional material about Fuscus; cf. *Suas.* 2.23 (also referring to matters of critical taste), 4.5. In each case the following theme, as promised, begins with a quotation from Fuscus; cf. *Suas.* 3.1, 4.1, 5.1.

No Greek declaimer had better success in this *suasoria* than Glyco. But the decadent passages were as frequent as the sublime. I shall let you sample both. My intention was to try you out by not adding my own views, and not separating the sound from the corrupt. It might have been that you praised the mad more. But that *may* happen even if I make a distinction. [123]

In the next *suasoria*, which opens with a quotation from Fuscus, Seneca pledges that he will allow his sons to evaluate for themselves the brillance of this very same declaimer (*Suas.* 2.10). But he immediately reneges by adding two damaging critical comments on Fuscus; one from Asinius Pollio and one of his own. [124] At the end of *Suas.* 2, Seneca mentions Fuscus and again reiterates his doubts on the critical taste of his sons, thereby neatly conflating both themes. [125] Here also Seneca marks his realization that they are now deeply under the influence of the stylistic faults prevalent in the schools, but he is confident that age, experience, and his own direction will point them to saner standards of style. The declaimer quoted directly after this discussion in the opening of *Suas.* 3 is Fuscus. Thus Seneca has associated the theme of the sons' developing stylistic judgment with this declaimer as an *exemplum*. [126] There is, then, a definite transition from *Suas.* 1 to *Suas.* 2 in this light, though indirectly expressed.

---

[123] *Suas.* 1.16; Winterbottom transl. On this theme see M. Lambert, "Alexandre le Grand, vu par Sénèque le Père," *LM* 10 (1974) No. 47, 6-13.

[124] *Suas.* 2.10; Winterbottom transl.:

I have mentioned this *suasoria* not because it contained anything very subtle that might stimulate you, but so that you could learn how brilliantly Fuscus spoke—or how licentiously: I shall not vote on that issue. It will be up to *you* to decide whether you think his developments self-indulgent or lively. Asinius Pollio used to say this was sport, not advice. I recall that in my youth nothing was more familiar than these developments of Fuscus'; all of us, with differing inflexions of voice, used to intone them, each, as it were, in his own key. But now that I've got round to speaking about Fuscus, I will append celebrated little descriptive passages from all the *suasoriae*, even if nothing turns up that anyone but a speaker of *suasoriae* likes.

The last remark is quite acerbic. The force of the diminutive, "little descriptive passages" (*descriptiunculas*), may also be pejorative; cf. his use of *satiabo* (*Suas.* 3.7) and *ingeram* (*Suas.* 4.5)—he will "glut" his sons with Fuscus so that they will become tired of his *explicationes* and *descriptiones*. Cf. 2 pr. 1, 2.

[125] *Suas.* 2.23; Winterbottom transl.:

But so as not to craze you further, I will end this *suasoria* here, for I have promised to add developments by Fuscus. Their extreme ornamentation and effeminate rhythm may offend you when you reach my age. Meanwhile I am sure you will take pleasure in the very vices that will later grate on you.

[126] Seneca's remarks at the end of the third and fourth *Suasoriae* (3.7, 4.5) also reflect his literary judgments on Fuscus, and refer to the desire of his sons to learn more about this declaimer.

No direct transition exists linking *Suas.* 5 to *Suas.* 6; instead a rather general comment on a *sententia*:

> Here he [Gallio] delivered a very eloquent epigram, one worthy to be placed in oratory or history (*Suas.* 5.8).

The text plainly implies the inferiority of declamation to either history or oratory as a literary genre, an opinion directly stated in the *Controversiae* (1.8.16). We must look at this statement in view of the contents of the next *suasoria*. The theme is from Roman history, rather than Greek: "Cicero deliberates whether he should entreat Antony for his life." This *suasoria* proceeds normally and perhaps should really have ended in section 14. But in that section, Seneca begins a long digression from declamatory material which on reflection relates back to Seneca's closing words in *Suas.* 5.8 quoted above. At the beginning of the digression Seneca says that since this *suasoria* is concerned with the events of Cicero's last days, it would be relevant to show how various *historici* dealt with his memory (*Suas.* 6.14). The remainder of the *suasoria* (*Suas.* 6.14-27) consists of extracts from or discussion about literary treatments of Cicero's last days.

Seneca is obviously trying to divert the attention of his sons from declamation to what he believes are more worthy modes of literary expression. [127] In the digression Seneca provides examples from three types of literature: oratory (6.15), history (6.16-25), and epic (6.25-27). When introducing the long fragment of an epic poem by Cornelius Severus, Seneca says that of all the very eloquent men who wrote on the subject, none lamented the death of Cicero more effectively (*Suas.* 6.25). This is an important remark, and it recalls an earlier statement in which Seneca said that none of the Latin declaimers could describe a storm at sea as successfully as the epic poet Albinovanus Pedo (*Suas.* 1.15). Thus Seneca seems to have constructed an informal literary hierarchy at the top of which stands epic poetry, followed by

---

[127] *Suas.* 6.16; Winterbottom transl.:

> However, my dear young men, I don't want you to get depressed because I am passing from declamation to history. I will make amends to you: though I may perhaps make you give up the schoolmen once you've read these solid and truly powerful sentiments.

Cf. *Suas.* 6.27. The entire digression which follows on writers who treated the death of Cicero, in the company of his other remarks, is to be taken as a means to convince his sons to leave declamation behind for more substantial literary pursuits: "And, as I shan't be able to bring this about straightforwardly, I shall have to deceive you, like someone wanting to give medicine to a child. Take up your glasses" (*Suas.* 6.16; Winterbottom transl.).

history, oratory, and finally declamation. Certainly the specimens from the literary sources in *Suas.* 6 overwhelm those from the declaimers in both quality and the prestige of their origin. [128] By the end of *Suas.* 6 Seneca possibly believed that he had made his point, since the final *suasoria* returns exclusively to specimens from the declaimers. Or perhaps, though less likely, he returned to declamation because, as he humorously says in the transition to *Suas.* 7:

> If I stop at this point, I know *you* will stop reading where *I* abandoned the schoolmen; so, to encourage you to unwind the book right to the end of the roll, I shall append a *suasoria* on a subject related to its neighbour. [129]

As promised, the next *suasoria* concerns the last days of Cicero: "Antony promises to spare Cicero's life if he burns his writings: Cicero deliberates whether to do so." This is virtually the same theme disparagingly referred to in the previous *suasoria* (*Suas.* 6.14):

> All concede that Cicero was neither coward enough to plead with Antony, nor stupid enough to hope that Antony could be won over: all, that is, except Asinius Pollio, who remained the most implacable enemy of Cicero's reputation. And he actually gave the schoolmen a handle for a second *suasoria*—for they often declaim on the theme: "Cicero deliberates whether to burn his speeches on Antony's promising him life." Anyone must realise that this is a crude fiction. [130]

In this passage, Seneca twice uses a fairly disdainful term for rhetoricians, *scholastici.* Likewise, he suggests their inability to see through an obvious lie and their excessive eagerness to grasp for a flashy *suasoria* theme, whether true or not. [131] In all, he has implicity contrasted historians and declaimers, to the detriment of the latter. So also Seneca has linked the statement above with the closing comments of *Suas.* 6.27, and thereby to the entirety of *Suas.* 7 whose theme, popular among the *scholastici,* was a patently false historical situation.

---

[128] Among those quoted are the historians Asinius Pollio (6.15, 24), Livy (6.17, 22), Aufidius Bassus (6.18, 23), Cremutius Cordus (6.19, 23), Bruttedius Niger (6.20), and the epic poet Cornelius Severus (6.26).

[129] *Suas.* 6.27; Winterbottom transl.

[130] *Suas.* 6.14; Winterbottom transl. The Latin texts of the two variant themes are fairly close: *Deliberat Cicero an salutem promittente Antonio orationes suas comburat* (6.14). Cf. the theme of *Suas.* 7: *Deliberat Cicero an scripta sua conburat, promittente Antonio incolumitatem si fecisset.*

[131] Cf. Winterbottom I, viii, note 3.

The total effect is to stress quite forcefully the gulf between rhetoricians and literary people so tellingly brought out in *Suas.* 6.

In *Suas.* 7 Seneca has therefore returned to the artificial world of the declaimers, although the men quoted are clever and occasionally achieve eloquence on the topic of the immortality of literature. Seneca fittingly ends this *suasoria* with a series of anecdotes which relate the discomfiture of several declaimers who typify the foolish excesses of the schools (*Suas.* 7.12-14). Two of the incidents tell how declaimers who insulted the memory of Cicero were themselves punished by the orator's son when he was serving as governor of Asia (*Suas.* 7.13-14). The book ends with a judgment on an obscure declaimer: "Gargonius, most amiable of fools, said two things on this theme unsurpassed in stupidity even by himself..." [132] The discussion of Cicero, his son, and the foolish declaimers at the end of this *suasoria* therefore continues to reinforce the unfavorable comparison between declamation and the higher forms of literature stated in *Suas.* 6 and elsewhere.

Seneca is eager for his sons to engage in political careers, [133] and therefore they must necessarily first become accomplished courtroom speakers and then political orators; thus the anthologies' inverted order of composition: The quasi-legal *controversiae* first, followed by the deliberative *suasoriae*. Seneca frequently alludes to the defects of declamation as a preparation for courtroom pleading, and also to the necessity for a discriminating style. As we have seen in this analysis of the *Suasoriae*, aside from their political careers, Seneca wanted his sons at the appropriate time to redirect their literary energies from declamation to more substantial genres, and therefore not to follow the example of many others who were content to expend their talents on these schoolboy exercises. [134]

Even with the loss of the preface to the *Suasoriae* where we might have expected fuller treatment, the body of the first book as a whole effectively contrasts declamation with the more worthy genres of literature. Seneca also juxtaposes the artificial style and the frequent foolishness of the declaimers, notably Fuscus, with the more solid and enduring authors. Although introduced in the first *suasoria* (1.15),

---

[132] *Suas.* 7.14; Winterbottom transl.

[133] Cf. 2 pr. 3-4. The Annaei must be understood as an extremely ambitious political clan, a point well made in Ferrill's study.

[134] Cf. his remarks in 10 pr. 1 where he rhetorically confesses tedium with the undue concentration on declamation.

this aspect becomes most pronounced in the final two themes. United also by similar subject matter and a transitional statement, these two final *suasoriae* are filled with contrasts which serve to demonstrate quite effectively the differences between declamation and true literature. Here Seneca is being consistent with the judgment expressed in the *Controversiae*: although declamation is a useful and entertaining exercise, it is useful only insofar as it prepares for more serious work. Over-emphasis on the exercises is decidedly harmful and leads to serious faults; carried to excess, it is a frivolous pursuit for a mature man (10 pr. 1).

Seneca clearly recognized, especially in the case of Fuscus, that his sons' critical standards of style had not yet risen to his own level. This topic figures prominently in the first five *suasoriae*. Seneca is attempting to direct his audience to higher standards of style and more serious literary ambitions. He has therefore unified both in content and structure the first book of *Suasoriae,* while restating and redefining the themes, goals, and methods of his earlier work, the *Controversiae.* Both works then are not merely haphazard collections of rhetorical reminiscences, but, given the limitations of the anthology format, well-crafted and planned pieces of literary commentary and criticism.

5. Controversiae *and* Suasoriae: *Sources*

In the first preface Seneca makes a sweeping assertion that he is relying solely on his memory for the specimens to be presented (1 pr. 1-5); most observers have uncritically accepted this account:

> What you ask is something I find agreeable rather than easy. You tell me to give you my opinion of the declaimers who have been my contemporaries, and to put together such of their sayings as I haven't yet forgotten, so that, even though you were not acquainted with them, you may still form your own judgement on them without trusting merely to hearsay. Yes, it *is* agreeable for me to return to my old studies, to look back on better years, and simultaneously to remove the sting of your complaint against Time—that you were unable to listen to men of such reputation. (2) But by now old age has made me regret the loss of many of my faculties. It has dimmed my eyesight, dulled my hearing, made my strong muscles tired: but among these things I mention it is memory, of all parts of the mind the most vulnerable and fragile, that old age first assaults. I do not deny that my own memory was at one time so powerful as to be positively prodigious, quite apart from its efficiency in ordinary use. When two thousand names had been reeled off I would repeat them in the same order;

and when my assembled school-fellows each supplied a line of poetry, up to the number of more then two hundred, I would recite them in reverse. (3) My memory used to be swift to pick up what I wanted it to; but it was also reliable in retaining what it had taken in. Now it has been undermined by age, and by a long period of idleness—which can play havoc with young minds too: to such an extent that though it may be able to come up with something, it cannot make any promises. It is a long time since I asked anything of it. But now, since you require it, I will see what it can do, and pry into its recesses with every care.

To some extent I am quite hopeful: whatever I entrusted to it as a boy or young man it brings out again without hesitation as though new and just heard. But things I have deposited with it these last years it has lost so entirely that even if they are repeatedly dinned into me, I hear them each time as new. (4) Hence enough of my memory is left for your purposes—for you aren't asking me about speakers you have heard yourselves, but about those who came before your time.

Be it as you wish, then: let an old man be sent to school. But I must ask you not to insist on any strict order in the assembling of my memories; I must stray at large though all my studies, and grab at random whatever comes my way. (5) I shall, perhaps, distribute over a number of passages epigrams which were actually spoken in one *controversia*: I don't always find what I want when I'm looking for it—but often what escaped me when I was searching for it comes to me when I am on some other tack. Some things, that I cannot quite catch as they hover before me only partly visible, suddenly come up clearly when I am relaxed and at leisure. Sometimes, even, an epigram that I have long hunted in vain comes at the wrong moment and is a nuisance when I'm occupied with some serious business. I have got, therefore, to adapt myself to the whims of my memory, which for some time has obeyed me only on sufferance. [135]

But there are serious problems in accepting Seneca at his word here. First of all, the text itself is contradictory. He states that he could

---

[135] I pr. 1-5; Winterbottom transl. Citations of those accepting Seneca's total reliance on memory are conveniently collected in Charles W. Lockyear, Jr., *The Fiction of Memory and the Use of Written Sources: Convention and Practice in Seneca the Elder and Other Authors* (Diss., Princeton 1970) 8-13. Some, however, have varying degrees of skepticism at Seneca's sweeping assertion and suspect that there must have been at least some reliance upon written sources; cf. Bornecque 28-29; Otto Immisch, "Wirklichkeit und Literaturform," *RhM* 78 (1929) 114-115; Winterbottom I, x, note 1. The only sustained and systematic analysis of Seneca's sources, however, is Lockyear's dissertation. He maintains that Seneca's assertion of reliance upon memory is a conventional literary fiction, and that many written sources are referred to or hinted at by Seneca himself. Cf. the summary in *DA* 32 (1971) 1491 A.

recall without delay everything he heard as a youth, while elsewhere admitting that he could relate specimens only as they occur to him at random. [136] Throughout the passage he is decidedly apologetic about the deteriorating state of his memory, but nevertheless posits it as the sole source for a work which includes quotations going back eighty years, which reproduces the words of over a hundred men, and which originally formed the equivalent of about 1,000 Teubner pages. No doubt Seneca did have an excellent memory and was acquainted with mnemonic techniques (1 pr. 17-19). Other instances of great memory feats in antiquity are recorded, and we are familiar with the basics of an elaborate mnemonic system supposedly invented by Simonides. [137] In practice, however, this method was extremely cumbersome and difficult to use. Quintilian therefore rejects it and suggests a more natural method of memorization (11.2.24-51). Although *memoria* was one of the five cardinal aspects of rhetoric, in reality it was the least important of them. [138] The descriptions of Simonidean mnemonics do not in any way transmit a true picture of memory capabilities in that period. Memory was as difficult for the ancients as for us, and few used any specialized system.

If we take Seneca at his word in 1 pr. 1-5, the composition of the *Controversiae* and *Suasoriae* would unquestionably constitute one of the greatest memory feats in recorded history. Here is a man who, three-quarters of a century later, could reproduce lengthy verbatim quotations heard only once in a crowded hall. Reason dictates that the uncritical acceptance of his total reliance on memory as a source, either in whole or even in a large part, must be rejected. And if we are convinced that he is not inventing or recasting quotations, then the inevitable conclusion is that Seneca was dependent upon written sources. If sufficient evidence can be found of written sources readily available to Seneca, and if there are grounds to believe that his stated reliance on memory is a conventional literary fiction, then with an even greater degree of assurance we can assume the use of written sources and

---

[136] 1 pr. 3, 5; cf. Lockyear (above, note 135) 7-8.

[137] Callim. fr. 71; *Ad Her.* 3.29-35; Cic. *De Or.* 2.299, 351-354, 360; Quint. 11.2.11-23; cf. L. A. Post, "Ancient Memory Systems," *CW* 25 (1932) 105-110; Caplan note (b) *ad loc., Ad Her.* 3.28; France B. Yates, *The Art of Memory* (London 1966); Harry Caplan, "Memoria: Treasure-House of Eloquence," in Anne King and Helen North (eds.), *Of Eloquence: Studies in Ancient and Medieval Rhetoric* (Ithaca 1970) 223-226, and authorities there cited. Cf. Lockyear (above, note 135) 17ff.

[138] Lockyear (above, note 135) 22-23.

therefore be reasonably sure that his quotations are substantially accurate. [139] Indeed, the text does contain many references to written sources. Nevertheless, scholars have all but neglected these and preferred to credit Seneca's memory.

But why would Seneca draw such a misleading picture of his sources in the first place, and why the great vehemence both in the first preface and elsewhere for sole reliance on memory? [140] Lockyear successfully argues that Seneca is indulging in a literary fiction conventional in antiquity. First, memory was recognized as a rhetorical virtue, and Seneca felt compelled to demonstrate his proficiency in it to be credited with rhetorical ability and training. [141] Next, Lockyear traces the importance of oral tradition and the beginnings of the literary fiction of a powerful memory, especially in the Platonic dialogues and their further development in Xenophon, Cicero, Gellius, Athenaeus, and Macrobius. [142] The three latter-named authors are especially important since their claim to be compiling their anthologies from memory is patently fictional. All three transmit considerable information on their sources, and the actual works are cited upon which the speakers depended for their statements. Lockyear then returns to Seneca, excerpting and classifying the references to his written sources, and then indicating other possibilities less directly mentioned. [143] He does, however, qualify the extent of the memory

---

[139] Written sources would be available to others and would discourage the blatant falsification or inaccurate rendering of quotations. Seneca himself aimed for accuracy (1 pr. 11).

[140] Besides the emphatic statements in 1 pr. 1-5, throughout the anthologies Seneca frequently uses the verb *memini* ("I remember") or similar equivalents when introducing a quotation; e.g., 1.1.22; 1.2.22; 1.7.15; 2.1.34; 2.2.9. He will also use *aiebat* ("he used to say"), *dixit* ("he said"), or equivalents, to give the impression that he is directly reporting something which he had heard. In one instance he states unequivocally that he had heard one *sententia*: *ipse enim audivi* ("for I myself heard ..."). Here he is probably attempting to tell us that at least in this case he *really* was there (9.2.23). While this may be true on occasion, his recall must have been aided.

[141] Lockyear (above, note 135) 23.

[142] *Ibid.* 27-157.

[143] *Ibid.* 158-190. He first establishes that there was wide publication of declamations and speeches prior to the time in which Seneca wrote (158-166). Then he categorizes the references in the anthologies to written sources under three headings of descending probability of actual use: I, definite statement (references to written works of Junius Otho, Cassius Severus, Votienus Montanus, Cestius Pius, Asinius Pollio, Scaurus, and Menestratus) 166-178; II, Senecan statement and corroborative evidence (written works of Arellius Fuscus, Latro, Junius Gallio, Calvus, and Hybreas) 178-186; and III, strong indications, but inconclusive (possible references to written works of Capito, Gorgias, Albucius, and, with less certainty, Labienus) 186-189.

fiction, since obviously Seneca did have a good memory and would have been able to draw upon it for a small proportion of the material. [144]

By establishing that Seneca depended upon written sources, Lockyear has also helped to settle a problem vexing Senecan scholarship for generations: whether or not we can rely on the accuracy and authenticity of the specimens. [145] For if Seneca was relying on memory alone, the authenticity of the excerpts would be gravely suspect. On the other hand, reliance upon written sources, as established by Lockyear, argues for fidelity of transmission, and thus we can be rather reasonably sure that Seneca's extracts faithfully portray stylistic characteristics. In turn, scholarship on Silver Age stylistics may now use the elder Seneca as a primary source with confidence.

Written sources available to Seneca were abundant. There was a long tradition of publishing judicial and political speeches in Rome reaching back to the elder Cato. Seneca himself makes it clear that published speeches of several men who figure prominently in his works were available. [146] Declamations were also published or circulated privately on a small scale. His own statements clearly show that Seneca had before him circulated declamations of Cestius, Montanus, Scaurus, Menestratus and perhaps Pollio. [147] The declamations of Albucius, a

---

[144] *Ibid.* 191-194.

[145] *Ibid.* 13-16.

[146] Thus, Cassius Severus (3 pr. 3-4; cf. Quint. 6.3.78; 8.3.89; 10.1.22, 116; 11.1.57; Tac. *Dial.* 19, 26; Suet. *Aug.* 56; *Gaius* 16; Lockyear [above, note 135] 168-170) and Votienus Montanus (*Contr.* 9.5.15-16 [Seneca quotes from his speech in defense of Galla Numisia] ; cf. 9.6.18). Scaurus published seven speeches (10 pr. 3; cf. Quint. 5.12.10) and some unspecified *libelli* which might have been declamations; cf. Bornecque (ed.) II, 564, note 237; Lockyear (above, note 135) 176-177. On Calvus, see 7.4.7; cf. Malcovati *Oratorum Romanorum Fragmenta Liberae Rei Publicae* (Torino 1955) 492-500; Lockyear (above, note 135) 185. On Pollio, see *Suas.* 6.15; cf. Quint. 1.8.11; Lockyear (above, note 135) 174-176.

[147] Cestius, cf. 3 pr. 15. His students memorized his declamations, and so written versions must have been available; cf. Lockyear (above, note 135) 173-174. In addition to his speeches Montanus also wrote or compiled a work which contained *sententiae* and literary judgments (9.6.18). Seneca tells us that he never declaimed, but Montanus may have written out the exercises and not performed them (9 pr. 1), since Seneca says that he never declaimed, but a goodly number of quotations from his declamations are preserved in the *Contr.* Scaurus also probably published declamations; cf. above, note 146; also Bornecque 145; Lockyear (above, note 135) 176-177. There is an obvious reference to a written source in the case of Menestratus, and it is an old one (*Suas.* 1.13). Pollio's *sententiae* and colors appear throughout Seneca's works, although Seneca could not have heard him often (4 pr. 2-3) ; thus it is likely that some of his declamations may have been circulated. Pollio's criticisms of the declaimers derive from an unknown source (cf. 2.3.19; 2.5.10; *Excerpta* 4.6 *extra*; 7 pr. 2; *Suas.* 2.10).

well known rhetorician and author, were also in circulation for Seneca's
use. Quotations from him are numerous, even though Seneca did not
hear him often. [148] Additional evidence also points to written declamations as sources. Seneca analyzes a transition from the *prooemium*
of a declamation to the narration in a manner which strongly suggests
that he had a text in front of him (1.1.25). In the same section he
analyzes, though in less detail, a similar transition by Gallio whose
published declamations we know were available to Seneca, as also were
those of Latro. [149]

Other works on declamation existed which also could have served
as sources. Junius Otho, a declaimer quoted by Seneca, wrote a work
on colors in four books. Seneca was familiar with it, and offers an
unfavorable review (2.1.33; cf. 1.3.11). Each book in Otho's work was
probably arranged by declamation themes, since this would be the
most convenient organization, and Seneca's use of Otho may be
reflected in a variety of statements Seneca makes on colors, such as
"nearly all used..." or "only one...," all of which suggests a compendium was before him. [150] Similar works may have existed on divisions,
since a parallel situation to the colors exists, and perhaps on *sententiae*. [151]

---

[148] Quotations may have been culled from his own notes or those of listeners.
[149] On Gallio see 10 pr. 8: *Monstrabo bellum vobis libellum quem a Gallione
vestro petatis. Recitavit rescriptum Labieno Pro Bathyllo Maecenatis ....* Bornecque (ed.) note *ad loc.* says that the reference is undoubtedly to a declamation.
Gallio's declamations were certainly published (cited in Quint. 9.2.91; cf. 3.1.21)
and were still popular in the time of Jerome (Bornecque 175). Later references
to Gallio's style argue for direct access to written versions; cf. Statius *Silv.*
2.7.32; Tac. *Dial.* 26; Sidonius *Ep.* 5.10.3; Lockyear (above, note 135) 184-185.
Latro wrote out his declamations before delivery (1 pr. 14, 17-18; cf. 1 pr. 23).
As his best friend, Seneca must have had access to these written versions; he
could hardly have memorized the great quantity of material from Latro otherwise
(e.g., the long quotation in 2.7.1-9; cf. Bornecque 29). Declamations were circulated
under Latro's name, though inaccurately ascribed; therefore genuine ones were
probably also in circulation (10 pr. 12). Quintilian quotes Latro from a source
independent of Seneca (Quint. 9.2.91; cf. *Contr.* 2.3: the same theme is mentioned, but the Quint. quotation is missing in Seneca). Hybreas, a Greek, may
also have published his declamations. Seneca quotes him fairly often although
he never came to Rome (Bornecque 172) and we have no evidence for Seneca
visiting Asia Minor. Cf. Lockyear (above, note 135) 186.
[150] E.g., 1.7.14; 1.8.8; 2.4.7, 9; *Excerpta* 4.6 *extra*; 7.1.20; 9.2.21.
[151] Cf. 1.6.8; 1.7.11; 1.8.7; 7.5.7; 7.7.10; 10.1.10; 10.5.12. Numerous references
occur to *sententiae* which were widely quoted. This suggests the existence of
anthologies; cf. Lockyear (above, note 135) 162. He also argues for the possibility
that the *explicationes* of Fuscus were drawn from written sources (*ibid.* 178-181;
cf. *Suas.* 2.10; 4.5). It is difficult to say exactly what these were; perhaps some
sort of *belle dicta* taken from descriptions.

Seneca focusses a great deal of critical attention on figures of speech. Gorgias, a speaker mentioned once, compiled a collection of figures in four books with illustrations taken from Asian and classical speakers. [152] This work could very easily have been an additional aid, especially useful for the numerous quotations in Seneca of Greek rhetoricians, many of whom never came to Rome.

Commentarii, circulated privately or publicly, have all but been neglected in the investigation of Seneca's sources. [153] These were speakers' notes where the most elaborate portions were regularly written out in full, while the rest was outlined (Quint. 10.7.30). *Commentarii* were preserved in family archives, and were used as a basis for the publication of actual speech texts, or were themselves published— though in edited form. [154] Declaimers inevitably followed the practice of orators and so also used *commentarii*. Seneca refers to them in the most unambiguous terms as source material in common circulation:

> Indeed, I think I shall be doing a great service to the declaimers themselves, who face being forgotten unless something to prolong their memory is handed on to posterity; for in general there are no extant drafts [*commentarii*] from the pens of the greatest declaimers, or, what is worse, there are forged ones. [155]

Because of their obviously wide publication, Seneca must have had access to the *commentarii* of many declaimers. In addition, those unpublished and held privately could easily have been available to him because of his close friendship with many of the declaimers mentioned in his works. [156]

Another important source for the collection were the notes taken

---

[152] 1.4.7. (This is the man who taught Cicero's son in Athens during 44 BC.) P. Rutilius Lupus adapted the work into Latin; cf. Quint. 9.2.102-106; 9.3.89; Kennedy *ARRW* 337, 338 and note 49. Lockyear (above, note 135) 177-178 thinks that Rutilius is a possible source for Seneca.

[153] Lockyear only alludes to them briefly (*ibid.* 16, 165).

[154] The practice was an old one, going back at least to the elder Cato; cf. Cic. *Sen.* 38; Kennedy *ARRW* 58. *Commentarii* were probably arranged into codices (*ibid.*). The speeches of Crassus might have been known only through these (*ibid.* 85). On the publication of *commentarii* see Quint. 4.1.69; 10.7.30-32; Tac. *Dial.* 23, 26; on their use in writing history see Kennedy *ARRW* 287-291.

[155] I pr. 11; Winterbottom transl. Cf. 3 pr. 6; Quint. 10.7.30. *Commentarii* could also denote a schoolboy's lecture notes (e.g., Quint. 2.11.7; 3.6.59), but here the meaning is unambiguous.

[156] These connections would remain strong between the families even after one of the principals had died. Some declaimers, e.g., Latro, did not use *commentarii* at all (he wrote his declamations out in full, but memorized as he wrote; I pr. 17-18).

by members of the audience at declamation sessions. Latro's pupils must have been especially dependent on these since his only means of instruction was the delivered speech; he disdained lectures and the laborious correction of drafts (9.2.23). Quintilian's students likewise took extensive notes, but they published them, to their master's ever-lasting regret (Quint. 1 pr. 7-8). In addition to recording striking expressions and outlines of division, students probably recorded summaries or quotations from the criticisms delivered following each declamation. [157] As a schoolboy, Seneca himself also took notes which he must have referred to in reproducing the references to and quotations from his schoolmaster Marullus. [158] Adults present at the declamation sessions likewise took extensive notes, especially for studying and imitating the style of an acclaimed rhetor (7 pr. 4-5). Other internal evidence supports use of personal notes or those of friends. A number of speakers quoted by Seneca declaimed either very rarely or only in private. [159] In addition Seneca frequently records the reactions of other audience members and their criticisms of particular aspects of a declamation. This type of information must have been taken down at the time it was delivered. [160] The occasional descriptions of delivery also seem to be first-hand impressions recorded in a notebook. [161] Here too, Seneca need not have relied on his own notes, but as in the case of the *commentarii*, he may have had access to notes of friends and acquaintances, or even published notebooks similar to the collections attributed to Quintilian. [162]

Other sources are referred to, but are difficult to categorize. Calvus, who died about 47 BC, is quoted on the difference between oratory

[157] Quint. (2.11.7) preserves a description of the contents of an average schoolboy's notes.

[158] 1 pr. 22, 24; 1.1.12, 19; 1.2.2, 17 etc. Ovid often imitated or adapted Latro's work; he also probably relied upon notes (2.2.8; cf. 9.6.11, 12).

[159] E.g., Cassius Severus (3 pr. 7, 18), Pollio (4 pr. 2, 3), Albucius (7 pr. 1), Montanus (9 pr. 1), and Labienus (10 pr. 4).

[160] E.g., 1.3.10; 2.1.36; 2.3.19, 22; 2.4.8; 2.5.19; 7 pr. 9. Cf. the comments of the various declaimers upon the colors of others (7.2.12; 7.5.11; 9.3.12; 9.5.10), and the accounts of applause (e.g., 2.3.19; 2.4.8; 7.2.9).

[161] See below, 132-134.

[162] The direct and accurate transcription of long passages during a performance was not exceptionally difficult since the use of short-hand was common and knowledge of it was not confined to professional secretaries (although these, too, might have been used). Cicero instructed some senators in the skill to record the Catilinarian debate in 63 BC. Cf. the discussion of D. R. Shackelton-Bailey (ed.), *Cicero's Letters to Atticus* (7 vols., Cambridge 1966) V, 351, note *ad loc.*, διὰ σημείων, *Att.* 13.32. The Emperor Titus was also well versed in shorthand (Suet. *Tit.* 3); see also Kees, "Kurzschrift" *P-W* XI, cols. 2217-2232.

and declamation (1 pr. 12). Seneca later quotes one of his poems and describes his delivery in vivid terms (7.4.6-8). It is hardly likely that Seneca witnessed his performances in person and so he may have relied either on an account from Pollio (who figures prominently in the anecdote) or perhaps on a lost work by Calvus himself.

Votienus Montanus published his speech in defense of Galla Numisia, but apparently Seneca also heard it in person, since he compares the written version with the speech as delivered (9.5.15-16; cf. 9.5.17). He also mentions other unidentified works by Montanus, at least one of which obviously included both literary criticism and *sententiae* (9.6.18).

Seneca was also familiar with Messalla's grammatical and rhetorical works (2.4.8), and perhaps these may have been the source of the few criticisms attributed to him. In addition to the sources already mentioned, Seneca obviously drew upon the standard literary classics of the day, including Homer, Vergil, Ovid, Cicero, Livy, and Sallust, among others [163]

6. Objectives

Seneca's objectives in collecting the two anthologies are closely tied to the problem of whether he was writing expressly for the benefit of his sons, as he himself constanly maintains, or whether he was indulging in a literary convention when he tied the composition to their urgent requests. As Janson has amply demonstrated, the mention of the dedicatee's request for a work was a conventional part of any literary preface, and it is in Seneca's prefaces that the vast majority of these references to his sons' urgings appear. [164] In this scheme, the dedicatee stands in for the general reading public when the writer feels that he must address it. [165] Thus the author lends his work the personal touch which a broader "dear reader" form of address so obviously lacks.

---

[163] Cf. the individual entries in the indexes of the standard editions of Kiessling, Müller, or Winterbottom. A rather obvious use of written sources occurs in *Suas.* 6.15-17, where Seneca quotes passages on the death of Cicero from a number of historians and poets. Since he was preparing to write a history of the civil wars, he must have been surveying the sources which he had gathered together.

[164] See Janson (above, note 48) 22, 50, 64, 116ff, 148-149. On the requests of the sons see, e.g., 1 pr. 1, 3, 4, 6, 10, 20, 22; 2 pr. 1; 4 pr. 1; 7 pr. 1, 9; 9 pr. 1; 10 pr. 1, 2, 4, 9; *Suas.* 6.16.

[165] Janson (above, note 48) 148.

6

The tone in which Seneca addresses his sons is that of a father to very young men just completing their rhetorical education and preparing for future careers. [166] This would indicate an age therefore of about 25 for the elder sons, and composition somewhere around AD 20. [167] Nevertheless, internal evidence dates the composition of the work to the mid-30's AD or even later. [168] Seneca therefore had moved back the dramatic date in order to make the conventional dictates of a prose preface believable. For if the audience knew that the sons were in their forties when he was dedicating this work on declamation, the whole conception might appear frivolous and unbelieveable. Thus Seneca did have a general audience in mind, and in order to follow the literary conventions and to satisfy the general reader's common sense, he addressed the dedicatees, his sons, as though they were at the age when the subject would normally be most attractive to them.

Such a conclusion does not rule out the possibility that Seneca may indeed have been writing in some measure at the behest of his sons and that they were still interested in the declaimers and the declamations of a past age. The repeated use of emphatic language in describing their requests for this material certainly must have had some reflection in reality. [169] Seneca constantly portrays the sons as interested in the declaimers they were unable to see, [170] and he makes a point throughout the works of delving into the character and talents of the men presented. Each of the sons had careers in which public speaking played an important role, and the interest we find expressed in memory, divisions, colors, and especially in good *sententiae* also must have had a factual basis. [171] The depth of Seneca's personal feeling expressed in the second preface to Mela and the paternal apprehensions about the careers of his other sons also indicate something more than a resort to prose preface convention. For this reason, and the ones enumerated above, we can conclude that Seneca had two

---

[166] Cf. esp. 2 pr. 3-5; also 1 pr. 19; *Suas.* 6.16. The sons are close friends with the younger Clodius Turrinus, whom Seneca describes in a manner reminiscent of Mela (10 pr. 16; cf. 2 pr. 3-5).

[167] Cf. Edward xxvi.

[168] Cf. the discussion below, 91-93.

[169] On the use of strong terms in such requests, see Janson (above, note 48) 117ff; on similar terms in Seneca see above, 54.

[170] 1 pr. 1, 4; 7 pr. 1; 9 pr. 1; 10 pr. 1, 2; cf. 1 pr. 11. With one pointed exception Seneca excludes those speakers whom he and his sons have witnessed in person (10 pr. 2).

[171] Cf. 1 pr. 19, 22; 2 pr. 5; 4 pr. 1; 7 pr. 9.

audiences in mind throughout; his sons, but more important, the general Roman literary public. [172]

The Decline of Eloquence: A Cure?

Thus, the audience: sophisticated and informed about the basics of rhetoric, and a good deal younger than Seneca himself. Through the *personae* of his sons, he was addressing the new generation of speakers they represented, one unacquainted with the eloquence of the Ciceronian and Augustan ages. And he tells us, it was since those "better years" that a perceptible decline in eloquence had occurred:

> A second advantage is that you can evaluate to what extent genius is vanishing every day and by what perversity of nature the progress of eloquence has been reversed. Whatever Roman eloquence has which may equal or surpass the boasts of the Greeks reached its height in the age of Cicero. All those geniuses who brought light to our studies were born then. Afterwards the art degenerated more each day, whether because of the profligacy of this age—for there is nothing so fatal to genius as profligacy, or, since the rewards of this most worthy calling had ceased, all competition was transferred to base pursuits flourishing with greater prospects of political advancement and profit, or whether because of some fickleness of the gods whose malicious law is consistent in everything, that when something reaches its peak, it falls back again to the bottom, indeed more quickly than it rose. [173]

Because of this decline Seneca is eager to provide his readers with a link to the golden age of public speaking which would otherwise be lost. At the time he was writing, Seneca was perhaps the only man qualified for the task by reason of his longevity, sound judgment, broad experience, and available sources. The citation of declining *ingenium*, (innate character and moral endowment) and its corruption by *luxus* (dissipation or profligacy), leads to a fuller and rather vivid description of a moral decline (1 pr. 8-10). No man, according to the ancient theory, can be an orator unless he is morally pure. [174] Bad character

---

[172] Cf. Janson (above, note 48) 50: "These lines, with their fine tone of parental solicitude and benevolence, are without doubt the most worth reading .... They also show that the dedication to his sons was made not only from formal convenience but reflected a real contact between father and sons."

[173] 1 pr. 6-7. Seneca is explaining to his sons the advantages of becoming familiar with samples of eloquence from the past. For a discussion of this important passage, see Sussman "Decline of Eloquence" *passim*.

[174] I.e., a *vir bonus*. The concept in Roman oratory goes back at least to the elder Cato, according to Seneca (1 pr. 9; cf. above, note 113).

not only results in laziness, plagiarism, and shoddy composition, but
also prevents, in the ancient view, the selection of proper models for
imitation, a cornerstone of Roman literary theory. [175] A decline of
morals therefore results in a generally lower standard of critical taste.
Whether this was the real cause is open to question. But Seneca had
correctly diagnosed a decline in taste whatever the reason might be. [176]
And of all the objectives motivating Seneca, we must assign a high
priority for the development of critical taste in his audience. [177]

Seneca mentions low morality as a cause of poor taste, but the
excesses of the schools and their inherent nurturing of extravagant
style receive far more attention. [178] The logical result of the distorted
tastes fostered in the schools was the growing gulf between declamation
and forensic oratory. Conceits and practices which would slip by or
even receive applause in a declamation hall could spell disaster in the
forum (7 pr. 6-7). Nurtured in the hot-house atmosphere of the
schools, the character of the declaimers themselves became weakened
and they found the rough give-and-take of a real court overpowering—
even Latro, who was probably the greatest declaimer of his day. [179]
Seneca was deeply concerned by the decline of taste and the rift between
declamation and oratory; for this reason he discusses both developments prominently in the most important part of the works—the
prefaces.

In the passage quoted above from the first preface, Seneca refers
obliquely to public oratory when he intimates that after Cicero's death
oratory declined because the rewards for eloquence diminished and men
turned their energies to base pursuits, perhaps delation or sycophancy,

---

[175] See esp. 1 pr. 10. The relationship of character to the selection of proper
models is discussed in Sussman "Decline of Eloquence" 202-205, 207-208.

[176] The prominent rhetorician Cestius openly admitted (9.6.12) that he said
foolish things just to win the applause of an audience which betrayed its poor
taste by preferring the styles of Cestius and Latro to those of far superior
orators such as Pollio, Messalla, and Passienus (3 pr. 14-15). The students of
Cestius would even prefer the master to Cicero if they did not fear being stoned
(3 pr. 15). The lack of taste in the audiences was apparent in their frequently
unrestrained applause (9 pr. 2; cf. 2.3.19; 7.2.9; Quint. 2.2.9-13), often completely
undeserved (e.g., *Contr.* 7.4.10). Bornecque (58) could not discover how audiences
expressed their displeasure, but theorized that with unrestrained applause so
common, its mere absence would be sufficiently damaging (cf. 7 pr. 9). On the
debasement of taste see also Quint. 2.5.10; 12.10.73-76; D'Alton 338; Sussman
"Decline of Eloquence" 204-205.

[177] Especially notable in the *Suas.*; cf. above, 70-75 *passim.*

[178] Seneca prominently emphasizes this point in the prefaces: 3 pr. 12-18;
7 pr. 6-9; 9 pr. 1-5; 10 pr. 12. Cf. 1.7.15; 1.8.16; Clarke 104-105.

[179] 9 pr. 3; cf. 9 pr. 4-5; Quint. 10.5.17-18.

which offered greater prospects of public office and profit. Seneca was thus the first observer to attribute the decline of eloquence to the change from Republic to Principate, and he was among the first Roman critics to recognize the interplay of political and historical influences on the development of human expression.[180] He fully appreciated the damaging effect on eloquence of repressing free speech; Seneca himself mentions the subject several times in regard to book burnings, and rails against the practice[181]

The topic of a decline in eloquence, discussed in the first half of the important first preface, recurs in the final and tenth preface, where it is coupled with a reference to free speech.[182] The repetition of this topic in the first and final prefaces is probably intentional, serving to keep the motif fixed firmly in the mind of the reader and to emphasize its thematic importance.[183] The concept of a decline in eloquence is therefore more encompassing than it may seem at first, since it embraces a decline in morals, style, critical taste, and opportunities for oratory, while demonstrating the growing artificiality of declamation and the educational system in which it reigned supreme. The most tangible result of these developments in declamation was the growing rift between court oratory and declamation.

Seneca is not echoing a tired commonplace when he laments the decline of eloquence; in fact, we should interpret his anthologies as a means of perhaps staving off further deterioration. He briefly theorizes

---

[180] Sussman "Decline of Eloquence" 195-202.

[181] 10 pr. 5-8; cf. 2.4.13; 7.3.9; 10 pr. 3; 10.5.22. See also younger Seneca *Ad Marciam* 1.3; Tac. *Agr.* 2; *Dial.* 27; *Ann.* 4.35; Suet. *Tib.* 61; *Gaius* 16; "Long." *Subl.* 44. Modern treatments include Gudeman's note *ad loc., Dial.* 40, *faces admovebant*; C. Forbes, "Books for the Burning," *TAPA* 67 (1936) 114-125; C. Starr, *Civilization and the Caesars* (Norton Lib. repr., New York 1965) 63-88. Significantly, Seneca blames the enemies of Labienus for the burning of his writings (10 pr. 5, 7) and studiously avoids mentioning Augustus who was probably the guilty party (cf. Griffin 14 and note 158). A third cause mentioned for the decline of eloquence, an inexorable process of growth followed by decay in all genres, is related to the proper use of imitation (cf. Vell. Pat. 1.17) but need not concern us here; see Sussman "Decline of Eloquence" 206-208.

[182] "Certainly it was to everybody's advantage that this cruelty [i.e., book burning] that turns on genius was devised later than the time of Cicero; for what would have happened if the triumvirs had been pleased to proscribe Cicero's talent as well as Cicero? .... How great is the savagery that puts a match to literature, and wreaks its vengeance on monuments of learning; how unsatisfied with its other victims! Thank god that these punishments for genius began in an age when genius had come to an end" (10 pr. 6, 7; Winterbottom transl.).

[183] The motif of decline is also implicit in another theme of the first preface, the *meliores anni* ("better years"); both recur in the tenth preface.

on the decline, but more concretely, he provides good and bad samples of eloquence to compare, reproduces the thoughts of other prominent men on the subject of declamation, and perceptively criticizes the efforts of many speakers. In general, Seneca tries to lend a sense of perspective to this relatively new fad of declamation. Neither a literary reactionary nor a lonely voice crying out for a total return to Ciceronian standards, Seneca recognizes the changed stylistic standards of a new age. He himself is greatly attached to some of the current and popular developments, especially the use of *sententiae*. But the excesses fostered in the schools greatly disturbed him. Although it was intended to be a preparatory exercise for school boys and an entertaining respite for Roman gentlemen, declamation began to overwhelm the more traditional literary callings. Seneca accepts its place as the cornerstone of the educational system, but he is not reluctant to present greatly contrasting points of view. [184] He himself points out that, in excess, declamation is a waste of time for grown men (10 pr. 1). Oratory, literature, and politics are the prime activities of a Roman gentleman, not these sterile though entertaining exercises.

Seneca's unmistakable preoccupation with the declining state of eloquence is evident; so also are his efforts to take remedial action. First and foremost was to bring to the attention of the Roman literary public the fact that eloquence had indeed declined. He himself had seen the process, and no reader of the first preface could fail to be unaware of his emphatic view that a decline had taken place. Many times literary developments are so gradual in occurring that they require a keen perception to recognize the fact. Not only does he expose the downward drift of eloquence, but he enumerates the ways in which it is happening. In a constructive mode, finally, he leads to some possible remedies: a complete reconsideration of the overriding influence of declamation in the educational system and a questioning of the relevance of the exercise to actual public speaking and literary creation. He champions the inculcation of sane critical standards of taste by examination of various examples of eloquence taken in a historical context, always looking back to great masters for inspiration, whether Cicero in oratory, Latro in declamation, or Vergil in poetry. In all, he tries to view literary style, whether of declamation or of other literary forms, in the greater historical context. Thus he rejects the

---

[184] Cf. Seneca's own comments on the importance of rhetorical training, of which declamation was an integral part (2 pr. 3), with the views reproduced of Cassius Severus (3 pr. 8-18) and Votienus Montanus (9 pr. 1-5).

crowd-pleasing artifices attractive to so many declaimers as ephemeral aberrations in the larger context of Roman eloquence. This sense of perspective gained over a long lifetime of observation and criticism forms the most valuable component of Seneca's criticism, and is precisely what he wishes to pass on to an audience which was not fortunate enough to have observed the course of eloquence for over three-quarters of a dynamic century in literary history.

Other objectives

Within the larger framework of arresting a decline in taste and style, Seneca mentions other specific goals in the first preface; recording his recollections of the famous declaimers themselves and preserving specimens of their speeches. He links these two objectives with the nurturing of his audience's critical taste:

> You tell me to give you my opinion of the declaimers who have been my contemporaries, and to put together such of their sayings as I haven't yet forgotten, so that, even though you were not acquainted with them, you may still form your own judgement on them without trusting merely to hearsay. [185]

We can well appreciate the interest of this newer generation in the older masters of declamation, especially since memories of them were fast fading and apparently little was recorded about them personally and artistically. For this reason the intensity of his sons' request is entirely understandable. Seneca transmits this information chiefly in the prefaces where he pens anecdotal critical portraits of the famous declaimers. Similar information, although to a lesser extent, appears also in the body of the *Controversiae* and *Suasoriae*. Seneca consciously attempts to distribute these portraits and glimpses throughout the works in order to provide relief from monotony and add new, unexpected material to whet the reader's appetite (4 pr. 1). Not only does he provide criticism, but in certain cases Seneca is also eager to correct false impressions which had arisen about the abilities of certain speakers, and to rectify erroneous ascriptions of authorship, whether through mistake or plagiarism. [186]

---

[185] I pr. 1; Winterbottom transl.

[186] I pr. 11. He points out also that Florus was the real source of a poor *sententia* ascribed popularly to Latro (9.2.23; cf. 10 pr. 12). Plagiarism was also a major problem at the time, one which Seneca thought symptomized the degeneracy of the age (1 pr. 10). Slavish imitation also bordered upon plagiarism (cf. 1.5.1; 2.1.28; 7.1.27; 10.4.19; *Suas.* 2.19; 3.7). In earlier, less corrupt days,

By far the greatest bulk of Seneca's works is neither criticism nor portraits of the declaimers, but rather specimens of their speeches. These may range in extent from a short phrase or sentence to six and a half Müller pages (Latro; 2.7.1-9), but are on the average fairly short—two or three sentences. Without question the examples are the most important component of the *Controversiae* and *Suasoriae*; it is with their preservation and critical use that Seneca is primarily concerned. Rather startling at first are the lack of selectivity and obvious repetitiveness in these examples. Side-by-side are passages of great eloquence and of simpering mediocrity. On occasion we find samples of plainly foolish, overwrought, and patently artificial prose. Even more unsettling is his common practice of passing over these with no critical comment at all, particularly in the *sententiae* sections. This is not necessarily a sign of hastiness or a lack of critical discrimination on Seneca's part. Far from it. In the very beginning of the work he makes no claim to selectivity; he suggests that he will recall virtually everything worth remembering in a particular declamation. [187] Thus he selects striking examples of speech, and not necessarily just what is excellent, for his audience can learn, as he himself repeatedly maintains, from inspecting both the good and the bad, and also in the process sharpen their own critical abilities. [188] By recording this vast volume of quotations, Seneca has transmitted to his readers a valuable portrait of the state of eloquence in the time of Augustus and Tiberius, and has challenged them to sift the good from the bad.

As we have seen, others had tried a similar task. Apparently Seneca felt that none had measured up to it, and so he sensed an obligation to compile his own collection of specimens. [189]

A subsidiary motive for producing these anthologies was a form of Roman literary nationalism. Eloquence was not solely the possession of the Greeks, as Seneca demonstrates in his comparison of Sallust to his Greek predecessor. [190] Indeed, Seneca believed that Cicero

---

when audiences were more discerning, such rampant plagiarism could not succeed (*Suas.* 2.19). Roman declaimers regularly copied the Greeks, but Seneca defends Latro on this count—perhaps a little too protectively, in the name of friendship (10.4.21). See also 7.3.9; 9.1.13; 9.3.12; 9.6.11; 10.4.20, 25; 10.5.20, 26; *Suas.* 7.14.

[187] 1 pr. 1; cf. 1 pr. 5-6; 2.4.12; 9.2.27.

[188] 2.4.12; cf. 9.2.27; *Suas.* 1.16; 2.10; 2.23.

[189] One writer, Junius Otho, produced a work on colors which Seneca did not like (2.1.33; cf. 1.3.11, above, 80).

[190] 9.1.13. The attribution of the original Greek to Thucydides is mistaken; cf. Winterbottom note (3) *ad loc.*

and his contemporaries equalled or surpassed the Greeks in oratory. [191] Seneca's friend Latro was even more vehement in his nationalism; he considered the Greeks of little value and disregarded them (10.4.21). One can see in Seneca's criticisms of the Greek declaimers little reluctance on his part to pass on uncomplimentary remarks. [192] The reason is important. The Greeks invented and perfected the art of rhetoric and looked down upon Roman practitioners as upstarts. But in oratory the Romans earnestly believed that in Cicero they could match the best Greece had to offer. [193] And in declamation they surely felt that they had surpassed their teachers.

There is also more than a hint of Spanish regional pride in the composition of the *Controversiae* and *Suasoriae*. Not only were the Annaei members of the rising class of provincial gentry, but they were from an area which had stimulated a long and bitterly held prejudice in the capitol city. [194] The inhabitants of the Spanish provinces were commonly thought of as violent, blood-thirsty barbarians, and *nouveaux riches*, who lacked real culture and polish. There was a germ of truth to this belief, but Spain could also boast of great centers of learning and more than its share of talented writers. [195] In his works Seneca presents numerous Spanish declaimers and authors, some of exceptional ability. The most notable is Latro, considered by Seneca the best declaimer of all. [196]

7. Publication and Date of Composition

In his old age Seneca desired to establish a literary reputation for himself. But publication of the *Controversiae* and *Suasoriae* was

---

[191] I pr. 6; cf. I pr. 11; 10 pr. 11; 10.4.23; *Suas.* 7.10.

[192] He is careful, however, to give a Greek his due. Although not without faults, Seneca places Fuscus, a Greek, among the best four declaimers (10 pr. 13). Cf. Sochatoff "Theories" 350-351; Weinrib 94-96. A survey of Bornecque's index of declaimers amply demonstrates his rather impartial outlook.

[193] Cf. Quintilian's famous remarks on Roman elegy and satire (10.1.93); also his comparisons of such writers as Sallust, Livy, and Cicero, with their Greek counterparts (Quint. 10.1.101, 105ff).

[194] On anti-Spanish prejudice in Rome see H. de la Ville de Mirmont, "Les Décalamateurs Espagnols aux Temps d'Auguste et de Tibère," *Bull. Hisp.* 14 (1912) 341-349.

[195] On this see Griffin 12-13.

[196] 10 pr. 13; a second member of the tetrad, Gallio, was also probably of Spanish birth (cf. Bornecque 173; Griffin 11-12: Fuscus was a Greek and Albucius was from Gaul). The first portrait of a declaimer in the prefaces to the *Contr.* is of the Spaniard Latro (I pr. 13-24), as is the last, of Clodius Turrinus, *pater et filius* (10 pr. 14-16).

deliberately delayed until after his death as his son's comments clearly indicate:

> If I had already published the works which my father wrote and wished to have published, he would have sufficiently seen to the fame of his own name. [197]

Shortly after finishing the anthologies, or perhaps concurrently, he began a history of Rome from the beginning of the civil wars, to which the younger Seneca's biography of his father, *De Vita Patris*, was probably the preface. In it his works are referred to in an apologetic manner which betrays apprehension at releasing the *Histories*; perhaps they were unfinished, but clearly the anthologies were ready for publication and his serious purposes indicate that he did indeed want these published. It is tempting to place the date of publication early in the reign of Gaius (AD 37-41) when freedom of speech was nurtured and one could praise the formerly banned works of Cremutius Cordus and Cassius Severus. [198] We can be assured that both anthologies were published, since they have survived and were sufficiently popular to be excerpted during the latter years of the Empire. There is also some evidence that other writers of the early Empire were familiar with the works of Seneca. [199]

Because of numerous internal references we can assign the date of composition to the period of about AD 37-41. Thus Seneca was in his early nineties while writing these works, and, surprisingly, lived to write a historical work afterwards. He refers to M. Aemilius Scaurus in the past tense; we can accordingly place the composition of this passage after AD 33, when Scaurus died. [200] Cassius Severus, who probably died in AD 37, is referred to in terms suggesting that he was already dead. [201] Seneca mentions the demise of the Sejanians

---

[197] *De Vita Patris* (fr. xv Haase). Cf. Kennedy *ARRW* 324 and note 31; Griffin 11; below, 137 and note 1.

[198] Griffin (11) points out that the *Contr.* and *Suas.* would not have been altogether pleasing to Gaius since Seneca praises Vergil and Livy; the Emperor had considered removing the works of both men from the libraries (Suet. *Gaius* 34).

[199] Cf. the discussion of the *altum silentium* on Seneca above, 18; below, 155ff.

[200] 1.2.22. Cf. Bornecque 143; Weinrib 149. Italo Lana, *Lucio Anneo Seneca* (Torino 1955) 86 maintains that this passage must have been written after the death of Tiberius. Since Seneca wrote the *Contr.* and *Suas.* in that order, he must have maintained what must be a frantic schedule for a man in his nineties. He would have had to compose the *Contr.*, *Suas.*, and *Histories* in a period of three or four years (i.e., AD 37-41). Weinrib 140 note 2 is skeptical of the pace.

[201] Bornecque 24-25; cf. Griffin 4 and notes 43, 44; also p. 11.

(9.4.21), [202] and in the tenth preface delivers a long and eloquent tirade against book burning (10 pr. 5-7). These subjects were sensitive, and in the later years of Tiberius the remarks on book burning could be especially dangerous. Both passages support a composition date, or at least intended publication after the death of Tiberius in AD 37.

Written after the *Controversiae* (2.4.8), the *Suasoriae* contain many more contemporary references. This suggests that Seneca compiled the *Controversiae*, which only contain a few, shortly before the death of Tiberius, and that the *Suasoriae* were written afterwards. Seneca speaks of Sejanus in a way possible only after his demise in AD 31 (*Suas.* 2.12), and mentions the extinction of the Scaurus family, an event datable to AD 34. [203] Other references in *Suas.* 3.7 point to a composition date (or projected publication date) after the death of Tiberius. [204] At the same time Seneca was contemplating or actually writing the *Histories*. The incomplete state of the *Suasoriae* and the great interest there expressed in history might indeed have arisen from Seneca's impatience to proceed with the more important work. As he drew near the end of his life, Seneca may have decided to leave the *Suasoriae* unfinished and devote his full energies to a more ambitious and challenging project.

---

[202] All the modern texts of Seneca from Kiessling through Winterbottom accept the crucial reading *Seianianos* in 9.4.21.

[203] *Suas.* 2.22. Cf. Dio 58.24; Tac. *Ann.* 6.29; Suet. *Tib.* 61; cf. Duff 38-39.

[204] Bornecque 24; Griffin 4, 11. The work was most probably written after AD 37.

CHAPTER FOUR

SENECA ON ELOQUENCE

1. *Overview*

The term "eloquence" is a better description of Seneca's critical interests than the more confining "rhetoric" or "declamation." Although his works primarily consist of declamation extracts, Seneca frequently includes samples from other genres for critical contrast and comparison. He believed that no single genre and no single language had exclusive reign over eloquence. Therefore we find in the anthologies a relatively large number of extracts from history, epic poetry, oratory, and comedy, while a fair proportion—mostly from declaimers—is in Greek. Seneca does not theorize abstractly on the nature of eloquence; he merely attempts to show how some have failed or succeeded in attaining it. In this he may have been constrained by the limits of his own intelligence and training or by the nature of the works themselves. Seneca's criticism is intuitive; he believes that common sense and experience can reveal whether an utterance is flawed or eloquent.

There is also very little abstract theorizing on the arts of oratory and declamation, although he does attempt to place certain developments such as the decline of public speaking and the growth of declamation in their historical perspective. [1] In only one instance does he attempt a significant statement on the *ars dicendi*, but here he is unoriginal, merely quoting the elder Cato's definition of an orator as a "morally good man, skilled in speaking." [2] Seneca subscribed wholeheartedly to this theory and pursued its implications in the indivisible relationship he envisioned between a man's character and his performance as a speaker.

The *Controversiae* and *Suasoriae* are basically works of literary criticism. In the beginning Seneca says that he intends to pass judgment on the declaimers of his day and to transmit samples of their expression (1 pr. 1). He is confident that his audience will benefit through inspection of the extracts and will also recognize an important literary

---

[1] 1 pr. 6-7, 12. Cf. his comments on division (1.1.13) and the teaching of rhetoric at Rome (2 pr. 5).

[2] *Orator est, Marce fili, vir bonus dicendi peritus* (1 pr. 9). Cf. above 67, note 113.

development; the decline of eloquence since the age of Cicero. [3] At certain points Seneca will consider the achievements of various men at some length but in so doing he confines himself to general terms. In a few instances he will linger over a phrase or sentence, but his analysis, if one may call it that, is usually couched in generalities. More often he will simply reproduce the specimen with little or no comment at all or quote criticisms made by others. Nevertheless, even in their surviving tattered state, the works are large. In sum there exists a considerable amount of critical commentary, which, when analyzed, allows a reconstruction of his basic rhetorical theories. [4] The most fruitful and coherent parts of the works are the prefaces in the *Controversiae*, since they focus upon the achievements of selected speakers or present their views on contemporary declamation. Scattered elsewhere are primarily remarks directed to specific divisions and colors.

Although Seneca's critical outlook substantially reflects the influence of Cicero, his activities as a critic are important historically. Seneca was a champion of stylistic common sense and simplicity of expression in an age of opposite tendencies. His basic views and Ciceronianism served as a link between the days of that orator and the end of the first century AD when Quintilian argued for a return to more classical modes of expression. [5] Seneca was not, however, a reactionary in style. Although he greatly admired Cicero and the speakers of that day, he accepted the inevitability of stylistic changes, and these he sought to direct in accordance with his standards of good taste. In addition, Seneca refined and adapted certain of Cicero's critical ideas and techniques for use in a different age of literary development.

2. *Critical Tools and Method*

Seneca's literary portraits and general comments upon the merits of a particular utterance are familiar devices of ancient literary criticism. But in certain areas of their use he has made some unusual modifications. He rejects, for example, the conventional use of the terse critical label for describing an author and his style. [6] A symptom

---

[3] 1 pr. 6. Other subsidiary motives underline the critical nature of the works; e.g., providing a historical perspective on the growth of declamation, proper ascription of works to their authors, and the prevention of plagiarism. See the discussion of his motives for gathering the anthologies above, 83ff.

[4] Briefly summarized in Sochatoff "Theories" 345-354.

[5] See Atkins 153.

[6] Cf. D'Alton 542-543.

of the contemporary tendency towards rigid categorizing in criticism, these labels often became commonplaces. The better ones centered upon the most striking aspect of a writer's style:

> It is all to the good if an author's predominant quality ... can be grasped within the narrow limits of a single epithet or phrase. We could well do with more labels such as "curiosa felicitas," "lactea ubertas," and "immortalis velocitas," which seem inevitable in their appropriateness. [7]

Nevertheless, in an age sadly lacking in critical talent, the majority of those coined were lifeless and frigid. [8] In a sense Seneca may have realized his own limitations in declining to use labels. [9]

If effective labels were beyond his grasp, Seneca atoned for this deficiency with the *sententia* critical summary. In these he frequently coupled analysis of a man's style and his psychological qualities, often with a touch of the ironic or unexpected for added point. At times he places several side-by-side, achieving a terse, staccato effect. Among the more successful creations is his description of Labienus as a man with a "more bitter brain than tongue," *homo mentis quam linguae amarioris* (4 pr. 2) and his depiction of Haterius who "kept his genius under his own power, its regulation under someone else's," *in sua potestate habebat ingenium, in aliena modum* (4 pr. 8). Less descriptive, but more humorous is his characterization of Sparsus as "a sane man among the school men—and a school man among the sane men," *hominem inter scholasticos sanum, inter sanos scholasticum* (1.7.15). [10]

The *sententia* summary is an important component of the longer critical portraits which occur primarily in the prefaces. [11] Seneca supplements these with amusing and vivid anecdotes which illustrate his criticism. In the portraits he attempts to include all the noteworthy parts of a speaker's performance, but avoids wherever possible reliance upon purely technical terminology. Each man is measured against

---

[7] *Ibid.* 543.

[8] Cf. *ibid.*

[9] For example, the occasion when he compares the brevity of Sallust and Thucydides; the situation begs for a label (9.1.13; cf. Quint. 10.1.102).

[10] Some other examples of rather effective critical *sententiae* occur in 1.1.25; 2.1.25, 33; 2.2.12; 2.5.20; 2.6.13; 3 pr. 2; 4 pr. 1, 7, 8, 9, 11; 7 pr. 2-7; 7.1.20; 7.4.8; 7.5.11; 9.2.26, 27; 9.4.17; 9.5.15, 17; 10 pr. 3, 4, 9, 11, 16; 10.4.23; 10.5.22; *Suas.* 1.16; 2.10. Series of critical *sententiae* occur, for example, in 2 pr. 1; 3 pr. 7; 7 pr. 1; 9.2.26.

[11] Most especially in the sketches of Latro (1 pr. 13-24), Haterius (4 pr. 6-11), and Albucius (7 pr. 1-9). In the body of the works, the portrait of Ovid is justly famed (2.2.8-12).

Seneca's personal standards of rhetorical taste which are more flexible than those of most ancient critics. His entire approach in the portraits derives from the model of Cicero's *Brutus*, although he rarely lapses into the mechanical and dogmatic criticism so typical of his predecessor. [12] Seneca's good humor, the restricted scope of his investigation, the indulgence freely granted to men of talent, and his conscious efforts to make the portraits interesting, prevent them from lapsing into frigid critical exercises. [13]

Even in the longer portraits he does not feel obliged to comment upon every aspect of the speaker's art. Instead, Seneca prefers to concentrate on a very limited number of characteristics which make each speaker unique; for example, the rugged constitution and *subtilitas* of Latro, the diligence of Cassius Severus, the contrasting emotional states of Pollio and Haterius, and the insecurity of Albucius. Thus he is sensitive especially to the personality of the speaker, and, at times, to his native qualities of voice, size, and strength. Style receives equal attention, especially figures of speech and diction, although the comments are predominantly non-technical. [14] Seneca shows less enthusiasm for the subject of argumentation, one which would embrace both division and colors. The various critical topics treated do not occur in any special order, and the same one might occur in several different places.

Seneca's practices in the composition of these critical portraits are best illustrated in the treatment of Albucius (7 pr. 1-9). A per-

---

[12] Cf. D'Alton 543-544.

[13] D'Alton (*ibid.*) criticizes the lack of the personal note in ancient critics generally, although he recognizes some of the important critical achievements of Cicero in describing certain men such as Crassus, Antonius, Calidius, and Hortensius. D'Alton (544) adds: "But his judgments on many other orators are of the routine character that leaves us unsatisfied. They show little in the nature of a personal reaction to the specific qualities of their eloquence, and fail to explain the relation between the man and the orator." On the other hand (in the case of his discussion of Lysias), D'Alton (*ibid.*) praises Dionysius as a critic because of his enthusiasm for the subject, which, to D'Alton, proves that this critic attained a personal feel for the author and could thus penetrate more deeply to a finer appreciation of the man's style and the reasons for his success. In contrast to Cicero in the *Brutus*, Dionysius also provides samples of the subject's work—a useful practice. One wonders whether Seneca was at all familiar with the Greek critic. The criticism in both shuns excessive praise or condemnation of an author, but, rather, aims at a balanced discussion of virtues and vices; cf. Grube 207.

[14] On figures; e.g., 1 pr. 23, 24; 4 pr. 7; 7 pr. 3, 6-9; 10 pr. 9-10. Diction; 2 pr. 1-3; 3 pr. 7; 4 pr. 7, 9; 7 pr. 2-6; 10 pr. 2. Argumentation; 1 pr. 22; 3 pr. 2; 7 pr. 1-3; 10 pr. 15.

vasive theme is the effect of certain personality traits upon the performance of Albucius as a speaker. When carried away by emotion
he would rise from his seated position; his vanity and ostentatiousness
were apparent from his practice of speaking for hours if a large
audience were present (7 pr. 1). Nevertheless, he lacked self-confidence,
and this caused a lack of proportion in his speeches since he was
afraid to leave out any possible line of argumentation (7 pr. 1-2).
A shy, sensitive man, Albucius was unsure of his abilities in general,
especially diction (probably with good reason; cf. 7 pr. 3-6) and extemporaneous speech (7 pr. 2). In the course of this portrait, Seneca
touches upon two important subjects, imitation and concealment of
artifice. He frowns upon the fickleness of Albucius in choosing
exemplars for imitation; infatuated with novelty, he changed his models
radically; therefore his style did not progressively improve with age
and experience as it should have (7 pr. 4-5). Although Seneca praises
the ability of Albucius to speak in a manner that did not display
obvious preparation (7 pr. 3), his lack of self-confidence caused him
to overemphasize this. In order not to seem "a man of the schools"
(*scholasticus*), Albucius employed common and vulgar words to excess
(7 pr. 3-4).

Lack of self-confidence appears to be at the root of several other
problems. Albucius experienced constant agony over what he should
say (7 pr. 3), and distrust of his own abilities (7 pr. 5) caused
anxiety which led to mental depression: "He was a gloomy, anxious
declaimer, one who was concerned over his eloquence even after he
had spoken—so much so that he was never free of anxiety." [15] Anxiety
about suffering insult for his use of figures caused Albucius to with-
draw from the courts after the disastrous oath figure incident (7
pr. 6-8).

In the portrait of Albucius, Seneca pays more attention to style
than to invention, arrangement, delivery, or memory. Diction is treated
at length, especially the proper manner of employing common or
vulgar words (7 pr. 2, 3, 4, 5, 6). Seneca shows great concern over
the judicious use of rhetorical tropes and figures. In Albucius he
found a useful example of a speaker who inserted these into speeches
too freely and inappropriately. The point is well illustrated in a
series of anecdotes and witty comments (7 pr. 6-9). The addition of
the latter material adds color to the criticism and a note of humor

---

[15] *Tristis, sollicitus declamator et qui de dictione sua timebat, etiam cum
dixisset: usque eo nullum tempus securum illi erat* (7 pr. 6).

to a basically dry subject. Throughout the discussion Seneca does not attempt to follow a logical order in treating the various aspects of the *officia oratoris* or the character of Albucius. [16] Implicit in this sketch is the artificiality of the world of declamation, and the inability of even a superior declaimer to conduct an ordinary legal case successfully. The recurring topic of Albucius' lack of self-confidence gives a sense of unity to the entire preface and, in identifying the pervasive role of this fault, Seneca has effectively tied together the effect of character upon performance.

In the fourth preface Seneca employs a variant of the critical portrait when he compares and contrasts Pollio and Haterius. Formally termed σύγκρισις, it was a common technique in ancient literary criticism and biography, [17] and especially helpful in illuminating the more important attributes of each man. Cicero experienced success with the method, especially in his frequent comparisons of Antonius and Crassus, Crassus and Scaevola, and Sulpicius and Cotta. [18] Some non-Roman critics from the Augustan age, Dionysius and probably Caecilius, saw the advantages of σύγκρισις and exhibited even more felicitous results. Seneca may have been familiar with the works of these two men, but it is more likely that he was influenced by Cicero's example. On the whole, Seneca's one experiment with the comparative portrait was quite successful; unfortunately no others exist in his works. The theme of the fourth preface is the contrasting psychological endowments of Pollio and Haterius, especially the effect of grief upon their speaking. Pollio declaimed shortly after the death of his son in a stern, pugnacious manner, while Haterius broke down in tears during a declamation which reminded him of his son who had died many years before. Although each man's emotional state and speech were totally opposite, nevertheless both spoke eloquently—one vigorously, the other heatedly and emotionally. [19]

On occasion Seneca resorts to the use of simile or metaphor in

---

[16] Cf. the portrait of Cassius Severus which may serve as an example; matters relating to invention (specifically, argumentation through use of emotion), 3 pr. 2; arrangement, no mention; style, 3 pr. 2, 4, 7, 18; memory, 3 pr. 6; delivery, 3 pr. 2, 3, 4, 5, 6.

[17] Cf. D'Alton 183-184 and numerous citations there; also Atkins 40, 107, 129-130, 243-244, 292, 319-321, 331-336; Grube 207, 209-211.

[18] See D'Alton 183ff and references there cited.

[19] Cf. Seneca on Lesbocles and Potamon, *Suas.* 2.15. A germ of this comparative method appears in 2 pr. 1-2 where Seneca investigates the effect of Arellius Fuscus and his faults upon his student Fabianus, and Fabianus' efforts to rid himself of these shortcomings.

his criticism. To stress the necessity for proportion, he is fond of
pointing out the magnitude of limbs relative to the body (1 pr. 21;
2.3.15; 7 pr. 2), a comparison found also in Cicero (*De Or.* 3.119).
Seneca likens the eloquence of Haterius to a great, though muddy
river, [20] but is perhaps more original when he faults the style of
Fabianus for lacking a "keen fighting edge." [21] While the use of
simile and metaphor could bring welcome variation and added point to
literary criticism, Seneca had not mastered their use, and employs
them infrequently.

Most of Seneca's criticism consists of one or several critical terms
applied to a facet of a speaker's performance or expression. This is
Seneca's basic method in the body of the works, and the terms nearly
always accompany actual samples of the speaker's expression. The key
to effectiveness in this is the employment of a precise, descriptive
critical vocabulary. Since Seneca studiously avoided technical and
rhetorical terms wherever possible, he resorted to the common storehouse of words. In an extremely useful work, Bardon has identified
in Seneca's critical vocabulary areas of success and originality but also
numerous deficiencies. [22]

A handicap to all Latin critics was the prior existence of a precise,
copious, and specialized vocabulary in Greek. Since Roman rhetoric
was directly derivative of the Greek, in order to express a concept
already well defined by his predecessors a Roman critic faced the
choice of transliterating the Greek term or finding Latin equivalents.
The latter were frequently imprecise and required further explanation;
indeed, the problems associated with translating Greek rhetorical and
literary terms always plagued the Romans. [23] Thus along with the

---

[20] 4 pr. 11 : a commonplace in ancient criticism; cf. Callimachus *Hymn to
Apollo* 108; Horace *Sat.* 1.4.11 (on Lucilius); *Ep.* 2.2.120-121; Quint. 10.1.94.
See Grube 236 and note 2, 237; also C. O. Brink, *Horace on Poetry* (Cambridge
1963) 159 note 3.
[21] *Pugnatorius mucro*, 2 pr. 2. He also likens the eloquence of Latro to a large
building (1 pr. 21). Augustus uses a vivid metaphor when comparing Haterius to
a runaway wagon which needs brakes applied: *Haterius noster sufflaminandus
est* (4 pr. 7; cf. Winterbottom note *ad loc.*). The most common metaphor in the
works describes style in terms of mental or physical health with the various
derivatives of *sanus*; these occur over a score of times. See below, 136 and note 169.
[22] Henry Bardon, *Le Vocabulaire de la Critique Littéraire chez Sénèque le
Rhéteur* (Paris 1940). The work includes a helpful lexicon of Seneca's critical
terms along with major cross references to standard Latin authors.
[23] Cf. D'Alton 206. For example, a number of Latin terms might commonly
be used to express a Greek term, although not one of them brought out all the
nuances of the original.

other Latin critics, even the highly nationalistic author of *Ad Herennium*, Seneca found the use of Latinized Greek terms unavoidable. [24] Many of these Senecan usages are the first occurrences in Latin, [25] but it would be foolish to conclude that he himself first transferred those words, since he is undoubtedly reflecting the new vocabulary of the declamation halls. Therefore we are probably unable to credit Seneca with any degree of originality in this sphere.

In his Latin terminology we find that Seneca uses a number of rather effective terms which Cicero avoided, especially *lascivus, inaequalitas*, and the various forms of *facundus*. [26] He is also fond of poetic words in criticism, some used with notable success, as *amabiliter* (1.1.25), *decenter* (e.g., 2.4.7), *culte* (e.g., 4 pr. 10), *mordax* (7 pr. 8), *nasutus* (*Suas*. 7.12), and *praedulcis* (*ibid*.). Among others the phrase *vigor orationis* is also effective and perhaps original. [27] The critics and rhetoricians of the day liked to invent personal adjectives for describing types of expression peculiar to certain speakers or writers; Seneca may have coined *Publilianus* (for the comic poet Publilius Syrus) following the lead of Scaurus who coined *Montanianus* (for the speaker Votienus Montanus). [28]

Seneca probably displayed originality in extending and modifying

---

[24] On his nationalism cf. D'Alton 205 and note 3 with citations there. On the necessity of using Greek terms see *Ad Her*. 4.10; cf. Varro *Academ*. 1.6.24; Cic. *Or*. 211; also D'Alton 205-206; Bardon (above, note 22) 90-91; Bonner 64-65.

[25] The great wealth of these are symptomatic of an ever increasing specialization in rhetorical theory, itself occasioned by the predominance of declamation in the educational system. Even a partial list of these occurrences demonstrates the extent; cf. Bardon 90ff; Bonner 64-65:

anthypophora (1.7.17)
cacozelos (*Suas*. 2.16; 7.11)
epiphonema (1 pr. 23)
ethicos (2.3.23; *Suas*. 1.13)
hexis (7 pr. 2)
idiotismos (2.3.21; 7 pr. 5)
metaphrasis (*Suas*. 1.12)
phantasia (*Suas*. 2.14)

phrasis (3 pr. 7; 7 pr. 2)
problema (1.3.8)
schema (1 pr. 23; 1.1.25, etc.)
scholastica (1 pr. 12; 2.3.13; 3 pr. 12, etc.)
thema (1.2.14; 7.5.12, etc.)
thesis (1 pr. 12; 7.4.3)
tricolum, tetracolum (2.4.12; 9.2.27)

[26] Bardon 90-94 further discusses Seneca's originality in basic critical vocabulary. In the analysis of Seneca's critical vocabulary we will most often do so in terms of similarities to and departures from the Ciceronian standard. Although others (e.g., Lucilius, Terence, the anonymous *Auctor ad Herennium*, and Varro) had preceded him, nevertheless Cicero's was the most extensive, influential, and creative contribution to Latin critical vocabulary; cf. D'Alton 206-207.

[27] 10 pr. 5; for others cf. Bardon 90-94. His lexicon of critical terms in Seneca (*ibid*. 11-62) may be consulted for additional occurrences of the various words discussed here.

[28] 7.2.14; 7.4.8; cf. 9.5.17.

the usage of some words for critical purposes. [29] Certain of these
were demanded by the new developments in rhetoric, as for example
inflectere in the sense of modifying a *sententia*; Cicero used it only
for the modification of a single word. [30] Other novel usages include
vafre, referring to a speaker's artfulness, and *civilis* in the sense
of "simple." [31] Seneca adopts Ciceronian usages, but with a different
emphasis, as with the adjective *vocalis*, which Cicero applies to the
orator, but Seneca to the description of a *sententia*. [32]

The principal merit of Seneca's critical vocabulary is the reliance
placed upon picturesque, imaginative, and descriptive terms. Undoubtedly this type of vocabulary grew out of declamatory style which itself
possessed these qualities, and demanded critical terms to match. We
find in Seneca's works some very evocative verbs describing or relating
to speakers: [33] *abstinere manus* (10.4.18); *decurrere* (4 pr. 7); *discur-
rere* (2.2.9); *insanire* (e.g., 10.5.27), *torquere* (1 pr. 18); *tumere*
(9.2.26). To describe literary or rhetorical effects he uses equally
vivid verbs: *evanescere* (9.2.24), *fluere* (4 pr. 11), *insanire* (*Suas.*
1.16). Figurative nouns used in a novel critical manner are *calor* (e.g.,
7 pr. 1; 10 pr. 3), *corpus* (9.2.26), *cultus* (e.g., 3 pr. 2), *luxuria*
(2 pr. 2), and *sordes* (7 pr. 4); to these we may add the adverbs
animose (e.g., *Suas.* 2.12), *furiose* (e.g., 10.5.21, 23), *sane* (e.g.,
10.5.21), and *valenter* (7.7.10). Seneca portrays literary efforts as
asper (e.g., 7.2.13), *citatus* (4 pr. 9), *effusus* (e.g., 2 pr. 1), *emollitus*
(7.4.8), *improbus* (7.5.14), *inaequalis* (3 pr. 18), *luxuriosus* (*Suas.*
2.10), *tumultuosus* (9.2.23), *vegetus* (*Suas.* 2.10), and *vividus* (2.6.12).
He characterizes the qualities of a speaker with equally evocative
adjectives: *acidus* (10.5.22), *amarus* (4 pr. 2), *capax* (2 pr. 4), *comptus*
(2.2.8), *cultus* (7 pr. 5), *horridus* (7 pr. 5), *strictus* (4 pr. 3), and
vitalis (1.1.22).

Seneca's vocabulary derives much of its vigor from terms relating
to sensory impressions: *acidus* (10.5.22), *se adligare* (10.5.18), *amarus*
(4 pr. 2), *asper* (e.g., 3 pr. 18), *calor* (e.g., 7 pr. 1), *solidus* (e.g., 2
pr. 1), *splendidus* (e.g., 2 pr. 1), *suavitas* (3 pr. 3). He is especially
fond of describing the voice in terms which are visual (e.g., *infuscatus*,
1 pr. 16), tactile (*obtusus*, 1.7.18; *solidus*, 3 pr. 3), gustatory (*dulcis*,
3 pr. 3), or auditory (*surdus*, 1 pr. 16). In his attempt to be concrete

---

[29] Bardon 95-100.

[30] *Ibid.* 95.

[31] *Ibid.* 97; among other examples cited are *se antecedere, tumide,* and *exsuctus.*

[32] Cf. *ibid.* 98 for many other similar examples.

[33] *Ibid.* 99-100. Cf. D'Alton 545.

Seneca uses words which suggest various physical states; e.g., *detorquere* (9.3.12), *exilis* (e.g., 2 pr. 1), *exucus* (7.5.15), *fluere* (e.g., 2 pr. 2), *sordidus* (e.g., 3 pr. 7), *strictus* (1.1.24), *tumultuosus* (9.2.23), and *vacuus* (3 pr. 7). His descriptions of *sententiae* especially confirm a strong tendency for imagery: [34] *amabilis* (9.3.10), *aperta* (7 pr. 2), *dulcis* (*Suas.* 7.12), *excitata* (10 pr. 15), *insidiosa* (*ibid.*), *praedulcis* (*Suas.* 7.12), *solida* (*Suas.* 6.16), *belle sonans* (7.4.10), *splendida* (7 pr. 2), *tumultuosa* (9.2.23), *vividior* (2.6.12), and *vocalis* (7 pr. 2).

Bardon points to a number of deficiencies in Seneca's critical vocabulary, but they are not as serious as he would have us believe. [35] Seneca's use of technical rhetorical terms is found imprecise, and to support this general conclusion Bardon develops at length the confusion evident in his use of *quaestio* for *tractatio* to describe the development of the argument of equity. [36] Bardon admits that such errors were fairly common and that Seneca may have been merely reflecting current usage. [37] However, there was a genuine debate on how these terms ought to be used, one which Seneca himself alludes to. [38]

In Seneca's critical vocabulary Bardon observes a decrease in the number and variety of certain word usages in comparison to the *Ad Herennium* and Cicero's rhetorical works. [39] Indeed, there is a sound basis for such a criticism. Nevertheless, the very different natures of oratory and declamation could account for these changes. Some of the examples adduced are not especially convincing. Bardon points out that in Seneca's works *sententia* has lost its specialized usage to signify the spirit of the law as opposed to the literal interpretation (*sententia* vs. *scriptum*). [40] But during the early Empire this concept was included under the heading of *aequitas* vs. *ius*; and further, the

---

[34] *Ibid.* 53.

[35] Bardon's methodology has been questioned in a number of reviews; cf. J. Marouzeau *REL* 18 (1940) 203-205; L. Laurand *REA* 44 (1942) 154; A. Cordier *RPh* 17 (1943) 220-222; J. van Ootegehen *LEC* 12 (1943) 228-231; C. J. Fordyce *CR* 60 (1946) 129. While it is not my intention to indulge in polemics, since his is the standard work on the subject, the conclusions he draws should be modified or refuted where necessary.

[36] Bardon 68-77.

[37] *Ibid.* 76-77.

[38] 1.1.4; cf. Marouzeau above, note 35. He concludes that Bardon's evidence does not conclusively show that the use in certain instances of *quaestio* for *tractatio* is faulty. He also questions Bardon's ability to state that Seneca either used the vocabulary of the schools or did not try to remedy the confusion in contemporary usage.

[39] Bardon 78-84.

[40] *Ibid.* 82-83; cf. *Ad Her.* 2.13, 14; Cic. *De Inv.* 1.55; *De Or.* 2.110. Bardon also mourns the loss of the meanings "idea" and "sentence."

anthologies were mainly concerned with the specialized meaning of *sententia* as a terse epigram. If Seneca had employed the additional range of usages, he might have confused his audience. [41] Also cited is his failure to use the term *altercatio*; but the word does appear, and in its proper sense. [42] Elsewhere Bardon (p. 85) points out that Cicero used five times as many adjectives to modify *vox* than Seneca did. While indeed true, and while a number of Cicero's adjectives are more descriptive, the implication that Seneca has a relatively limited critical vocabulary is faulty. Only a small portion of the anthologies are Seneca's own words, and this total is small indeed when compared to the great Ciceronian corpus. Thus normal changes in terminology, the differences between genres, and the relative amount of literary remains must be considered in comparing the critical vocabulary of Seneca with that of his predecessors.

An essential component of Seneca's method and approach was his refreshing lack of dogmatism. Such an outlook totally opposed the stultifying tendency of Hellenistic and Roman rhetoric towards increasing complexity and reliance upon strict rules. The rhetoricians of the period were predominantly men of little cultural breadth or creativity who felt more comfortable in dealing with narrow technicalities. [43] These specialists could not regard any expression as eloquent if it violated even the most insignificant rule of the myriad which had developed. Since he was an amateur, Seneca could state that genius requires critical indulgence and, within reason, should not be confined by strict rules:

> Nor am I one of the very harsh critics who examines everything according to the strict rules. On the contrary, I think one must pardon many things for men of genius; yet only faults should be pardoned, not monstrosities. [44]

This attitude reflects Cicero's in *De Oratore* and places Seneca in the most productive current of ancient literary criticism. [45] Seneca

---

[41] Cf. Bardon 82-83.

[42] Bardon 86; cf. 10 pr. 2. The word describes the part of a court speech involving a swiftly paced debate between counsel for both sides. He cites as the standard passage for its meaning Cic. *Brut.* 164; actually, a better reference would be *Att.* 1.16.10; cf. Quint. 2.4.28.

[43] Cic. *De Or.* 2.133; 3.54, 75. Cf. D'Alton 149-152.

[44] 10 pr. 10; cf. his remarks directed against a quibbling grammarian, *Suas.* 2.13; also D'Alton 545; Sochatoff "Theories" 354.

[45] On Cicero see D'Alton 149-150 (and numerous citations there), also 79, 121 and note 4, 333; Grube 196. On the other ancient critics see e.g., Cic. *De Or.*

thought that technically flawed expression could achieve eloquence and that one could redeem faults with excellence in other areas of speaking, as Haterius did:

> There was much you could reprove—but much to admire .... But he made up for his faults by his virtues, and provided more to praise than to forgive .... [46]

In his attempt to account for the contemporary state of eloquence, Seneca looked at the historical background. His long life span enabled him to witness personally the very great changes in oratory and declamation from the last dying gasps of the Republic to the principates of Tiberius and Gaius. He also displayed a profound appreciation of the ever-growing intimacies between rhetoric and literature. [47]

Seneca's historical approach probably was influenced by Cicero in two areas. The orator appreciated in a rudimentary fashion the influence of political environment on literature. [48] More importantly, however, Cicero enunciated the cardinal precept that genres develop slowly, and its corollary that not only envisions progress from crude beginnings, but also admits the possibility of eventual decline. [49] Seneca briefly describes and analyzes the changes in oratory and declamation which he had witnessed during his life (1 pr. 6-12; cf. 10 pr. 7). The position of these remarks lends added significance; they occur in the first preface, the most important portion of the *Controversiae*. [50] The anthologies taken as a whole also demonstrate through examples

---

1.23, 146; 2.75; 3.70, 81, 92, 121; Quint. 2.13.16-17. On the similar attitudes of Augustus, cf. Quint. 1.6.19-20; Suet. *Aug.* 86ff; Gell. 10.24.2; Philodemus, in Christian Jensen, *Philodemus über die Gedichte, fünftes Buch* (Berlin 1923) 51 (XXII, esp. 24-30); younger Seneca *Ep.* 114.13; Tac. *Dial.* 18 (Aper speaking); "Longinus" 35, 36.

[46] 4 pr. 11; Winterbottom transl. Cf. Grube 111, 246 and note 2, 247, 343, 351.

[47] See Bonner's useful chapter, "Some Indications of Declamatory Influence on the Literature of the Early Empire" (149-167); also below, 153 and note 3.

[48] See the account of D'Alton 191-202.

[49] The cardinal principle: *nihil est enim simul et inventum et perfectum* (*Brut.* 71); cf. Quint. 9.4.5; 10.2.7-8; 10.3.4; 12.11.25; D'Alton 191. Cicero was undoubtedly influenced by Greek critics in this area, certainly in the artistic simile (e.g., *Brut.* 70), and was probably following a similar criticism of Greek oratory; cf. D'Alton 191-203 *passim*, esp. 192. Although Cicero lived during the height of Roman oratory, he was aware of the possibility of a full cycle in which it might decline and die (*Tusc.* 2.5; cf. D'Alton 202 and references there cited). D'Alton 546 considers Cicero's application of historical method as possibly his greatest contribution to Roman criticism; cf. esp. *Brut.* 70-76; *De Or.* 2.92-96; also Atkins 40-41; Grube 179.

[50] Cf. above, 51 and note 50.

the changed state of eloquence since the age of Cicero, and pointedly attempt to document a decline (1 pr. 6, 11; cf. 10 pr. 7). Again, in the first preface Seneca offers three possible explanations for this decline of eloquence; a deterioration of morality, the change of the political system, or an ineluctable fate which decrees that a rise to perfection is followed by an accelerated decline (1 pr. 7). He therefore has viewed these developments historically and delved superficially into the causes. Seneca was the first Roman critic to declare openly that a decline had occurred, and he deserves credit for even this brief attempt to ask why, especially in the realm of political influences. [51]

The crucial first preface also contains an account which traces the growth of declamation since the days of Cicero in which Seneca analyzes the changes of terminology applied to the exercises. [52] If, however, he deserves credit for his broad historical overview, Seneca also inspires some disappointment as did his predecessor, Cicero. [53] For one, there are grave errors in the analysis of declamatory termino-logy. These are unpardonable since Seneca was an interested observer of declamation during the period in which these changes were occur-ring. [54] Although we may consider the speculations on the reasons for decline to be original and thought-provoking, nevertheless he expands upon only one, the deterioration of morality (1 pr. 8-11). We receive only the barest of hints at how the changed political system may have influenced the decline of eloquence. The idea of an inevitable cycle surely deserved further treatment, particularly in its relationship to imitation. [55]

Seneca is on shaky logical ground indeed when he says that inspection of the quotations provided will prove how much eloquence has declined since Cicero. Although he does attempt to include material from both declaimers and orators, the form of the works dictates a great pre-ponderance of specimens from the former. This is hardly a sufficient basis for determining how much, if at all, eloquence had declined. Moreover, the material is not chronologically presented, and throughout, the eloquent is mixed with the vapid and corrupt. Thus the evaluation of Seneca's historical approach has two sides: praise for a sense of

---

[51] Cf. Sussman "Decline of Eloquence" *passim.*

[52] 1 pr. 12; cf. the discussion of this passage and its inadequacies above, 6-10.

[53] On Cicero's shortcomings see esp. D'Alton 546.

[54] As Seneca himself tells us (1 pr. 12): ... *nam et studium ipsum nuper celebrari coepit: ideo facile est mihi ab incunabulis nosse rem post me natam.*

[55] Cf. Sussman "Decline of Eloquence" *passim.* Discretion may have been responsible for the muted treatment of the political theme.

chronological perspective and several flashes of penetrating insight, but disappointment at defects in observation and an unwillingness to dig more deeply and develop his ideas.

In the previous examination of Seneca's technique for creating critical portraits, we briefly touched upon perhaps the most worthy element of his critical method: his preoccupation with each individual's personality and psychology, and the effect of these upon speaking performance. He also realizes that there is no one royal road to eloquence; therefore different speakers could achieve this goal in totally different ways. [56] For the want of a better term, we can call this entire outlook "individualism," one marking a departure from the main stream of ancient literary criticism which was primarily partisan and objective. [57] The majority of critics were chiefly concerned with the finished product rather than its creator, and they tended to react in absolutes of either excessive praise or reproach. One exception to the general neglect of personal character was the *vir bonus* tradition which stated that only morally good men could attain eloquence. Although there was some opposition to this simplistic notion, [58] it was a commonplace. In part the wide acceptance of the theory stemmed from the great reliance on *ethos* in argumentation and the attempt of rhetoricians to make their art morally respectable in the struggle with philosophy for domination of the educational system. The corollary of the *vir bonus* dictum says that style is the mirror of the man—*talis hominibus fuit oratio qualis vita*, another commonplace which nearly without exception also referred to moral character only. [59] Unfortunately most ancient critics, unquestioning heirs to dogmatic and formulaic conventions, failed to pursue the implications of these two concepts and consider the other traits of character, mind, and genius which influence literary creation. [60]

Seneca firmly believed in the *vir bonus* definition, and he articulates it passionately in the first preface. [61] He also probably subscribed to

---

[56] As in the cases of Pollio and Haterius, both treated in 4 pr.

[57] Grube 344 (on "Longinus"). Cf. D'Alton 201.

[58] Notably, Philodemus; cf. Grube 200.

[59] The younger Seneca *Ep.* 114.1 refers to it as a proverb; the rest of the letter is an exposition of the doctrine; cf. D'Alton 537-538 and citations there; A. Michel, "Le style, c'est l'homme même...," *REL* 50 (1972) 247-271.

[60] Cf. *ibid.* 210, 538. Cicero at least recognized the importance of individuality in a broad manner of speaking, especially in the sketches of certain speakers in the *De Or.* and *Brut.* Others were Caecilius, Dionysius, and "Longinus."

[61] 1 pr. 9; cf. 1 pr. 8-11; also 2.5.18; *Suas.* 2.22.

the *talis oratio qualis vita* corollary later expounded by his son. [62]
Since he was an amateur, Seneca could be flexible. With the example
of Cicero to stimulate him, and prompted by his own shrewd common
sense, he was able to take a broader view which the professionals,
absorbed in narrow technicalities, could not. These two commonplaces
of ancient theory may well have been the clue that the totality of a
man's character profoundly influences artistic creativity; at least Seneca
found it necessary to delve into character in the various critical portraits.
This factor marks the essential difference between the mechanistic
criticism of his contemporaries and the sounder, more productive
approach of a "Longinus."

The critical portrait of Albucius, analyzed above, is a good example
of the manner in which Seneca links speaking performance to character.
As in most of the other portraits, he attempts to isolate one or two
major character traits responsible for the salient attributes of the
speaker. In the case of Albucius, Seneca stresses that speaker's lack of
self-confidence and demonstrates its effects in a variety of ways.
There is, however, a risk of oversimplification in such a portrait because
the dictates of space do not allow Seneca to pursue other character
traits at any length.

The succinct portrait of Haterius (4 pr. 6-11) is especially effective. [63]
In it Haterius emerges as a more complex figure than the stern and
rather one-dimensional Pollio. Seneca says that Haterius spoke passionately and emotionally under the influence of grief (4 pr. 6). An
accomplished extemporaneous speaker, he was the only Roman able to
achieve the characteristic Greek sense of ease and fluency. But Haterius
spoke too rapidly and was unable to restrain his own volubility (4 pr.
7). For this reason he stationed a prompter in the audience (4 pr. 8).
Haterius' disposition of the arguments in division was not coherent
because excess emotion caused him to neglect the rules. Since he spoke
so quickly he sometimes used unsuitable words (4 pr. 9) and made
slips which lent themselves to obscene interpretations (4 pr. 10-11).
Seneca's portrait thus emphasizes a key personality trait—his lack of
self-control, and this in turn affected many aspects of his speaking.
It appeared most notably in the free rein Haterius gave to his emotions
during delivery. At times it led to eloquent expression. On the other
hand, to his lack of self-control Seneca implicity assigns several grave

---

[62] E.g., 4 pr. *passim*; 7.4.6; *Suas.* 2.17; cf. younger Seneca *Ep.* 114 *passim*.

[63] Ben Jonson found it so; he translated it virtually word for word into English
and applied it to Shakespeare. Cf. below, 170-171.

faults: excessively fast delivery, prolixity, and sloppy argumentation. Haterius was unable to control the *impetus* within him (4 pr. 9; cf. Tac. *Ann.* 4.61); his poor word choice was a result of his torrential pace. The several manifestations of his lack of self-control dominate the portrait, and the reader leaves with a heightened awareness of the major qualities of his speech, both good and bad, which emanated from this personality quirk.

A similar preoccupation with one or two idiosyncrasies of character appears in several other portraits. The long portion devoted to Latro (1 pr. 13-24) directs attention to this declaimer's lack of moderation. Latro engaged in excessively strenuous recreation (1 pr. 14-15), indulged in erratic work habits (1 pr. 13-15), while he totally neglected his voice training and health (1 pr. 16-17). Nevertheless his rugged constitution and great energy rescued him from serious harm, except for poor eyesight and a bad complexion (1 pr. 14, 15, 16, 17). Although Seneca deals at some length with Latro's memory (1 pr. 17-19) and *subtilitas* (1 pr. 20-24), very little is said about style and therefore no attempt is made to link it to his character.

The rather brief portrait of Fabianus in the second preface attempts to relate how a calm, philosophical temperament from which all emotion had been banished affected this declaimer's speaking. He achieved greater success in *suasoriae* since these did not require emotional fervor in delivery. His style and manner of delivery, according to Seneca, mirrored his temperament:

> ... a sort of unselfconscious sheen played upon his unaffected style. As he spoke, his expression was gentle, and, like his calm character, relaxed. He did not strain his voice or exaggerate his movements as the words flowed out, so it seemed, unbidden. Of course, the fact was that his character was by now placid and peaceful. He had suppressed genuine feelings, banished afar anger and grief, and was no good at pretending to feel what he had escaped from. He was better suited to *suasoriae*. No-one described more lovingly the characteristics of places, the courses of rivers, the positions of cities, the character of peoples. He never stopped for lack of a word: a generous flood of speech flowed round everything in a swift and easy stream. [64]

Both portraits demonstrate Seneca's interest in the effect of emotion on speaking. If genuinely felt, it causes within the speaker a tension

---

[64] 2 pr. 2-3; Winterbottom transl. The sketch of Cassius Severus (3 pr.) is difficult to interpret in this light because it is concerned primarily with the vast differences between declamation and court oratory. Severus is provided as an

or commitment which can result in eloquent expression. Thus Pollio and Haterius both speak eloquently under the influence of grief; the violence and passion of Calvus are reflected in his style and success in pleading (7.4.6-8). Although Cassius Severus could arouse emotions in an audience at will (3 pr. 2), he was more effective when really angered and forced to improvise (3 pr. 4, 5). On the other hand, in submitting to Stoic doctrines, Fabianus had banished all extremes of emotion from his personality and thus lacked the combative spirit required for success in *controversiae*. He was unable to generate emotions in others because he lacked them himself. But there was an important exception. Whenever the material of a speech allowed for the commonplace reproach of contemporary morality, a theme that would be dear to the heart of any Stoic, Fabianus became inspired (2 pr. 2). In company with the best ancient critics, Seneca believed therefore that sincere emotion was required of a speaker to inspire the corresponding feelings in others. [65] Although noted for his laziness and poor speeches, Scaurus excelled when he enticed his opponents into the *altercatio* (a point by point debate between the two opposing lawyers), in which he conducted himself more in the fashion of an emotionally involved litigant than a defense attorney (10 pr. 2-3). This *calor* did not appear in the published versions of his speeches and therefore Seneca wishes that all of his writings were burned by decree of the Senate, not just the seven orations it proscribed. [66] Thus even a speaker who was not

---

example of an excellent court speaker but poor declaimer, even though he had all the attributes necessary for success (3 pr. 7). Thus the preface is not so much the investigation of a man and his style, but rather why a fine orator failed as a declaimer. The ninth preface, on Votienus Montanus, is incomplete. What remains is primarily a quotation from him attacking declamation as a preparation for court oratory. The tenth preface is a series of thumbnail portraits. One of the more interesting is of Scaurus. Seneca focuses upon his laziness and its effect on his speaking (10 pr. 2-3). The violent temperament, excessive courage, and free speech of Labienus (10 pr. 4-7) resulted in a prominent display of his Republicanism, and thus a multitude of enemies who arranged for the burning of his books. Preferring not to outlive his works, he committed suicide. Little is said of his style or delivery except that he was very eloquent. Musa's lack of judgment caused him to speak foolishly and inappropriately (10 pr. 9, 10). Clodius Turrinus was diligent to a fault and thus blunted his natural power (10 pr. 14-16). The engaging portrait of Seneca Grandio (*Suas.* 2.17) describes a man with a passion for largeness in all matters, who, while declaiming, would physically extend himself in the attempt to appear larger than he was.

[65] Arist. *Poet.* 1455 a 32; Cic. *Or.* 132; *De Or.* 2.189-196; Horace *A. P.* 99-113; Quint. 6.2.26-36; younger Seneca *De Ira* 2.17; "Longinus" 9; cf. D'Alton 128 and note 2.

[66] 10 pr. 3; cf. Cicero's description of Galba, *Brut.* 93; also Quint. 6.2.26. The relationship between truly felt emotion and the achievement of eloquence

technically very competent could attain eloquence on occasion when moved by strong emotion.

3. *Formal Criticism*

Seneca's critical approach is hardly comprehensive. In the various portraits he selects only the most striking qualities to comment upon, while in the vast body of the anthologies his criticism is either non-existent or confines itself to generalities. Scattered here and there is a wide variety of technical comments, but in no one place does he pause to give us his own theories of rhetoric. If, on the other hand, his criticisms are grouped under the traditional five parts of rhetoric and analyzed, some coherent standards emerge.

Invention

Invention is primarily concerned with determining the crucial issue upon which the case rests (*status* or *stasis*), [67] and then assembling the appropriate arguments for proof and refutation. Argumentation is a broad subject including physical evidence, formal arguments (often addressed to probability based on this evidence or on examples from the past), and appeals to emotion (*ethos* and *pathos*). Since declamations were fictitious cases, the speakers could not introduce direct evidence in the form of contracts, eye-witness reports, or physical traces of the alleged act, although a speaker might refer to these indirectly. The lack of attention to primary evidence in declamation would have been a grave educational defect were it not for the deeply held mistrust of such evidence in real courts. The practices of suborning witnesses and falsifying contracts or physical remains were widespread and juries habitually preferred logical arguments based on probable human action in the circumstances, supported by commonplaces and appeals to emotion.

The division of a declamation was an outline of the formal argumentation, a part of the speech which regularly occurred after the narration

---

probably springs from the greater vigor of mental conception in a highly aroused emotional state; cf. Cic. *Part. Or.* 6.20; Quint. 6.2.29-33; on the concept in "Longinus," cf. Grube 344. An audience would be more impressed when it detected a genuine emotional state in the speaker and could therefore be more confident in the speaker's honesty and forthrightness. Figures and other rhetorical artifices of style are an attempt to recreate artificially the natural vigor and ornamentation called forth under the influence of deep emotion; cf. D'Alton 112ff.

[67] See above, 40 and note 21.

in a judicial speech. It differed from the outline of a court speech since usually only one side of the case was presented at a session. Thus the declaimers had to proceed through a larger number of *staseis* and arguments in support of each in order to anticipate the opposition. Since it provided more practice and was more complex, division might form a good preparation for judicial argumentation. [68] One of the best declaimers of the age, Latro, delivered a synoptic outline of his division before speaking in order to allow the audience to follow more easily (1 pr. 21).

The better declaimers were very proficient in division, [69] but it required skill and care which others were unable or unwilling to muster; some believed that argumentation did not allow sufficient scope for stylistic embellishment. For this reason Montanus criticizes declaimers who neglected division altogether (9 pr. 1); on the other hand Seneca faults others who made it too complex (7 pr. 1, 2). The goal in division was to attain *subtilitas*—the precision and clarity characteristic of Latro. [70] The omission of a formal division altogether was permissible in cases which hinged on a question of fact or, in one instance, where the declaimer could treat the argument as a philosophical topic. [71]

Seneca was persuaded that the division must be appropriate to the case and the situation (7.4.3; cf. 9.1.12). The doctrine of propriety in argumentation receives more scrutiny in the *Suasoriae* where, with some humor, Seneca discusses the manner of presenting a deliberative question before an absolute ruler, in this case Alexander. [72] He reproduces the advice of Cestius and adds several topical Roman anecdotes to illustrate its general applicability. Cestius says that in a free state one does not argue in the same manner as before a king. Even among kings there are differences; some may tolerate the truth

[68] On the value of division as a preparation see *Decl. Min.* 270; Bonner 39. The complexity was responsible for some distaste: 1 pr. 21, 22; 2.2.12; 7.5.8; 9 pr. 1, 2; cf. Quint. 7.1.41.

[69] See Bonner 74.

[70] 1 pr. 21; 1.1.13; 7 pr. 1; cf. Lewis A. Sussman, "Early Imperial Declamation: A Translation of the Elder Seneca's Prefaces," *SM* 37 (1970) 139, note 10; Winterbottom, note (1) *ad loc.* 1 pr. 20. In the division sections of the *Contr.* Latro appears 36 times; his nearest rival (Gallio) only 14 times. Latro's manner of division was Seneca's critical standard.

[71] A case involving a question of fact is termed a *controversia coniecturalis*; 7.3.6; cf. 7.7.10; 9.6.10; Quint. 4.2.8; also Quint. 2.4.26; 3.6.15; Kennedy *ARRW* 326. A philosophical question was called a *thesis* (*Contr.* 7.4.3; cf. 1.3.8; 1.7.17; 7.6.18).

[72] *Suas.* 1.5-8. On this anecdote and the question of *decorum* see below, 130-131.

more easily, others must be flattered but in a way suggesting due respect and not sycophancy.

The doctrine of propriety was vital to *ethos*, the effective and believable portrayal of character as an adjunct to persuasion. Since in many cases declaimers assumed the part of an actual litigant and not a colorless attorney, great care had to be exercised to ensure that the character, behavior, and emotions were appropriate. [73] Declaimers were known to weep, and in two such instances Seneca commended the eloquence of the presentation (4 pr. 6, 11; 9.4.21). Thus even an extreme emotion was allowable, provided it suited the circumstances. *Ethos* was in a sense vital to arousing *pathos*, for if the speaker's own emotional state was not believable, he could hardly expect to instill a similar feeling in his audience (2 pr. 2). Seneca genuinely admired one who could manipulate the emotions of his listeners (3 pr. 2; cf. 7 pr. 3; Quint. 6.2.20ff).

Colors were important adjuncts to argumentation, but considered as separate entities. [74] Therefore while they appeared most frequently in the argument itself, colors could occur in the narration (e.g. 7.1.20, 21), or indeed in any other part of a speech. But exactly where they should be was a matter of concern to some critics. Seneca reports Pollio's suggestion on the matter and probably concurs with it:

> ... the *color* must be displayed in the narration and pursued in the argumentation. People do not act wisely who use up all the resources of a color in the narration; it meant putting more than was required in the narration and less than was required in the proofs. [75]

Seneca's criticism of colors is consistent with his usual common-sense approach. He prefers more subtle ones than the silly, overworked specimens common in the schools. [76] Declaimers should avoid colors which are far-fetched or in bad taste since these could harm a case. [77]

---

[73] Ovid was attracted to *suasoriae* which emphasized this aspect; 2.2.12; cf. 2.3.23; 2.4.8; *Suas.* 1.13. See also Quint. 3.8.51-53; 4.1.47; Bonner 52-53.

[74] 1.5.9; 7.1.21; 7.5.8; 7.6.17. See above, 41-43.

[75] *Contr. Excerpta* 4.3 *extra*; transl. after Winterbottom. Cf. Bardon 96, who also cites 2.6.7; 7.1.21; 10.2.13-15, 17, to which add 7.1.20.

[76] Bornecque 101-102 gives a series of examples; cf. Bonner 56. Seneca rightly condemns a number of patently foolish ones; 1.3.11; 1.4.20; 2.1.33; 9.4.22; cf. Petr. *Sat.* 10; Quint. 4.2.94. Among the more outlandish colors listed in Bonner 56 are omens in dreams, supernatural manifestations, and overriding emotions. See also the example above, 42.

[77] 1.6.9; 10.5.18. See also 2.5.18; cf. 2.3.19; 7.1.20, 21; 9.1.15; 9.2.28; 10.5.18. Paradoxically, he remarks that a color of Gorgias was inept, though charming: 1.4.7; cf. 7.7.14; 9.2.20.

A certain sense of decorum in their use was advisable; thus Passienus
recommends simply accusing a step-mother, but not vilifying her
(7.1.20). But Seneca in this instance could excuse a lapse if emotional
fervor carried the declaimer away (*ibid.*). We can sense his regard
for Latro's colors. These, when examined separately, were rough
and harsh; but integrated into his speeches they succeeded in overwhelming the judge, not just persuading him. [78] Pollio argued for
colors that were straightforward, direct, and believable (*Excerpta*
4.6 *extra*), and probably spoke for Seneca as well. In all, Seneca's
critical standards for colors seem noticeably higher than most of his
contemporaries. [79]

Commonplaces and famous examples (usually historical) were aids
to argumentation although, like colors, they were not necessarily
confined to that section of a speech. [80] These useful devices provided
the declaimers with narrative stock pieces which they could insert
at the appropriate time in any number of different speeches. Familiar
ones concern a variety of subjects, including cruelty, adoption, the
vicissitudes of fortune, wealth, moral corruption, or the faults of
famous generals. [81] There seems to have been a standard logical way
of progressing through them; Seneca comments on its absence in the
school declamations of Ovid. [82] Speakers had a ready repertoire of
commonplaces and when the situation demanded they recited them
almost mechanically. But Seneca thought that great care was necessary,
since the audience might become offended if the commonplace were
inappropriate. In support, he recalls a declamation delivered by Latro
when he inserted a commonplace on adoption insulting to both Augustus
and Agrippa, who were listening. [83] A sense of moderation was

[78] 10 pr. 15; cf. 7.2.13, where a declaimer used a color that was also apparently
harsh, but, nevertheless, successful; see also 1.8.8.

[79] See Bornecque 37, on 7.2.11 and 7.5.11. An anthology of colors collected by
Junius Otho receives a poor review from Seneca; see above, 80ff. Quintilian
devotes much attention to the use of colors; his critical views generally agree with
Seneca's (see esp. Quint. 4.2.88ff).

[80] Indeed, they could serve as colors (e.g., 1.8.12, 16; 2.1.29; 9.6.18-19;
10.4.17-18) or a part of the argument itself as a *quaestio* (e.g., 7.3.7). Commonplaces could be expressed in *sententia* form (e.g., 2.4.4) or as various kinds of
figures (e.g., 7 pr. 7).

[81] E.g., 1.2.8; 1.8.16; 2.1.29; 2.7.1, 7; 9.2.19. The more important commonplaces are conveniently indexed in Winterbottom 11, 635, s.v. "commonplaces."

[82] 2.2.9. It is interesting that Latro borrowed a hackneyed commonplace from
the *scholastici* which Ovid further revised, shortened, and adapted for his poetry
(2.2.8; cf. Ovid *Am.* 1.2.11-12).

[83] 2.4.12-13; cf. the commonplace oath figure used by Albucius—it was suitable
for a declamation, but not for an actual court case (7 pr. 7; cf. 7.5.12-13).

necessary in the use of commonplaces. Seneca approvingly refers to Latro's usual good sense; as a rule he limited the number and length of those introduced, but not the spirit of his delivery (7.7.10).

Arrangement

Seneca labels the opening of a speech the *principium* or *prooemium.* [84] He seems unsympathetic to the use of figures here (*Suas.* 7.14) and finds an overly dry delivery of the *prooemium* unsuitable (2 pr. 1). If the situation warranted, it could be dispensed with altogether (2.1.23).

Seneca is more concerned with the narration (*narratio*) and does not hesitate to provide long excerpts or even an entire one (1.2.7-8; cf. 2.1.3). Characteristically these specimens consist of short, staccato sentences lacking internal subordination and connectives to the sentences preceding or following. Nearly all the declaimers quoted are therefore conforming to the convention that a narration must be clear, easy to follow, and convincing. Seneca believed that the narration could also be omitted if the case demanded. [85]

The formal argument of a case generally followed the narration; its outline was the division. [86] In certain types of cases even deletion of the division (and thus the formal argumentation) was acceptable to Seneca. In the previous treatment of division we have already seen how complex the internal structure of arguments became; in general Seneca is wary of this development (1.1.13). An argument could contain a defense (of the client) and an accusation (of the opposition); the proper order of these was debated. Seneca agreed with Fuscus that the accusation should come first, followed by the defense, then the peroration (7.5.7). A man with some feeling for psychology, Seneca realized that people are more inclined to favor a defense, and that it would be more persuasive to have this impression fresh in their minds at the conclusion of the speech. Some speakers mixed the defense and accusation; they followed through a series of points comparing their side to the opposition. Seneca thought that such a comparison could prove dangerous to the weaker side: "…it is inexpedient to come to close grips; details that are not matched together are more easily hidden." [87]

---

[84] As *principium*: 2 pr. 1; 3 pr. 10; 7.1.20; *Suas.* 7.14. As *prooemium*: 1.1.25; 7.1.26; 10.1.13.

[85] He does not criticize its deletion: 1.4.8; cf. 1.2.19; 2.1.23.

[86] Cf. above, 59 and note 81.

[87] 7.5.7; Winterbottom transl. Cf. his note (1) *ad loc.*

In Roman courts the prosecution normally spoke first. Yet declaimers speaking as prosecutors and delivering a narration appropriate to an opening speech often included in their arguments a refutation, thus giving the impression of a reply. [88] This practice, which Seneca does not fault, points to a very clear distinction between the practices of the school and the courts. Presumably it allowed the students more practice. But eventually this inclusion of the refutation spread to the courts themselves. [89]

The digression or *excessus* was the literary gem of a declamation. It could occur within the argument but usually preceded it and followed the narration. [90] These digressions were often descriptive; geography and storms were favorite subjects. [91] Seneca regularly refers to these with the word *descriptio*, and does so in a manner suggesting that it was in practice a conventional part of a speech. [92] In *suasoriae* descriptions were an essential component; therefore, because of his excellence in descriptions, Seneca thought that Fabianus was especially well-suited for these exercises (2 pr. 3). Nearly every one of the *Suasoriae* in the concluding portions contains material from digressions. Seneca also preserves extracts from some descriptions in the *Controversiae*; three especially vivid ones are a torture scene (2.5.4, 6), a storm (7.1.4, 10-11), and a drunken orgy (9.2.4-14 *passim*).

There was a strong tendency as descriptions became more like commonplaces to insert them with little regard for their appropriateness; Seneca found this distasteful, [93] but he fails to denounce some of the more seamy examples. [94] Perhaps he realized that as a showpiece, descriptions sometimes required very picturesque treatment, to the point of vulgarity. A varied vocabulary was requisite for success

---

[88] See Clarke 92-93, 105; therefore they are answering absolutely imaginary objections from imaginary opponents (cf. Quint. 4.2.28; 5.13.50; 6.1.42; 7.1.38). In certain *controversiae* this was a popular way to handle a case (*Contr.* 10.5.12; cf. 7.5.7).

[89] 9 pr. 2; cf. Clarke 105.

[90] Quint. 4.3.1ff. Cicero thought it should be interwoven in the argument (*De Inv.* 1.97). Cestius placed one in the narration (7.1.27).

[91] D'Alton 507-508; Bonner 58-59. See *Suas.* 1.1, 2, 4, 15; 2.1, 8; 3.1, 2. They also occurred in the *Contr.*: e.g., 1.3.3, 7; 7.1.4, 10-11; *Excerpta* 8.6. A complete listing in found in Winterbottom's index, 11, 636, s.v. "descriptions." See also above, 62.

[92] 1.4.8, 9; 2 pr. 1; *Suas.* 3.4; cf. 9.2.21; *Suas.* 3.7; Bonner 58.

[93] 7.2.14; 9.2.21. Many were commonplaces; cf. Winterbottom I, xii and note 3. Seneca often just relates that a set description was used, but does not bother to quote from it (e.g., 1.4.2; 2.1.26; 9.6.18; *Suas.* 2.8, 14; 3.2; cf. 6.10).

[94] E.g., 9.2.4ff; but see Quint. 4.3.2.

(7.1.27), although excesses were to be avoided (2 pr. 1). A poetic prose style was conventional in description [95] and the sought after effect was smooth and flowing, not sententious (2 pr. 3; cf. 9.2.21).

Seneca labels the conclusion of a speech the *epilogus*. [96] There is little critical comment on this part, apparently because he totally agrees with the ancient conventions which required a concentration of emotional effort and appeal (7.4.6; cf. 7.4.8) and few people violated the rules. He did object, however, to effeminate prose rhythms for achieving emotional effects (7.4.8). The *epilogus* should leave a favorable impression upon the audience, and he therefore ruled out an accusatory tone in it (7.5.7).

The arrangement of a speech was not always apparent to the audience, in part because the declaimers consciously attempted to effect transitions as neatly and as effortlessly as possible, often with a *sententia* or figure. [97] Seneca found the *sententia* transition elegant (e.g., 7.1.26), especially one case where the *sententia* was also a figure (1.1.25).

Seneca does not seem very concerned with a speaker's arrangement, provided it was sensible and appropriate to the situation. Therefore, his comments on the topic are few, and on one occasion when listing the parts of a speech he does not even marshal them in proper order. [98] He praises the pointedness and unity in the individual speech divisions of Cassius Severus, yet Tacitus tells us that this same speaker totally disdained matters of arrangement (*Dial.* 26). Grossly negligent arrangement was not overlooked by Seneca, but he did not consider it an especially vital matter. Thus he spared Severus because his emotion and heated extemporaneous delivery served to overshadow his faults (3 pr. 2-6). Haterius neglected proper arrangement more noticeably (4 pr. 9), but on balance Seneca delivers a favorable assessment of his speaking abilities (4 pr. 11). His genius compensated for the faults and Seneca, who refused to consider every rhetorical rule sacred (10 pr. 10), did not regard Haterius' unconventional arrangement as a very serious deficiency. But the arrangement of Albucius was so grotesque that Seneca rightly censured him. Albucius rambled on so

---

[95] Imitiations of Vergil were popular, if not always successful (7.1.27; *Suas.* 3.4-5; 4.4-5; cf. *Suas.* 1.2; 2.20).

[96] 1.7.15; 3 pr. 10; 4 pr. 8; 7 pr. 2; 7.4.5, 6, 8; 7.5.7; 9.6.11, 12, 13.

[97] 1.1.25; 1.8.1; 7.1.26. Ovid, a master of the art of transition from one story to another in the *Met.*, consistently and usually quite successfully employs *sententiae* to link tales which are otherwise only tenuously related to each other.

[98] ... *principia, argumenta, narrationes aride dicebantur, in descriptionibus extra legem omnibus verbis dummodo niterent permissa libertas* (2 pr. 1).

excessively that he rarely completed a *controversia*; he piled argument upon argument, and confirmed proofs with new proofs (7 pr. 1). Each *quaestio* was constructed as if it were a speech entire with all the conventional component parts. Seneca finds this anomaly to be totally inconsistent with good sense. [99]

Arrangement was so stereotyped that this alone could account for Seneca's lack of interest. The structure used by the declaimers, if not conventional, was hardly artistic enough to elicit much comment in the first place. [100] To observers and declaimers alike it was the clever *sententia*, subtle division, and ingenious color which were most attractive.

Style

Of all the parts of rhetoric Seneca was most concerned with style. In the prefaces he tends to speak of style generally, saving more specific comments for the body of the works. Following the theories of Theophrastus, Roman critics thought that good style consisted of attaining four virtues: correctness, clarity, ornamentation, and appropriateness. [101]

Correctness, expression in accordance with the accepted usage and grammatical rules of the language, was the most basic. [102] The standard of speech was the Latin of the educated upper class in Rome. The criteria were high, for even so careful a writer as Livy drew Pollio's scorn for Paduan provincialism (*Patavinitas*) in style. [103] Although Seneca considered Latro the best declaimer (10 pr. 13), the speech of this Spanish declaimer received a similar criticism from Messalla:

> Messalla was indeed a man of the most painstaking nature in every field of learning, but as a custodian of Latin speech he was extremely diligent. Consequently when he heard Latro declaiming

[99] 7 pr. 2; cf. Tac. *Dial.* 19 and Gudeman's note *ad loc., mille argumentorum gradus.*
[100] Cf. W. C. Summers, "Declamations Under the Empire," *Proc. Class. Assoc.* 10 (1913) 94.
[101] A useful discussion of the subject of style is found in D'Alton, Chap. II, "Aspects of the Problem of Style," 68-140. Rome's best speaker accepted the headings of Theophrastus (Cic. *Or.* 79), and we may well assume that Seneca followed his lead. There were some slight variations on the scheme of Theophrastus in the various Latin critics, but apparently all relied upon him; cf. D'Alton 77ff.
[102] Or simply, *Latine.* See *Ad Her.* 4.17 and Caplan (ed.) note (f) *ad loc.;* Cic. *De Or.* 3.37ff; *Brut.* 258ff; *De Opt. Gen. Dic.* 4; cf. Arist. *Rhet.* 1407 a 19 — 1407 b 25; D'Alton 78.
[103] Quint. 1.5.56; 8.1.3; cf. Kennedy *ARRW* 307 and note 8.

he said, "He is eloquent—in his own language." He conceded
Latro's genius, but criticized his expression. [104]

Evidently Latro's Latin usage was not always strictly correct; Seneca
(through Montanus) records an occasion when he began a speech
with a solecism (9 pr. 3; cf. Quint. 10.5.18). A proponent of correctness in speech, Seneca could make allowances dictated by common
sense or usage. In the *suasoria* where the three hundred Spartans sent
to Thermopylae debate whether or not to retreat, he successfully
refutes the arguments of a quibbling grammarian. Displaying flexibility
on the role of absolute grammatical correctness as opposed to sense
and context, Seneca reveals the ability to grasp the undefinable essence
of effective expression:

> There occurs to me a thought on the same sort of subject spoken
> by Cornelius Severus. Considering that it concerns Romans, it
> perhaps betrays excessive cowardice. He represents solidiers dining
> when battle has been proclaimed for the following day, and says:
> > "Stretched on the grass,
> > They said: *This* is my day."
> He put over in the most choice manner the emotions of men on
> a razor-edge of suspense; but he took too little account of the
> greatness of the Roman spirit: for they dine as if despairing
> of the morrow. How great was the spirit of those Spartans!
> *They* were incapable of saying: "This is my day."
> The grammarian Porcellus used to brand as a solecism Severus'
> saying in this line "this is my day" instead of "our day," when
> he had represented more than one as speaking. Here Porcellus
> was finding fault with the best feature of an excellent epigram.
> Change it to "our day," and all the elegance of the verse will
> disappear: for its propriety lies in this phrase, which is taken
> from the common idiom, "this is my day" being virtually a proverb.
> If you look to the sense, anyway, not even a grammarian's pedantry
> (which should be kept away from all superior intellects) will
> maintain its ground: they didn't all speak together as in a choir
> under the direction of a grammarian, but each individual among
> them said: "This is my day." [105]

A second requisite virtue of style is clarity. Seneca knew that an
overly abrupt style led to obscureness of expression (2 pr. 2). Many
of the ancient critics recognized this danger in concise style, never-

---

[104] 2.4.8; cf. *Suas.* 6.27; also Cic. *Pro Arch.* 10.24; Bonner 64.

[105] *Suas.* 2.12-13; Winterbottom transl.; cf. Quint. 1.5.36. Seneca's views here
reflect those of Augustus (Quint. 1.6.19; Suet. *Aug.* 86ff; Gell. 10.24.2). The
younger Pliny reports criticism of a speaker whose only fault was that he had
none (*Ep.* 9.26.1; cf. Quint. 10.4.4).

theless brevity was a much sought after effect, especially in *sententiae*. [106] Believing that they were obstacles to clarity, Seneca repeats Livy's harsh assessment of vulgar or archaic words often used in the attempt to attain a severe style. If one must depart from the mean, Seneca considered fullness of expression preferable to compression since it is easier to edit out unnecessary words than to add them (9.2.26; cf. Quint. 2.4.5-6).

Ornamentation was the means by which ordinary prose could be transformed into artistic expression. According to the ancient theory, this, the most difficult virtue of style to attain, was achieved through the employment of figures, judicious word choice, and composition (the careful disposition of words within a sentence and appropriate prose rhythm). In his general comments on ornamentation, Seneca selects the middle of the road in its use and identifies at least one instance when striving for excess ornamentation led to poor judgment and faulty style. [107] However, oranmentation was a chief attraction of declamatory displays, one demanded and applauded by audiences. The declaimers therefore became preoccupied with ornamentation at the expense of argumentation, and speakers transferred this habit to the forum. [108] Even Pollio, an austere stylist, was more florid in his declamations than his speeches and Seneca accepted this as normal when kept within reasonable bounds. [109]

Rhetorical figures were an indispensable element of declamatory ornamentation; only the "dry declaimers" avoided their use (2.1.24). The great number found in the anthologies attest to their popularity. [110] Nevertheless the entire subject was very complex, as Quintilian's treatment reveals. [111] Although Seneca is not averse to using figures himself, he tends to avoid the very specialized nomenclature attached to them. [112] In the *Controversiae* Seneca frequently calls attention to the

---

[106] See D'Alton 477-478, and ancient sources there cited.

[107] 4 pr. 10; cf. 2 pr. 1; *Suas.* 2.23.

[108] 9 pr. 1, 2; cf. Philostratus *VS* 586; D'Alton 212.

[109] 4 pr. 3; cf. Quint. 2.10.10-12.

[110] Bonner 66-70 gives a convenient collection and classification of those found in Seneca. The term "figure" here will also include tropes, since it was always a matter of great difficulty for ancient theorists to distinguish between them; Quint. 9.1.1ff; cf. Ad Her. 4.42ff; Kennedy *APG* 298-299.

[111] Quint. 8.6 (tropes); 9.1-3 (figures); cf. D'Alton 106-114.

[112] He uses, for example, the terms *anthypophora* (1.7.17) and *tetracolon* (9.2.27), but usually prefers to term a figure as such (*figura*) or use the Greek word, *schema*, leaving technical identification to the reader (e.g., 1 pr. 23; 1.1.25; 2.1.23; 2.3.18, 22; 2.4.9, 10, 11; 9.2.22; 9.6.14; 10.4.18; cf. 2.1.24; 4 pr. 7). Seneca perceives a broader definition of figures—one which encompassed shaping a part

misuse of figures. His deep concern is understandable since the declaimers were inclined towards excesses in ornamentation and frequent lapses of stylistic judgment. Of all the speakers mentioned, Latro is his model for the employment of figures. Prior to use at some time when a declamation might appropriately require them, Latro painstakingly composed and perfected an array of figures (1 pr. 23). To him figures were a device of argumentation, not just an ornament:

> "He (Latro) said that figures were not invented for the sake of display, but rather as an aid, so that something which might offend one's ears if said openly might creep in stealthily and indirectly" (1 pr. 24).

Latro's concealment of his carefully prepared figures was a major component of his *subtilitas* (1 pr. 23-24); he declined using unbelievable figures, but approved those which damaged the other side, not which simply amused the audience (1.1.25).

Other declaimers also successfully used figures as, for example, Cestius (2.4.9) and Albucius (7 pr. 3; cf. 2.5.17), but many came to grief and the reasons Seneca records are instructive. Although otherwise a competent speaker Moschus ruined his style by constantly expressing himself in figurative language. Seneca severely criticized this lack of restraint and termed his speech "not figured, but distorted" (10 pr. 10). In the excesses of a speaker such as Moschus we can identify the overwhelming desire of many declaimers to please an audience which demanded striking figures; the many and elaborate Gorgianic figures in Seneca's collection attest to a contemporary infatuation with display. [113] Musa was representative of this pandering trend; his metaphorical figures were so inflated that Seneca suggested a sound thrashing for the man (10 pr. 9-10). In so doing Seneca did not think he was being unduly harsh, since in the same context he admitted that he was no stickler for the rules and gladly made allowances for men of genius. [114]

Although he reproduces many figures in his works, Seneca rarely

---

or even the whole of a declamation (1.1.15 and Winterbottom note *ad loc.*; cf. 1.2.16; 2.1.23; 2.3.18; 2.3.22; 2.4.9, 11; 2.5.17; 2.6.6; 9.6.14; 10.4.18; also 7 pr. 3 and Winterbottom note (1) *ad loc.*). His manner of dealing with the terminology of figures is important evidence for Seneca's non-technical, non-pedantic approach to criticism.

[113] See D'Alton 212 who cites especially 2.4.12; 10 pr. 9; *Suas.* 2.16. There are many other instances; cf. Bonner 66-70.

[114] On incredible and overly imaginative figures cf. Quint. 8 pr. 25; "Long." 16.4; D'Alton 444; Atkins 229.

pauses to criticize or analyze them technically except in the broadest
terms. Thus while he speaks of the bizarre hyperboles in the style of
speakers such as Musa, he will normally pass over similar expressions
with no comment. 115 Seneca's practice is similar when it comes to
alliterations, at least one of which has been called a "horror of Ennian
proportions":

> "Non possum," inquit, "pati sine patre." Me autem sine te putas
> pati posse? Quemquam autem patrem putas pati sine liberis
> posse? 116

Several entertaining anecdotes centered on the faulty use of figures
with the general criticism implicit in the humor. One such concerns
Haterius who, while defending a freedman on the charge of homosexual
relations with his patron, unwisely extended the meaning of the word
officium ("duty"), and therefore became the butt of many jokes.
Haterius said:

> "Losing one's virtue is a crime in the freeborn, a necessity in a
> slave, a duty for the freedman." The idea became a handle for
> jokes, like, "you aren't doing your duty by me" and "he gets in a
> lot of duty for him." As a result the unchaste and obscene got
> called "dutiful" for some while afterwards. 117

Albucius also suffered great embarrassment after the unwise use of
a figure in court which caused him to retire completely from the
legal profession (7 pr. 6-7). The reason Seneca discerns is enlightening:
in declamations Albucius could use figures with impunity and not
worry whether they were appropriate to the situation (7 pr. 8).
Another anecdote regards the various uses of Vergil's metaphorical
phrase *plena deo*, and draws its humor from the various ways in
which the leading literary men of the day applied it. 118 While Seneca
expresses no real criticism of the figure except for mentioning Gallio's
appropriate use of it, the anecdote demonstrates (as did the one
above about Haterius) how quickly an unusual figure might attain a
reputation.

A common figure in which Seneca displays some critical interest
is the repetition of the same idea in different words. Some speakers

---

115 E.g., 10.4.5; cf. Bonner 70. The overuse of hyperbole resulted in much of
the *tumor* and bluster so characteristic of declamatory style; cf. 10.4.2; *Suas.* 2.17.

116 2.1.37. Alliterations of the letter "p" were particularly popular; see Bonner
66, who cites 1.1.6; 1.5.1; 1.6.12; 1.7.8; 2.2.7.

117 4 pr. 10; Winterbottom transl.

118 *Suas.* 3.5-7. The expression does not appear in our surviving texts of Vergil;
cf. Winterbottom note (2) *ad loc., Suas.* 3.5.

were guilty of excesses in this. Haterius realized his tendencies and stationed a freedman in the audience to signal him when to move on (4 pr. 7-8). Votienus Montanus, an orator, lacked Haterius' prompter but Seneca thought that the more ample boundaries of real oratory could in some degree mask the excessive handling of one idea in different ways; in the relatively limited scope of a declamation this fault stood out noticeably (9.5.15). Montanus would indeed say something well; but, dissatisfied, he would proceed to repeat the idea in many different ways. Seneca concluded that his major vice was ruinous over-repetition (9.5.17). For this reason Scaurus used to call Montanus "the Ovid of the orators" since the poet also did not know when to leave well enough alone (*ibid.*). Seneca applauds the general conclusion Scaurus drew: "to know how to stop is as important a quality as to know how to speak." [119]

An essential ingredient of the pointed style was antithesis, frequently in the form of an isocolon. Some of the examples preserved in Seneca are artfully crafted and testify to the care applied to their composition. But a number also exist which are clumsy and suggest that many declaimers introduced them solely for the purpose of contrast, and frigid ones at that. [120] Two part antitheses occur more commonly in Seneca than the three member ones. [121]

Seneca does not have much praise for tri- or tetra-cola because of the manner in which declaimers abused them. He slightingly refers to the tricolon as "this brand-new sickness" (2.4.11-12) and criticizes speakers for padding both tri- and tetra-cola in order to fill out the framework of the figure without contributing to its sense (9.2.27).

Word play (*paronomasia*) occurs commonly in Seneca's works and, although interested in its origins, he does not wholly approve of this figure. [122] He traces its use to Cicero, Laberius, and the writers of Atellan farces (7.3.9). A variation of word play also elicits criticism—the contrast of a simple verb with its compound, as in *peribit ergo quod Cicero scripsit, manebit quod Antonius proscripsit?* [123]

---

[119] 9.5.17 (Winterbottom transl.). On this point see also W. C. Summers (above, note 100) 99; T. F. Higham, "Ovid and Rhetoric," in N. I. Herescu (ed.), *Ovidiana* (Paris 1958) 40-41.

[120] Cf. Bonner 67-68.

[121] See Norden *AK* I, 289; Bornecque 109; Bonner 67.

[122] 7.3.9; cf. Quint. 9.3.69ff. For further examples and references see Bonner 60-70.

[123] *Suas.* 7.11; cf. Bonner 70, who cites a similar example in 7.7.3. A frequent occurrence was the contrast of different forms of the same verb; e.g., *tu exorasse*

Numerous other figures appear in the excerpts of the declaimers, but the opinions and samples looked at provide a fair idea of Seneca's attitude towards their use. He is obviously not as concerned with technicalities as he is with conveying to his reader a sense of good judgment and proportion in employing figures; they must contribute to the case and not just demonstrate the speaker's stylistic refinement.

The common sense and emphasis on propriety so evident in Seneca's remarks on figures also characterize his thoughts on diction. Thus he opposes the use of gaudy or artificially long words solely intended to make a speech seem more impressive. [124] Seneca appreciated the limitations of Latin when compared to Greek, a richer and more subtle tongue. Nevertheless he astutely recognized that Latin could be more vigorous and direct. [125] Perhaps the relatively narrow vocabulary Seneca noticed in some was partially inherent in the language itself. Cestius, by birth a Greek, had a limited storehouse of Latin words, but abounded with ideas; his greatest difficulties occurred in descriptive passages which required a wider, more picturesque vocabulary (7.1.27). In his *explicationes* Cassius Severus likewise had more ideas than words (3 pr. 7), but in his case a discriminating sense of diction came to the rescue. Albucius generally exercised good diction (7 pr. 2), although sometimes he was guilty of poor word choice in the attempt to conceal his preparation (7 pr. 3). Latro composed his speeches rapidly, and Fabianus delivered them copiously; both practices could understandably result in poor diction, but in their cases word choice did not suffer (1 pr. 17-18; 2 pr. 3). Thus even limited vocabulary and swift composition or delivery did not inevitably result in poor diction.

Seneca believed that antique and obsolete words ought to be avoided since they 'caused obscurity (9.2.26). Although guilty of such usages, Haterius did not insert these words purposely, but in the swift flow of his speech he could not exercise sufficient care. Even the rapidity

---

te dicis, ego te exoratum puto (2.3.17; cf. 1.1.3, 5; 2.4.6; 7.1.15). Bonner (*loc. cit.*) also discusses plays on words with similar sounds, although not etymologically related.

[124] 2 pr. 1; *Suas.* 2.17. On *verba grandia* see Atkins 157-158 and Bonner 64; cf. Horace *AP* 97; Persius 3.45. A useful treatment of Seneca on diction is found in Sochatoff "Theories" 348-349.

[125] On the relationship between the two languages, see 1 pr. 6-7; 2.6.12; 4 pr. 7; 7 pr. 3; 9.1.13-14; 10.4.23. Cf. Cic. *Nat. Deor.* 1.8; *Pro Caec.* 51; *De Fin.* 3.51; Lucr. 1.136-139, 832; 3.260; younger Seneca *Ep.* 58.1; Quint. 3.6.97; Pliny *Ep.* 4.18; Gell. 2.26; D'Alton 203-204; Sochatoff "Theories" 350-351.

of delivery could not conceal these old words, many of which were used by Cicero but had soon dropped out of vogue. [126]

Seneca faulted the use of obscene or low vocabulary. [127] Albucius was a notable offender who, we are told, did not realize that the splendor of his speech was polluted by the filth which he added (7 pr. 3-4). In contrast to the case of Haterius, his word choice was not accidental, since he stated that there was no word which could not occur in a declamation. His reason was simple: he wished to avoid being typecast as a *scholasticus* at any cost (*ibid.*). Latro, with whom Seneca usually agrees, opposed this notion and maintained that uncouth words must always be avoided (7.4.6). Indeed, the entire issue of how to employ colloquialism properly was difficult. Seneca kept an open mind on the question. Although he can express disapproval, more often his unfavorable criticism of colloquial speech resulted from improper handling rather than rigid bias:

> The pursuit of vulgarism is one of the virtues of style that rarely succeeds; one needs great restraint and the right moment. His [Albucius'] record in the employment of this quality was variable; he was often successful, often a flop. And it is not surprising that a virtue so close to a fault should not be easy to master. But no-one employed this trick more appropriately than my friend Gallio. Already in his youthful declamations he could use this manner fittingly and suitably and with propriety: I used to be the more surprised because a tender age normally shuns everything that resembles vulgarity, let alone vulgarity itself. [128]

Ovid was careful with his language according to Seneca, but exhibited poor word choice at times—and realized it himself, as did his friends. He knew his faults, but nevertheless loved them. [129]

From his own practice and a chance comment plainly Seneca accepted the common practice of coining new words where necessary. [130] To

---

[126] 4 pr. 9. On the use of antique words see W. C. Summers (ed.), *Select Letters of Seneca* (London 1913) xlii; Sochatoff "Theories" 348; cf. Quint. 2.5.21; 8 pr. 31; Tac. *Dial.* 23. Additional references and discussion are found in D'Alton 81.

[127] 1.2.23; 4 pr. 9; cf. Petr. *Sat.* 118; but Quint. 2.10.9; 8.3.23.

[128] 7 pr. 5-6; Winterbottom transl. Cf. 3 pr. 7; 4 pr. 9; 7 pr. 3-4; 10 pr. 2; cf. Cic. *De Or.* 3.150; younger Seneca *Ep.* 114.13-14; Quint. 8.3.17ff; Suet. *Rhet.* 6; Summers (above, note 126) xlii-xliv. See also 1.2.23; 2.3.21; 7.5.9; 7.6.21. Colloquialism did detract from *gravitas* (10 pr. 2). The views of Seneca find a parallel in Quintilian, who favored temperate use (1.5.5; 2.10.9) but felt that *sermo vulgaris* alone was insufficient, and required elevation through judicious word choice (12.10.43). See also D'Alton 80, 393-394.

[129] 2.2.12; cf. younger Seneca *Ep.* 114.1; Quint. 10.1.98, 130.

[130] 7.6.21; cf. in general Bardon 90-100.

him words were therefore only a tool of expression; when they did not fulfill this purpose for any reason, their value was lost. The ideal declaimer would then have a diction that was neither obscene nor excessively colloquial, but one that was carefully chosen and appropriate (3 pr. 7).

Seneca does not seem greatly concerned with the technicalities of composition, the general critical term applied to artistic word placement, sentence structure, word order, and prose rhythm. [131] Three major faults were associated with this aspect of style: (1) abruptness, caused by excessive use of short and disjointed sentences, (2) rarity of balanced periodic sentences, and (3) employment of faulty prose rhythms. In the criticisms he does address to composition, Seneca rarely comments on the first two points. Thus, while he frequently reproduces successions of short, choppy sentences, he seldom directs attention to this type of sentence structure, and then only in exceedingly extreme cases (e.g., 2 pr. 2). Seneca wholeheartedly embraced the pungency and point of the new Silver Age style. Quotations such as the following are common:

> He had done nothing wrong. He loves a whore—something that often happens. He is a youth; wait, he will reform and marry. [132]

Seneca is comparatively silent on the subject of periodic sentences although he reproduces a number of examples and composes them himself. [133]

The proper arrangement of words was a necessity in achieving pleasing prose rhythms, but this did not mean the wholesale transference of poetic meters to prose. [134] Seneca is generally favorable

---

[131] See Gudeman's (ed.) note *ad loc., hians compositio,* Tac. *Dial.* 21; cf. *Ad Her.* 4.18; Quint. 9.4. The Latin term *compositio* is equivalent to the Greek σύνθεσις τῶν ὀνομάτων.

[132] *Nihil ... peccaverat; amat meretricem; solet fieri: adulescens est, expecta, emendabitur, ducet uxorem* (2.4.10; Winterbottom transl.). Cf. Norden *AK* I, 283; Bornecque 124-125; Bonner 65. The Emperor Gaius may be referring to such style in his famous "sand without mortar" comment (Suet. *Gaius* 53; but see below, 156-157.

[133] Periods were thought especially useful in descriptive passages and numerous examples are quoted; e.g., 1.3.1; cf. Bonner 66.

[134] See Quint. 9.4.45ff; Atkins 275-276; Clarke 42. Euphony was necessary in ordering words (Quint. 9.4.32ff), but Quintilian opposed arbitrary rules of placement (9.4.24ff). Many prose writers affected poetic inversion of customary word order; see Quint. 2.4.3; Pliny *Ep.* 7.9.8; cf. D'Alton 444. The quotations reproduced by Seneca are, according to one observer, only "sporadically clausulated"; see Winterbottom I, xix and note 2. The anonymous excerptor tried to improve the prose rhythms in the original text.

to the use of rhythmical sentence endings (*clausulae*), but harshly criticizes padding with nonsensical phrases to achieve this effect. [135] He also disapproves of closing rhythms with a preponderance of short, choppy syllables, a fault which he usually refers to with various forms of *frango*. [136] Even more distasteful were soft and effeminate rhythms, apparently those which combined short choppy rhythms with the use of liquid consonants and the letter "m." Such usages must have enjoyed great popularity since even the vigorous Calvus occasionally employed them. [137] Seneca observed in his lifetime a decline of proficiency in prose rhythm. While the Asianists of the age were fond of rhythms characterized by an excessive number of short syllables, the *scholastici*, probably influenced by the Atticists, virtually neglected this aspect of composition. [138]

Since they are stylistic ornaments in sentence units, Seneca's criticism of *sententiae* can be considered under composition. As we have already seen, the Romans were fond of them, and when he came to arrange his extracts, Seneca devoted the most space to *sententiae*. In contrast to the sections of divisions and colors it is remarkable that Seneca did not choose to insert criticism in the *sententiae* portions; his critical attitude towards them must be gleaned from chance comments in the prefaces and color sections. [139]

Seneca's criticisms of *sententiae* are rarely technical; he exhibits the generalized reaction of an amateur enthusiast rather than the detailed analysis of a professional *rhetor*. A survey of the critical adjectives applied to *sententiae* confirms this impression. Although Bardon faults their lack of specificity and the omission of more analytical tools of criticism, the adjectives used are for the most part vivid, descriptive, and effective. For example, we find such words as

---

[135] 7.4.10; 9.2.27; *Suas.* 7.12; cf. Cic. *Or.* 229-230; Summers (above, note 126) xxxvi. The better critics thought that the rhythms should be unobtrusive (Cic. *Or.* 209, 213, 218; "Long." 41).

[136] 7.4.8; 9.2.22; *Suas.* 2.23; 7.12. Cf. Quint. 8.3.57.

[137] 7.4.8; cf. 7.4.6; 9.2.22. Seneca refers to these usually with derivatives of *mollis* ("soft, effeminate") or once with *mitis* ("mild, gentle"): 2 pr 1; 7.4.8; 9.2.24; cf. 7.4.6. The choppy cadence arose from a majority of short syllables; cf. the quotation from Calvus which Seneca characterized as both *emollita* and *infracta*: *credite mihi, non est turpe misereri* (7.4.8). Such an excess was thought not only effeminate, but lacking the dignity required of elevated prose; cf. D'Alton 101-102.

[138] E.g., 1.4.5; cf. Quint. 9.4.65-66; Norden *AK* I 290ff; Bonner 66.

[139] He reports another's criticism once, however (1.5.3). Discussion of *sententiae* in the *Suas.* occurs primarily in the concluding sections.

amabilis ("lovely"), *audax* ("bold"), *celebris* ("distinguished"), *dulcis* ("sweet"), *excitata* ("animated"), *praedulcis* ("very sweet, luscious"), *vocalis* ("sonorous"), and *belle sonans* ("prettily cadenced"). [140] Further evidence of Seneca's non-technical approach is the frequent appearance of *laudata* ("praised") to describe a *sententia*; in such cases we may agree with Bardon that Seneca has not employed a sufficiently specific term. Other broad terms such as *nobilis* ("notable"), *splendida* ("brilliant"), and *bona* ("good") also appear. [141] *Dissertissima* ("very eloquent") expresses the highest regard attainable (e.g., 9.5.15; *Suas.* 2.11, 5.8), while *stultissima* ("very stupid") indicates the opposite. Seneca does not lack humor when applying the latter term:

> Saenianus said a very stupid thing: "The rich man always despised me, always counted me as dead." To rival Saenianus' saying, after this epigram *I* always counted Saenianus as dead. [142]

Seneca often applies a form of *corrupta* to *sententiae* whose content is foolish or inappropriate. [143] On other occasions he refers to similar expressions as *improba* ("outrageous"; 7.5.14; cf. 1.5.3) or *inepta* ("foolish"; 7.3.10), while attempts for overstrained point are considered puerile (*Suas.* 2.16; cf. 1.7.10).

In all his criticisms of *sententiae*, Seneca emphasizes not only stylistic refinement but also meaning and sense. But to achieve its intended effect he also thought that a *sententia* must be terse; thus a good declaimer should have more ideas than words (3 pr. 7). When comparing Thucydides with Sallust, Arellius Fuscus thought the Roman better since he could express the same idea in fewer words. [144] But Seneca perceived that excessive brevity could also prove dangerous since it might result in obscurity. [145] At the other end of the spectrum, inflating *sententiae* with superfluous verbiage was to be avoided (*Suas.* 1.16) and, similarly, the excess repetition of the same idea in different words (9.5.15-16). A variation of the latter practice was *echo*. Using this device, a declaimer would begin and end a speech

---

[140] See Bardon 53, 78ff, 112-113.

[141] For use of *laudo* and its derivatives, see 1.8.12; 2.6.12; 9.4.22; *Suas.* 6.10. On the other terms cf. Bardon 53.

[142] *Excerpta* 5.2 *extra*; Winterbottom transl. Cf. 1.4.12; 7.5.10.

[143] 7.1.25; 9.1.14; 9.5.17; *Suas.* 1.12, 13.

[144] 9.1.13; on brevity see also 1.1.25; 1.5.9; 2 pr. 2; 2.1.34; 2.6.13; 7.1.27; 10.5.26; *Suas.* 1.11. The quotation in 9.1.13 is not from Thucydides; on the identity of the Greek writer see Winterbottom note (3) *ad loc.*

[145] See Summers (above, note 126) xxxv-xxxvi; Bonner 54. Cf. younger Seneca *Ep.* 100.8; Quint. 10.1.130; 12.10.48; Tac. *Dial.* 20.

with the same *sententia*, pointedly calling attention to the fact. Seneca
recounts at length Cestius' witty and devastating remarks against
those who used *echo*, thereby suggesting strongly that Seneca himself
shared this low opinion of the device (7.7.19).

Seneca was wary about a general class of *sententiae* modeled after
those found in the comedies of Publilius Syrus which he refers to as
sententiae Publilianae (7.2.14; 7.3.8; 7.4.8). He reports that Moschus
termed their use "insanity," while he himself claimed that this type of
sententia had "infected" the minds of young people when they first
became popular (7.3.8). But Seneca balances his own harsh view with
the remarks of Cassius Severus, a great admirer of the playwright.
According to him, people only imitated the playwright's poorer qualities,
leaving aside those things "better expressed by him than any other
comedian or tragedian, Roman or Greek." [146] Severus provides three
examples which are both clever and true generalizations; for example,
"O life—for the wretched, long; for the lucky, short." [147] The young
declaimers passed over these worthy expressions for ones with a more
spicy content (7.3.8). With varying degrees of success, speakers also
turned to other poetic genres for inspiration. [148]

Seneca especially admires the qualities of liveliness and spirit, and
thus praises Cassius Severus for his animated *sententiae* (3 pr. 2;
cf. 2.6.12). Even with his non-technical vocabulary, Seneca effectively
points out which *sententiae* work, but rarely how or why. His standard
is the total effect upon the listener, and this he can only express in
generalities, though picturesque and evocative. There are, however,
some coherent themes in his criticism; the attraction of brevity, liveliness, and force, coupled with dislike of the inappropriate, the hyper-
bolic, the foolish, and the cute. Seneca also believed that there were
certain imponderables of style which allowed *sententiae* of dissimilar
qualities to achieve success. Thus Clodius Turrinus, a talented but
not great declaimer, authored *sententiae* which Seneca esteems because
they are "lively, wily, and pointed" (10 pr. 15). But Albucius, who
enjoyed the respect of Seneca and Pollio, authored *sententiae* of a
totally different sort: they were "straightforward and clear, adding
nothing hidden or unexpected; but were resounding and brilliant"
(7 pr. 2).

---

[146] 7.3.8; indeed high praise, but a common attitude as noted by Winterbottom,
note (2) *ad loc.*; cf. younger Seneca *Ep.* 8.8; *Tranq.* 11.8; Gell. 17.14.

[147] 7.3.8: *O vita misero longa, felici brevis!*

[148] See Bonner 138ff.

Of all the stylistic virtues, propriety is the most difficult to define. In part this is due to its broad application, denoting appropriate expression in the context of the speaker's person, the subject, and the situation. Propriety is a key ingredient of good style, but can also extend to argumentation, arrangement, and delivery. [149] The exercise of strict formulas to achieve propriety is nearly impossible; it requires common sense, good judgment, and the lessons of experience. In the analysis of the other parts of rhetoric we have, in effect, already been examining the role of propriety, and have seen how Seneca prefers to test performance through the use of commonsense standards. Thus Seneca has been applying the test of propriety all along, revealing that it is an essential ingredient of his critical theory. [150]

Seneca records at length the opinions of two declaimers which directly bear upon the broader view of propriety. In both instances he reveals his own understanding of the concept's wide application. Since he chose to include these sections and not in any way to refute them, we may assume that they express his own thoughts. The first instance is Latro's explanation of proper procedure in managing a defense by employing proper argumentation, diction, prose rhythm, but especially appropriate *pathos*. The case in question concerns a woman who became blind weeping for her husband who was captured by pirates. Her son plans to go off and ransom the man, but she demands that he stay, support her, or be imprisoned otherwise:

> Latro said the case for the mother should be put mildly and with restraint. "What she seeks is not revenge but pity, and she is at law with a young man so situated that in demanding his affection she obstructs it." He said, therefore, that one should abstain even from over-rough words, whenever this sort of theme comes up; the style itself should be toned down to match the kind of emotion we want to arouse. In the perorations we even make our voices break on purpose, bow our heads and ensure that the speaker doesn't clash with what he is speaking; moreover, epilogues are suited by a gentler rhythm. [151]

In the second passage Cestius outlines his precepts on how to manage argument in the *suasoria*, "Alexander deliberates whether to sail the

---

[149] Propriety as a virtue of style is but one aspect of the broader, more inclusive theory of *decorum*; see D'Alton 114-138.

[150] For example, one may examine Seneca's opinions on figures; see above, 120-124. As noted, he rarely touches upon technicalities, but is more concerned with proper use. Thus he will criticize excessive employment of them or injecting inappropriate ones.

[151] 7.4.6; Winterbottom transl.

ocean" (*Suas.* 1). This advice, discussed above under the topic of argumentation, is punctuated by several anecdotes from Roman history, and is remarkably long (*Suas.* 1.5-8). The entire section is a thinly disguised guide to arguing a case before an emperor, and conveys the absolute importance of propriety in presenting such cases. Crucial to his criticism is the proper deportment of the speaker (*ethos*), a topic on which Seneca himself elsewhere presents sensible advice. [152] But the majority of Seneca's remarks concern propriety in word choice, a topic treated under the virtue of diction. There we identified a great dislike for obscene language or thought, and concern over the proper employment of colloquial speech. [153]

Passing to matters less concerned with style, Seneca shows frequent concern over the unseasonable use of wit, particularly when not in keeping with the dignity required by the situation or when it could prove dangerous. [154] In argumentation one had to guard against expressing thoughts that might alienate the audience (2.4.13) or inserting historical commonplaces inappropriate to the case (7.5.12-13). Careful preparation in all phases of speech was necessary, but Seneca points out that it should not be made overly apparent to the audience. A glib speech could arouse suspicion since it suggests insincerity (7 pr. 3; cf. 1 pr. 2). The manner of delivery common to the courtrooms was thought improper for a school declamation (10 pr. 12), and in a court itself one must observe the conventional demeanor of the defending or prosecuting attorney (10 pr. 2).

Memory

Memory was probably the least important part of rhetoric. Most declaimers apparently did not make it a practice to memorize their speeches verbatim, although they might learn by heart such vital portions as the *prooemium* and conclusion. Notice of extemporaneous declamation in the anthologies is certainly not unusual. [155] Notes were commonly used, some quite elaborate (e.g., 3 pr. 6), and the manner of preparing a speech for delivery was undoubtedly similar to the methods described by Quintilian (11.2.27-51).

The length and prominence of Seneca's comments on memory in the first preface are misleading; they owe more to literary conventions

[152] See 2.4.8; *Excerpta* 4.5 *extra* (no. 1); 7.4.6; cf. 2.5.18.
[153] E.g., 1.2.21, 23; cf. the remarks on colloquialisms; 7 pr. 3, 4, 6, and above, 125-126.
[154] 3 pr. 4; 7.3.9-10; 9.4.17, 21; cf. 1.1.25; *Suas.* 1.5-6.
[155] Cf. below, 134 and note 165.

than to excessive concern over mnemonic techniques. [156] In an extensive passage he recounts some prodigious memory feats which he performed in his youth and describes the deterioration of these powers caused by the onset of old age (1 pr. 2-5). He also possibly attributes a contemporary neglect of memory to lowered moral standards (1 pr. 10).

Latro is Seneca's paradigm for excellence in memory and illustrates its great utility in public speaking. Although Latro wrote swiftly, he could learn a speech by heart while he composed it (1 pr. 17-18). He had excellent grasping and retentive powers; Latro retained and could instantly recall every declamation he ever wrote. His memorization of historical information, considered useful in argumentation, was outstanding.

Latro's memory was essentially a natural gift, but he supplemented it with mnemonic techniques. Seneca undoubtedly wishes to underline this point, since he repeats the thought twice (1 pr. 17, 18). He insists that the mnemonic system was easy to master, providing evidence in the form of several notable feats performed by Cineas, an ambassador of Pyrrhus (cf. Cic. *Tusc.* 1.59; Pliny *HN* 7.88), an anonymous listener at a poetry recitation, and Hortensius (cf. Cic. *Brut.* 301; Quint. 11.2.24). Seneca believes that memory is important, but that competence is partially innate. [157] The mnemonic technique to which Seneca refers is probably the cumbersome Simonidean method, one more effective than perhaps some modern detractors are willing to admit. Seneca's abhorrence of technicalities is again evident; he speaks of the memory system elliptically without either naming it or giving the slightest hint as to its operation (1 pr. 19).

Delivery

Seneca pays scant attention to gesture (*motus*), one aspect of delivery, and passes on only some general comments on voice (*vox*). [158] Nevertheless delivery was a vital part of rhetorical training and Quintilian rightly devotes a great deal of space to it. [159] The term

---

[156] 1 pr. 2-5; cf. above, 77 and note 138.

[157] In this he agrees with Cic. *De Or.* 2.355-356, 360, and Quint. 11.2.1.

[158] The Latin terms most often used for delivery are *actio* or *pronuntiatio*. Cf. Quint. 11.3.1 where he quotes Cic. *De Or.* 3.222 and *Or.* 55. See also Quint. 3.3.1; Bardon 12, s.v. *actio*; *ibid.* 49, s.v. *pronuntiatio*.

[159] 11.3.1-184. He retells the anecdote about Demosthenes, who, when asked what the three most important parts of oratory were, asserted them to be delivery, delivery, and delivery (Quint. 11.3.6; cf. 11.3.1-9).

declamation itself was originally the name of a vocal exercise; only later did it become more inclusive and therefore supplemented by other forms of voice training. [160] One exercise mentioned by Seneca and considered a conventional practice was going up and down through the equivalent of a singer's musical scale (1 pr. 16; cf. *Suas.* 2.10). Like memory, Seneca believed that a good voice was partially a natural gift, and partially acquired through training; a lack of practice and concern for health were detrimental to it (1 pr. 16). Seneca preferred the combination of a sweet but strong voice (3 pr. 3), finding a hoarse or dry intonation distasteful (1.7.18; 2 pr. 1).

The nature of declamation many times required the speaker to assume the appropriate character of the person represented. The term *pronuntiatio*, often used to convey the idea of delivery, occurs frequently in contexts which suggest a highly emotive or theatrical mode of delivery; Seneca approved of such a presentation providing it was not obtrusive. [161] Since no portion of the surviving text supports the notion, it is impossible to say if Seneca approved of the standard theatrical gestures associated with such a delivery. A lack of vehemence in bodily motion seemed unusual (2 pr. 2), and he disliked contrived poses intended to give an exaggerated impression of height (*Suas.* 2.17).

An excessively swift pace of delivery was a cause for concern in Haterius who, according to Augustus, "needed the brakes." [162] Within reasonable limits, however, Seneca thought that speed was both desirable and effective, perhaps because it revealed the deep emotional involvement of the speaker. [163] In one case, for example, Latro's *impetus* of speech kept his listeners in a state of astonishment; here, at least, Seneca is clearly conflating speed and emotion in delivery, both of which he admires (1.7.16). Thus he endorses the delivery of Cassius Severus who allowed nothing of a leisured pace in his presentations (3 pr. 2; cf. 3 pr. 7), and Seneca could conclude that this speaker

---

[160] Cf. above, 5.

[161] Cf. his remarks on Cassius Severus in 3 pr. 3: ... *pronuntiatio quae histrionem posset producere, nec tamen quae histrionis posset videri*, "... his delivery would have made any actor's reputation, without being at all reminiscent of an actor's" (Winterbottom transl.; cf. his note (4) *ad loc.*). See also 7.4.6; Quint. 2.10.13-14; 2.12.9-10; 3.8.51-54. Declaimers had to be as versatile as professonal actors; cf. Quint. 11.3.5; Pliny *Ep.* 2.14.12. See also above, 9.

[162] 4 pr. 7; cf. Winterbottom note (1) *ad loc.*; also 1.6.12; 4 pr. 9; Tac. *Ann.* 4.61.

[163] See Seneca's remarks, also on Haterius, 4 pr. 6—true emotion seems to have aided delivery. On Seneca's general approval of a swift pace of delivery see also 2 pr. 3; 7 pr. 2.

was better heard than read (3 pr. 3). An emotionally charged, rapid delivery was his preference, at least in *controversiae*; those who could not perform in this fashion had to look elsewhere for expressing their eloquence. [164]

The ability to speak extemporaneously received important notice. [165] The delivery of a declamation off-the-cuff must have been a feat requiring extraordinary presence of mind, memory, and general oratorical skill. The speaker would have to fabricate *sententiae* to please a critical audience, divide the argument, and contrive colors. At the same time he would be required to pay close attention to style and delivery. Because of the well-recognized difficulties in speaking extemporaneously, and because it appears more genuine, such a delivery has always commanded more respect than an obviously prepared or read speech. Seneca appreciated these factors and, as we have already mentioned, favored speeches which did not give the impression of elaborate preparation. [166]

Given the difficulties involved, one could hardly expect an extemporaneous delivery to equal a prepared speech. Yet Cassius Severus, who habitually prepared very carefully, actually spoke better when forced to deliver an extemporaneous speech; several others performed nearly as well. [167] Seneca admired this ability, but clearly regarded it as a stunt; he preferred thorough though unostentatious preparation. [168]

To summarize, the *Controversiae* and *Suasoriae* are more than a collection of extracts from declaimers; they are, and were intended to be, works of literary criticism. The methodology employed is basically conventional, although Seneca does rework or reject certain contemporary practices.

He declines to employ terse critical labels, then a customary and common critical tool. Instead he preferred the pointed and more flexible *sententia* description of a man and his works. Several or more such *sententiae* could, with the addition of other material, constitute the longer critical portraits found mainly in the prefaces. In

---

[164] As in the case of Fabianus, 2 pr. 2-3; cf. the discussion of the Vergilian phrase *plena deo* (*Suas.* 3.5-7).

[165] 2.5.20; 3 pr. 6; 4 pr. 7; 7 pr. 2; 9.3.13.

[166] Cf. 1 pr. 21, 24; 1.5.9; 7 pr. 3; 10 pr. 14. Seneca displays surprise at the excessively elaborate speech outline used by Cassius Severus (3 pr. 6).

[167] 3 pr. 6. On the others see above, note 165.

[168] Cf. Cic. *De Or.* 1.150. Quint. (10.6) treats the matter with his customary good judgment. Cf. Tac. *Dial.* 6; *Ann.* 4.61; Pliny *Ep.* 2.3.1-3 .

these portraits Seneca pays special attention to character and its effect upon style, a significant step in the predominantly mechanistic and objective ancient critical methodology. The sketches are studiously non-technical and selective; they examine in ordinary language the most striking attributes of personality and speaking performance.

On occasion Seneca uses similes and metaphors as critical tools; most of the criticism, however, consists of just one or several words applied to a sample of a speaker's work. This is Seneca's basic methodology in the body of the works. Although Bardon has found fault with his critical vocabulary, it is, nevertheless, quite effective, on occasion original, and nearly always picturesque.

In the overview, Seneca is a non-dogmatic observer, and possesses a broad historical perspective, although not necessarily an accurate or sufficiently detailed one.

Turning from methodology to content, in his various criticisms assembled under the five parts of rhetoric, Seneca displays throughout a moderate and sensible outlook. As the many cross references to Cicero and Quintilian attest, he is firmly in the mainstream of that critical tradition. In contrast to these two men, however, Seneca was an amateur in rhetoric and so exhibits studied indifference to technical terminology and rigid rules. His criticism most often reflects the total effect of a speaker's performance upon an intelligent listener; rarely does he examine something analytically. Indeed, he will often conflate in his comments several traditional virtues of style or even parts of rhetoric. In criticism directed at individual specimens of style, he prefers to speak in non-technical generalities regarding the success or failure of each specimen, whether in terms of style or contribution to persuasion.

Seneca's critical standard is effective and esthetically pleasing speech. Thus he admires argument which wins a case, not just applause; he prefers arrangement which is appropriate to the situation and balanced. A speech should be easily comprehensible and ornamented within the bounds of good taste; it should be sufficiently attractive, yet not ostentatious. Memory, a useful skill, is in part a natural gift which can be aided by mnemonics. Delivery should be appropriate to the person depicted and the surroundings; in *controversiae*, to be convincing, one should demonstrate some emotional fervor.

At the time he was writing, Seneca was an old man who had obviously been an interested observer of declamation and oratory for over two-thirds of a century—and a momentous century at that. In any person

of reasonable intelligence, such long experience should lead to a
heightened sense of taste, propriety, and common sense. In Seneca it
clearly did. A deeply held feeling for propriety (*decorum*) underlies
his criticism in nearly every area. But though important, this is but
one facet of a more universal outlook on rhetoric, one to which Seneca
repeatedly refers in a metaphorical fashion with various forms of
sanus, "healthy," and its negation. [169] Healthy, sound, and rational
expression is the ideal; any observer with common sense and experience
can discern what does and does not constitute such speech. Thus Seneca
does not always have to indicate whether a statement is good or bad;
in context, he thinks, it should be self-evident. Only the more striking
examples elicit comment. While this standard of sanity in expression
is implicit in the prefaces, words of the *sanus* group rarely appear
there. It is in the body of the works, while dealing with actual specimens,
where Seneca can point his finger to examples which are sane or insane.
Even more, speakers whose minds are not in a healthy state cannot
hope that their expression will be otherwise; man and style are one.
In this fashion, then, Seneca's call for rationalism in every part of
speaking, and his emphasis on the effect of character on performance
merge together in a coherent fashion.

---

[169] Words of the *sanus* group applied to speakers and their expression occur
in 1.7.15 (twice); 2.1.25 (three times), 26; 2.6.8; 7.6.24; 9.2.26 (three times),
28; 10 pr. 9; 10.4.22; 10.5.21, 24 (twice), 27; *Suas.* 1.12, 13, 16 (twice); 2.16, 17.
Synonymous phrases suggesting sanity or its opposite also occur; e.g., 3 pr. 18
(Severus speaking); 9.2.26 (Miltiades quoted); 10.5.27. Other uses of the *sanus*
group by people Seneca quotes are found in 7.3.8; *Suas.* 1.12. The metaphor was
not unique; e.g., Cic. *Or.* 99; *De Opt. Gen. Dic.* 8; *Brut.* 51; Hor. *Ep.* 2.2.122;
Petr. *Sat.* 3; Quint. 12.10.73; but as an effete virtue cf. Tac. *Dial.* 23; Pliny
Ep. 9.26.1.

CHAPTER FIVE

THE HISTORIES

In 1820 a fragmentary palimpsest biography of the elder Seneca by his son was discovered. From it we learn that he wrote a history of Rome from the beginning of the civil wars until nearly the day of his own death, early in the reign of Gaius:

> If I had already published whatever works my father wrote and wanted to have published, he would sufficiently have seen to the fame of his own name. For unless my filial devotion deceives me, and even the error arising from this is honorable, he would be considered among those who, because of their innate ability, have deserved to be famous by the mere titles of their writings. If anyone had read his *Histories* from the beginning of the civil wars, the point where righteousness declined for the first time, nearly up until the day of his own death, he would consider it important to know who the parents were of the man who [recorded] Roman events// .... [1]

---

[1] Haase fr. xv (Codex Vaticanus Palatinus 24); cf. Müller 548 n. 1.

Si quaecumque composuit pater meus et edi voluit, iam in manus populi emisissem, ad claritatem nominis sui satis sibi ipse prospexerat; nam nisi me decipit pietas, cuius honestus etiam error est, inter eos haberetur qui ingenio meruerunt ut puris scriptorum titulis nobiles essent. Quisquis legisset eius historias ab initio bellorum civilium, unde primum veritas retro abiit, paene usque ad mortis suae diem, magni aestimaret scire quibus natus esset parentibus ille, qui res Roma / / nas ....

On this fragment see O. Rossbach, "De Senecae philosophi librorum recensione et emendatione" (Insunt Senecae fragmenta Palatina edita a Guilelmo Studemund), *Bresl. Phil. Abh.* 2, 3 (1888) 1-184 (referred to hereafter as Rossbach "De Senecae"). Other studies relating to the elder Seneca's lost *Histories* and referred to frequently in this chapter (by author's last name) are: Paul Archambault, "The Ages of Man and the Ages of the World," *Revue des Études Augustiniennes* 12 (1966) 193-228; Jacqueline Brisset, *Les idées politiques de Lucain* (Paris 1964); L. Castiglioni, "Lattanzio e le storie di Seneca Padre," *Rivista di filologia e d'istruzione classica* 56 (1928) 454-475; A. Grisart, "Suétone et les deux Sénèque," *Helikon* 1 (1961) 302-308; F. Haase (ed.), *L. Annaei Senecae opera quae supersunt* (3 vols., Leipzig 1898-1907); I. Hahn, "Appien et le cercle de Sénèque," *Acta Antiqua* 12 (1964) 169-206 ("Appien"); *idem,* "Prooemium und Disposition der Epitome des Florus," *Eirene* 4 (1965) 21-38 ("Prooemium"); Werner Hartke, *Römische Kinderkaiser* (Berlin 1951); Friedrich Klingner, "Tacitus und die Geschichtsschreiber des 1. Jahrhunderts n. Chr.," *Museum Helveticum* 15 (1958) 194-206; Alfred Klotz, "Das Geschichtswerk des Aelteren Seneca," *RhM* 56 (1901) 429-442; Franz Joseph Kühnen, *Seneca und die römischen Geschichte* (Univ. Köln diss., München 1962); Otto Rossbach, "Annaeus," no. 16,

The *De Vita Patris,* as the fragment is called, is the only reliable evidence for the existence of the *Histories,* although traces of a deep interest in the writing of history exist in the anthologies. [2] In the works of Suetonius (*Tib.* 73) and Lactantius (*Div. Inst.* 7.15.14-16) are two passages ascribed only to a Seneca which are historical in content. Since Quintilian, who is usually thorough in such matters, does not mention that the younger Seneca wrote history (10.1.129), many have assumed that the two are fragments of the lost *Histories,* while others have vigorously disputed this claim. [3] Nevertheless, on the meager evidence of the *De Vita Patris* and the questionable fragments, the work has been conjectured to be a source for Lucan, Tacitus, Suetonius, Florus, and Appian. [4]

---

in Pauly-Wissowa, *Real-Encyclopädie,* vol. I (Stuttgart 1894) cols. 2237-2240 (Rossbach *P-W*); H. Schendel, *Quibus auctoribus Romanis L. Annaeus Seneca in rebus patriis usus sit* (diss., Greifswald 1908); Guilelmus Studemund, "L. Annaeus Seneca librorum quomodo amicitia continenda sit et de vita patris quae supersunt," *Bresl. Phil. Abh.* 2, 3 (1888) I-XXXII; Carlo Tibiletti, "Il proemio di Floro, Seneca il Retore e Tertulliano," *Convivium* n.s. 3 (1959) 339-342.

[2] He considered it a more substantial field than declamation (*Suas.* 5.8) and encouraged his sons to ponder it as a field of future endeavor. Although Seneca apologizes for introducing specimens from history in the collection, he confesses that he did this intentionally to whet their appetites for historical study (*Suas.* 6.16; cf. 6.27). History was useful for a declaimer (1 pr. 18), but Seneca thought the rhetorical exercises to be inferior forms of literary expression (1.8.16) and a stepping stone to more serious means of expression (2 pr. 3-4); cf. above 72ff. In general, see *Suas.* 6 *passim.*

[3] The references to the extensive literature on this question of their authenticity are conveniently listed in Schanz-Hosius II, 341. See also the more current bibliography (here primarily in reference to the Lactantius fragment) in Marion Lausberg, *Untersuchungen zu Senecas Fragmenten* (Berlin 1970) 3, n. 10. Grisart should be consulted on the Suetonius fragment.

[4] As a source for Lucan, see Brisset 35; Hahn "Appien," 197-198, 201; Rossbach "De Senecae," 168-169; Pierre Wuilleumier and Henri Le Bonniec (eds.), *M. Annaeus Lucanus: Liber Primus* (Paris 1962) 4. As a source for Tacitus, see Ronald Syme, *Tacitus* (2 vols., Oxford 1958) I, 277. Cf. the parallelism of thought between the elder Seneca and Tacitus on the fate of delators (*Contr.* 10 pr. 7 and *Ann.* 1.74) and those noted by C. Preisendanz, "De L. Annaei Senecae rhetoris apud philosophum filium auctoritate," *Philologus* 67 (1908) 105, note 101. As a source for Suetonius, see Grisart, *passim.* As a source for Florus, see Peter *HRR* II, CXVIII-CXVIIII; E. S. Forster, "Florus," in the *Oxford Classical Dictionary* (Oxford 1949) 365; and in the 2nd ed. (Oxford 1970) 442; *idem* (ed. and transl.), *Florus* (London 1929) xi; Tibiletti *passim*; Paul Jal (ed. and transl.), *Florus: Oeuvres* (2 vols., Paris 1967) I, xxix-xxx (with much citation), lxxxix; O. Rossbach, "Florus," *P-W* vol. 6, cols. 2761, 2765; Hahn "Appien," 172ff, esp. 174, 197. Castiglioni 460 asserts that the debt of Florus to Seneca is that of imitator to model. For Seneca as a source of Appian see Hahn "Appien" 196-206. Castiglioni 456-457 would like to attribute a number of historical references in the younger Seneca to his father's historical work, especially some which mention the imperial family.

The passage found in Suetonius is a vivid description of Tiberius's last moments:

> Seneca writes that conscious of his approaching end, he [Tiberius] took off the ring, as if to give it to someone, but held fast to it for a time; then he put it back on his finger, and clenching his left hand, lay for a long time motionless; suddenly he called for his attendants, and on receiving no response, got up; but his strength failed him and he fell dead near the couch. [5]

The attribution to only a Seneca, unqualified, has caused contention. The information in *De Vita Patris*, coupled with the knowledge that Seneca almost surely lived into the reign of Gaius, indicates that the *Histories* contained an account of this event. Therefore some assume that the passage is a fragment of that work. The other camp contends that the text is from a lost work of the son, since the ascription to a Seneca *sic nude* could only refer to him. Grisart has ingeniously challenged the latter argument, although hardly conclusively. [6] Thus the evidence is contradictory and, lacking further information, perhaps the problem is insoluble.

Lactantius preserves a text taken, again, from only a Seneca, in which Roman history has been divided into periods analogous to the different ages of man:

---

[5] Suet. *Tib.* 73; transl. from the Loeb ed. by J. C. Rolfe, *Suetonius* (2 vols., London 1914, rev. 1928):

Seneca eum scribit intellecta defectione exemptum anulum quasi alicui traditurum parumper tenuisse, dein rursus aptasse digito et compressa sinistra manu iacuisse diu immobilem; subito vocatis ministris ac nemine respondente consurrexisse nec procul a lectulo deficientibus viribus concidisse.

[6] In seeking to identify which Seneca is meant in the attribution of an anecdote in the Suetonius life of Vergil, Grisart argues that the Seneca mentioned in *Gaius* 53 must be the elder Seneca, and that the famous criticism there referring to Seneca's style as "sand without mortar" applies clearly to the format of the *Contr.* and *Suas.* The attributions to Seneca in the *Vita Vergilii* 28, *Tib.* 73, and *Gaius* 53 are all to a Seneca, unqualified. The first two are references to Seneca as a source; perhaps, Grisart thinks, the *Contr.* and the *Histories*. The third is a literary reference. But when referring to the younger Seneca in the *Nero*, Suetonius uses qualifiers which leave no doubt as to which Seneca is meant (*Nero* 7.1, *Annaeus, senator*; 3.5, 52.1, *praeceptor*). The use of these qualifiers, according to Grisart, is Suetonius's method of distinguishing between the two Senecas, and confirms that in *Tib.* 73, *Gaius* 53, and *Vit. Verg.* 28 the elder Seneca is meant. While there is some evidence that Suetonius was familiar with the works of the elder Seneca, Grisart's data are insufficient for establishing so sweeping a conclusion. Cf. W.-L. Lebek, "Zur Vita des Albucius Silus bei Sueton," *Hermes* 94 (1966) 360-372; also below, 166-167.

Not unsoundly did Seneca distribute the times of the Roman city into ages: The first was infancy, under King Romulus, by whom Rome was begotten, and brought up, as it were. Then came childhood, under the other kings, by whom she was increased and trained in many disciplines and institutions. But, when under the rule of Tarquin, she had already begun to grow up, so to speak, she did not bear the servitude, and, throwing off the yoke of proud domination, she preferred to obey laws rather than kings. And when the end of the Punic war came with that of her adolescence, then, finally with established strength, she began to flourish. When Carthage was removed, which for so long had been Rome's rival for empire, she stretched forth her hands toward the whole world on land and sea, until, with all kings and nations subjugated to her dominion, when material of wars began now to fail, she used her own strength and resources badly, and with these she exhausted herself. This was her first old age, when, torn with civil wars and oppressed with intestinal evil, she fell back upon rule by a single command, as though she had been revolved to another infancy. For when the liberty was lost which she had defended under the leadership and authority of Brutus, she grew so old that she was, as it were, not able to support herself without leaning upon the prop of those ruling. [7]

Here, too, the debate has raged for the same reasons. Even more so than the Suetonius passage, many believe that the quotation in Lactantius must certainly come from a historical work, [8] and therefore should be assigned to the elder Seneca. In addition, the younger Seneca displays a distinct aversion to historical writing, and it is therefore difficult to conceive of him writing a work which might contain such a passage. [9] Doubters maintain that this description of Rome's growth might just as easily have come from a lost philosophical work of the younger Seneca; in any event, they believe that Lactantius was so familiar with his works that a mistaken ascription would be impossible. [10] In support of their arguments they identify several close

---

[7] Lact. *Div. Inst.* 7.15.14-16; Mary Francis McDonald (transl.) *Lactantius: The Divine Institutes* (Washington 1964). See the discussion of this passage in Archambault 193-200.

[8] Cf. Sallust *Cat.* 10; *Hist.* 1, fr. 9, 11, 12, 16 (Maurenbrecher); Livy *Praef.* 9; Florus 1, *Praef.* 4-8; Vopiscus *Vita Cari* 2, 3; Ammianus 14.6. See Archambault 193-200.

[9] Remarked upon by Kühnen 18ff and esp. 20-27; cf. younger Seneca *QNat.* 3, *Praef.* 5ff; *Ep.* 83.13; *De Ira* 3.22.1. But on pp. 78ff, Kühnen attributes the Lact. fragment to the younger Seneca mainly because of the plain attribution to "Seneca" only, adding (pp. 85-86) that it does not necessarily have to originate in a historical work, but could be from a lost philosophical tract. Cf. Griffin 19.

[10] Kühnen summarizes these arguments well.

parallels in wording with extant works of the younger Seneca. Nevertheless, the style and thought of the son were deeply influenced by his father, and even if the work were from a lost philosophical treatise, the conception might ultimately have originated in the *Histories*. [11] Ascription of the fragment to either of the two Senecas on purely stylistic grounds is impossible; its style is uniquely Lactantian. [12]

Several remarks in the *Controversiae* coupled with the evidence in *De Vita Patris* reveal that a cyclical conception of human affairs intrigued the elder Seneca. [13] The representation and amplification of such an idea in Lactantius causes one to suspect that the elder Seneca is the source. Lactantius could easily have mistaken the son for the father, since the names are identical and confusion between the two may extend back very far. [14] But ascription to the elder Seneca can only be a conjecture in the absence of confirming evidence.

Thus, the problem of the fragments; confusing, divided, and ambiguous. No solutions are in the offing. In order to learn anything definite about the *Histories*, we must return to the text of *De Vita Patris*.

The younger Seneca chooses to mention six facts about the *Histories*: (1) the author was his father, (2) the inception point—the beginning of the civil wars, and perhaps the formal title, [15] (3) the coincidence

---

[11] Cf. below, 157-158.

[12] For discussion, see Hartke 393, 394, 395 (esp. note 4); Kühnen 78-79; Castiglioni 462ff; Hahn "Prooemium" 24ff.

[13] E.g., the elder Seneca's comments on the decline of Roman eloquence: *Deinde ut possitis aestimare, in quantum cotidie ingenia decrescant et nescio qua iniquitate naturae eloquentia se retro tulerit: quidquid Romana facundia habet, quod insolenti Graeciae aut opponat aut praeferat, circa Ciceronem effloruit; omnia ingenia, quae lucem studiis nostris attulerunt, tunc nata sunt. In deterius deinde cotidie data res est, sive luxu temporum — nihil enim tam mortiferum ingeniis quam luxuria est — sive, cum pretium pulcherrimae rei cecidisset, translatum est omne certamen ad turpia multo honore quaestuque vigentia, sive fato quodam, cuius maligna perpetuaque in rebus omnibus lex est, ut ad summum perducta rursus ad infimum, velocius quidem quam ascenderant, relabantur (Contr.* 1 pr. 6-7).
See also his discussion of the growth of declamation, where the closing statement clearly reveals the biological viewpoint: ... *ideo facile est mihi ab incunabulis nosse rem post me natam (Contr.* 1 pr. 12).

[14] The two Senecas have been constantly confused because of their names: both are Lucius Annaeus Seneca. See above, 19-20. It is indeed possible that confusion began at a very early date, perhaps back to Jerome; see Paul Faider, *Études sur Sénèque* (Gand 1921) 96 note 1; cf. Griffin 19. On the confusion between the two, see Grisart *passim*.

[15] E.g., Livy's *Ab Urbe Condita*, The elder Pliny's *A Fine Aufidii Bassi*, and Tacitus' *Annales ab Excessu Divi Augusti*.

of the inception of the civil wars with a decline of morality, (4) the termination date—nearly the day of Seneca's death, (5) by implication, the date of composition, and (6) the subject matter, Roman history (*res Romanae*). In addition, the wording provides hints concerning publication. From this information it is possible to reconstruct something of the *Histories* in very broad strokes.

1. *Scope*

The *Histories* dealt with Roman history from the inception of the civil wars very nearly to the day of Seneca's death in the early part of Gaius' principate (AD 37-41). Although the latter date can be determined to a fair degree of accuracy (*ca.* AD 39), a number of different points can be proposed for the beginning of the civil wars; the Gracchi, the Social War, Marius and Sulla, Caesar and Pompey. A qualifying phrase in the *De Vita Patris*, however, is crucial. It was a history "from the beginning of the civil wars, the point where righteousness declined for the first time...." (*ab initio bellorum civilium unde primum veritas retro abiit*). Seneca has therefore associated the outbreak of the wars, probably as an effect, with the beginning of moral decadence and luxury. Ancient writers, among them Sallust, Velleius, Lucan, Florus, Appian, Victorinus, and Ammianus, are nearly unanimous in assigning the inception of moral decay to the period encompassing the destruction of Carthage and Corinth in 146 BC, and they date the beginning of Rome's civil wars to the period of the Gracchi, shortly thereafter. [16] It is difficult to imagine that Seneca strayed from this conventional dating; he was a conservative at heart. [17]

---

[16] We should note an opinion held by at least one of the Annaei; cf. Lucan *Bell. Civ.* 1.158ff, esp. 173-182; also Florus (if we admit him into the family) 1.47.2; 2.1-2; cf. Rossbach *P-W* 2239. (On the apparent inconsistency between Florus 1.19 and his proem, see Hahn "Appien" 175.)

For this dating, see Sallust *Cat.* 10.1; *Hist.* 1 fr. 11, 12 (Maurenbrecher); cf. Wendell Clausen, "Notes on Sallust's *Histories*," *AJP* 68 (1947) 293-301, esp. 300; Hahn "Appien" 173, 203; Velleius 2.1.1-2; cf. 1.12.6; 2.2.2; 2.3.3; Pliny *HN* 33.150; Appian *Bell. Civ.* 1.2; Victorinus *In Rhet. Cic.*, in Halm *Rhet. Lat. Min.* (Leipzig 1863) 158, cf. Aug. *Civ. Dei* 2.18; 2.21; also 1.30; Orosius 5.8.2. The use of *primum* is decisive for identification of the date; cf. Rossbach "De Senecae" 162-163; *idem, P-W Suppl.* 1 col. 85; D. C. Earl, *The Political Thought of Sallust* (Cambridge 1961) 47. The Lactantius fragment also reflects this long established tradition.

One may interpret Tac. *Hist.* 1.1 as opposing this dating; he says that before Actium Roman history was written *pari eloquentia ac libertate*, but that afterwards, when *omnem potentiam ad unum conferri pacis interfuit, magna illa ingenia cessere; simul veritas pluribus modis infracta* .... Schanz-Hosius II, 341 also finds

2. Composition and Publication

The elder Seneca was writing the *Histories* early in the reign of Gaius; this dating helps to explain the appearance of such a historical narrative, [18] for under Augustus (towards the end of his rule) and Tiberius the authors of similar works were often punished and their books burned. [19] Thus the perils were real; Asinius Pollio thought it prudent to end his historical account at 42 BC, and even the young Claudius was dissuaded from narrating the more sensitive parts of the period after the death of Caesar. [20] Shortly after the accession of Gaius there was a brief period of optimism and *libertas*; the old histories, once banned or burned, were now republished, and a new one was written. [21] It was a propitious time for a project which had evidently been on Seneca's mind for a long time.

---

the Gracchan dating to be wrong; cf. Klotz, esp. 438. Weinrib 137 apparently takes the disappearance of *libertas* with the death of Brutus as the equivalent of the decline of *veritas* and therefore the starting point in accordance with the text of the Lactantius fragment — *amissa enim libertate*; cf. Castiglioni 458ff. However, decline was shown in the fragment after the destruction of Carthage when Rome's first old age began — *bellis lacerata civilibus atque intestino malo pressa* .... I find it hard to believe that the elder Seneca, who was obviously preoccupied with the notion of decline and equated it with the civil wars, would have this decline take place so soon before the reign of Augustus. ... *ab initio bellorum civilum unde primum veritas retro abiit* must surely go further back in the Republic, especially given the time and conditions (the Julio-Claudians were still reigning) in which Seneca wrote.

[17] Hahn's discussion of the scope of the *Histories* ("Appien" 176ff) is the most sensible. He argues that it must go back at least to the fighting between Marius and Sulla, or the *Bellum Sociale*, if not to the Gracchi, who could then be linked to the fall of Carthage; cf. Studemund 163; Rossbach *P-W* col. 2239; *idem, P-W Suppl.* 1 col. 85. Rossbach (throughout "De Senecae") rightly considers the mention of *unde primum veritas retro abiit* as a vital piece of evidence and more suitable to the times of the Gracchi than to the later civil conflicts. On the elder Seneca's conservatism, see the younger Seneca *Ad Helv.* 17.3-4.

[18] According to *De Vita Patris*, the elder Seneca was working on the *Histories* and also covering the period nearly up until the day of his death, which can be dated about AD 39 (cf. above, 23-24). Seneca may have begun work at the end of Tiberius' reign. In any event, from the tone of *Suas.* 6 and 7, and other remarks in his extant works, it is evident that he must have been considering writing history. Weinrib 151-153 maintains that his time schedule was so tight that he must have been writing the *Suasoriae* and the *Histories* at the same time.

[19] On book burning, see above, 87 and note 181.

[20] On Pollio see Peter *HRR* II, LXXXVIff. Claudius' voluminous work opened with the death of Caesar and resumed after the civil wars. The intervening period was too sensitive to be covered in any detail (Suet. *Claud.* 41). Claudius began the work when young and worked on it also while Emperor. See also Peter *HRR* II, CXX-CXXIII; Brisset 8.

[21] Suet. *Gaius* 13-16; Dio 59.24.4; younger Seneca *Ad Marciam* 1.2-4; cf. Ferrill 32-33.

Klotz has suggested that the *Histories* were never published, in large measure because of the dangers in releasing a work on recent events so sensitive, and thereby likely to irritate powerful people. [22] But as we have seen, Seneca was writing during a brief period of free speech. Moreover, the wording of the *De Vita Patris* indicates that it was not a pure biography but, rather, the publisher's introduction to the *Histories*. [23] Would the younger Seneca have published the introduction, and not the book? Or would he have mentioned the *Histories* at all, if they were as dangerous as Klotz believes? [24] The apologetic and modest tone of the *De Vita Patris* is also significant. The work lacked the *ultima manus* and may have been unfinished; Seneca was working on it almost until his death. The author himself was not a literary man nor a senator; therefore, some explanation was needed to explain how a man such as Seneca came to write history. Since his morals and politics were somewhat old-fashioned, the younger Seneca probably found it necessary to prepare readers for his deep conservatism in the introduction.

It seems unlikely in the first place that Seneca would write a politically outspoken work which could endanger the careers of his sons and the prosperity of the family, both of which he had carefully nurtured. Such a book would very likely be burned, banned, and the family disgraced.

The *Histories* were not intended for a limited private circulation. Seneca would hardly have undertaken such a great task without the

---

[22] Klotz 429, 440, 442; cf. his review of Schendel in *BPhW* 29 (1909) 1527; Eugen Westerburg, "Lucan, Florus und Pseudo-Victor," *RhM* 37 (1882) 48-49. Those who believe that the work was published include Weinrib 152-153; Peter *HRR* II, CXVIII; Faider (above, note 14) 177; Brisset 7; Ronald Syme, *Tacitus* (above, note 4) 1, 277; Rossbach *P-W* col. 2239; *idem, P-W Suppl.* 1 col. 85; *idem* "De Senecae," 164ff; Bornecque 14-15 (asserts that *De Vita Patris* indicates that the work had not yet been published, but does not preclude later publication; cf. Kennedy *ARRW* 324); Schanz-Hosius II, 340, 341, 398; Whitehorne 20; Schendel 48-50.

[23] The wording emphasizes the *Histories* and their content while mentioning the other works in an elliptical fashion. The *Histories* were so unlike the *Controversiae* and *Suasoriae* that they deserved a prefatory explanation of the author, his background, and how a municipal equestrian from Spain came to write an account of Roman history, especially since this field was usually considered the prerogative of the senatorial class. Among those favoring the *De Vita Patris* as an introduction to the *Histories* are Faider (above, note 14) 171; Schanz-Hosius II, 340, 398; Schendel 50. Rossbach "De Senecae" 162 maintains that it was not a *laudatio funebris* (in note 1), and also that it was published before the *Histories*, which followed shortly thereafter.

[24] Klotz 442; cf. Rossbach *P-W Suppl.* 1 col. 85.

prospect of eventual publication. Indeed, an epithet in Martial suggests that the work was well-known enough to be hinted at and understood. He tells us that eloquent (*facunda*) Cordova talks of its two Senecas and unique Lucan. [25] Clearly the transferred epithet *facunda* could not apply to an anthologist of declamatory specimens. The term is more appropriate to a historian whose works Martial, acquainted with the family, and others must have read or known about. [26] The most likely time for publication would be soon after the elder Seneca's death, although a later date cannot be ruled out.

3. Content

The *Histories* necessarily must have dealt extensively with the civil wars, some part of which Seneca himself lived through. During his impressionable childhood spent in Cordova, Seneca and his family were witnesses to and perhaps participants in some of the bloodiest fighting and the most intensely bitter civil discord. He pointedly refers to the *furor* of the period (1 pr. 11), and quite conceivably dwelled upon the horrors of civil war as did his grandson, who may have referred to the lost work. [27]

---

[25] *Duosque Senecas, unicumque Lucanum/facunda loquitur Corduba* (Martial 1.61.7-8).

[26] Another reference in Martial may be relevant: *Atria Pisonum stabant cum stemmate toto/ et docti Senecae ter numeranda domus* (4.40.1-2). If he is referring to the younger and elder Senecas and Lucan, we have the convergence of two terms typifying these three representatives of the Annaei: *facundus* (1.61.7-8) and *doctus*. *Facundia* could be exhibited in the law courts, or more so, in the Senate. It refers also to literature, including poetry and history. *Doctus* implies great learning and erudition. For this reason it seems inappropriate to apply such terms to a man whose published works were two anthologies of extracts from declaimers. However, they would fit a man who had written a history of Rome. That Martial expected these terms to be understood without further explanation would suggest that the *Histories* were published and well known. One must not overlook the possibility that in 1.61.8 Martial is speaking of the younger Seneca and one of his brothers (Novatus or Mela) and that in 4.40.2 he is referring to all three. But with our knowledge of the sketchy literary careers of the younger Seneca's brothers, one if not both of the references should bring to mind the elder Seneca. L. Friedländer (ed.) *M. Valerii Martialis: Epigrammaton Libri* (Leipzig 1886) in his notes does not attempt to identify the two Senecas of 1.61.7. But for 4.40.2 (*et docti Senecae ter numeranda domus*) he specifies the three Seneca brothers. While this is a distinct possibility, the parallel reference of 1.61.7 with its additional qualification of the poet Lucan again for a total of three seems to argue against Friedländer's interpretation. Cf. Faider (above, note 14) 29; he thinks that both Martial references probably point to the elder Seneca. Cf. above, 18, note 2; below, 160.

[27] The opening lines of Lucan's *Bellum Civile,* especially 1.1-32, are note-worthy. Cf. Eva Matthews Sanford, "Lucan and Civil War," CP 28 (1933) 124: "No

The period was filled with the deaths of many great and illustrious figures. In reporting these Seneca cannot have failed to employ the conventional summary character sketch, which briefly told of a famous man's personality, qualities, and achievements. Called *epitaphia*, they provided the writer with an opportunity to display his mastery of the terse *sententia* and rhetorical point. Seneca himself had studied the use of this device, and, in the *Suasoriae*, he briefly traced its development in Thucydides, Sallust, Livy, and contemporary writers. Following this brief analysis Seneca provides a series of five *epitaphia* on Cicero (*Suas. 6.22-26*).

The elder Seneca was an intensely moral man, and, not surprisingly, he almost surely molded the *Histories* on a moral theme—the decline of *veritas*. When qualifying the inception point of the work (*ab initio bellorum civilium*), the younger Seneca adds for the sake of clarity *unde primum veritas retro abiit*. As we have already seen, the phrase is meant to specify the very beginnings of Roman civil discord in the time of the Gracchi; *primum* surely indicates the first outbreak, while *veritas* means that this point was the beginning of Roman moral disintegration. The choice of the term *veritas*, one which must surely reflect his father's usage, is curious. The expected word would be the more inclusive *virtus*. Instead we find *veritas* in the sense of "righteousness, truth, and integrity." [28]

During the earlier Republic the term *virtus* in its proper sense was current; under the changed political conditions of the late Republic it had become a debased slogan with little meaning:

> The decline of the old tradition can be measured by the debasement of *virtus* itself into merely a conventional laudatory formula, requiring the support of extreme adjectives. As such, it is accepted by Cicero and used by him from his earliest letters and speeches to his latest. In the face of this debasement two courses were possible: to reassert the old tradition or to redefine it to suit the changed circumstances. Cicero, as an admirer of the old Republican tradition and, at the same time, a *novus homo*, followed both courses, and that either was considered necessary or even desirable again underlines the decline of the original ideal. Finally, while

single quotation, or even any moderate number of lines selected for the purpose, can demonstrate the extent to which the theme of the horror of civil war underlies the poem." She detects the deep and vivid impression of the wars—on a man born in AD 39; perhaps some of the color, emotion, and immediacy came from his grandfather's description in the *Histories*. See below, 160 and note 32.

[28] Tacitus's use of *veritas* in *Hist.* 1.1 is not a parallel; he is clearly referring to historical accuracy and candor.

accepting the conventional debased significance of *virtus* in his speeches, Cicero seems to have turned partly from the Roman tradition and sought his ideal standard more in the ideas of Greek philosophy. [29]

Seneca's use of *veritas* therefore reveals his awareness that *virtus* no longer adequately described the moral qualities with which he was concerned.

Various Latin writers personified or even deified *veritas*, but Seneca's usage seems unique, with the exception of a passage in Martial who describes a personified *Veritas* rising again from the Underworld after the oppressive reign of Domitian:

> Non est hic dominus, sed imperator,
> sed iustissimus omnium senator,
> per quem de Stygia domo reducta est
> siccis rustica Veritas capillis.
> Hoc sub principe, si sapis, caveto
> verbis, Roma, prioribus loquaris. [30]

The phrases *de Stygia domo reducta est* and *verbis, Roma, prioribus loquaris* suggest a cyclical conception of *Veritas* similar to the younger Seneca's description of the *Histories* (*unde primum veritas retro abiit*). Further, a concept of death and renewal—a biological cycle— is implicit in both passages. [31] *Veritas* is rural virtue incarnate, characterized by bluntness and candor. The mention of *siccis capillis* is significant; her hair does not reek with the perfumes which typify the extravagances of city dwellers. [32] We find a parallel sentiment in

---

[29] Earl (above, note 16) 38. See also the entirety of his useful chapter, "Sallust's Concept of *Virtus*" 28-40.

[30] Mart. 10.72.8-13: "No master is here, but a commander, aye, a senator most just of all [Trajan], by whose means rustic Truth with her unperfumed locks has been brought home from her abode by Styx. Under such a prince, if thou art wise, beware, O Rome, to speak the words thou didst before." Walter C. A. Ker (transl.), *Martial: Epigrams* (2 vols., London 1925).

[31] The use of the word *retro* in *De Vita Patris* points convincingly to a cyclical conception and the use of the biological metaphor. Cf. Horace's use of *retro*; *Fugit retro/levis iuventas et decor* ... (*Odes* 2.11.5-6). Thus, like Lactantius, Horace identifies *iuventus* (cf. Lactantius's *iuvenescere*) as the apex of the human cycle. The climb then reverses direction downward (*retro*); cf. Verg. *Georg.* 2.200; 4.495; *Aen.* 4.439; 9.539. An easily recognized parallel in thought exists between *Georg.* 1.199-200 and the elder Seneca's discussion of the decline of eloquence: *sic omnia fatis/in peius ruere ac retro sublapsa referri*; we may compare to this Seneca's wording: ... *sive fato quodam, cuius maligna perpetuaque in rebus omnibus lex est, ut ad summum perducta rursus ad infimum, velocius quidem quam ascenderant, relabantur* (1 pr. 7).

[32] Cf. Mart. 3.12.1; 3.63.4.

Seneca's denunciation of the luxurious and decadent manner in which
young men of his day were living. Their vices are precisely those
associated with urban living: laziness, dancing, singing, lust, effeminacy,
high-pitched voices, elaborate hair dressings, body depilation, and,
most serious of all to Seneca, dishonesty (1 pr. 7-10). The similarities
in both conceptions of *veritas* do not readily find parallels in Latin
literature and may suggest Martial's familiarity with the *Histories*.

The decline of morality was a theme closely related to the concept
of cyclical history.[33] In one version the cycle begins with a Golden
Age, followed by progressively more degenerate stages. The historical
view was therefore not one of progress towards an ideal state but
deterioration from it.[34] Out of the old Etruscan lore and perhaps
Eastern sources, but especially from Stoicism, came the idea of a new
cycle which began after the old one had run its course.[35] A third
concept, related to the cycle theory, was the metaphor of the various
ages of man applied to a nation's growth. Thus different stages of
national existence were likened to birth, infancy, childhood, young
manhood, mature manhood, and old age.

In the *Controversiae* Seneca reveals a strong attachment to the idea
of cyclical patterns in history; of the two references one surely suggests
a biological cycle (1 pr. 12; cf. 1 pr. 6-7). The younger Seneca's
description of the *Histories* confirms this interest in cycles and suggests that it was a unifying motif. The weight attached to *veritas* in the
De Vita Patris demonstrates a concern with the decline of morals
accompanied by a growth in luxurious living. In both there seems to be
a debt to Sallust, a writer whose style Seneca esteems greatly (9.1.13;
Suas. 6.21). This historian regarded the termination of the *metus
Punicus* as a cause for the decline of Roman morality; he implied that
foreign conquests aided in establishing domestic extravagance.[36] More
weight should be given to two writers who would almost certainly be

---

[33] The concept was widely held in antiquity; cf. Archambault 193-228; esp.
193-200.

[34] For references, see *ibid. passim*; also R. Häussler, "Vom Ursprung und
Wandel des Lebensaltersvergleichs," *Hermes* 92 (1964) 313-341.

[35] See Brisset 59.

[36] *Sed ubi labore atque iustitia res publica crevit, reges magni bello domiti,
nationes ferae et populi ingentes vi subacti, Carthago, aemula imperi Romani, ab
stirpe interiit, cuncta maria terraeque patebant, saevire fortuna ac miscere omnia
coepit* (Sall. *Cat.* 10.1). Cf. *Hist.* 1 fr. 11, 12 ,16 (Maurenbrecher); Vell. Pat.
1.12.5. Other parallels are listed by Ernout in his Budé edition of Sallust (Paris
1964) 64, note *ad loc., Cat.* 10.1. See also Hahn "Appien" 203.

familiar with Seneca's *Histories*; his grandson Lucan, and Florus, a possible relative. Both harbor a cyclical theory of history strongly tinged with moral coloring. [37]

The Lactantius passage is a melding of the biological, moralistic, and cyclical conception of events into a fairly eloquent though pessimistic summation of Roman history. The Seneca quoted has compared the stages of Roman growth to the ages of man, from birth to an old age during the civil wars, after which the cycle renewed itself into a new childhood under Augustus. The date for the beginning of the decline is the destruction of Carthage and the emergence of the Gracchi. When speaking of the decline of eloquence, the elder Seneca points to a malign fate as one possible cause; its law is immutable that when something rises to perfection it then sinks to the depths even more quickly (1 pr. 7). The idea is Stoic in origin. [38] The Stoics further believed that the end of a decline cycle was universal chaos, followed by renewal. [39] Following this pattern, as he probably was, Seneca may have likened the civil wars to this chaos, and brought about a renewal under Augustus. The inferences drawn upon the content of the *Histories* therefore arouse suspicion that the Lactantius passage may be a genuine fragment; but if it comes from the younger Seneca, he may well have been indebted to his father for the conception.

---

[37] See Lucan *Bell. Civ.* 1.67-97, 158-182; cf. Brisset 49, 59-60; B. M. Marti, "The Meaning of the Pharsalia," *AJP* 66 (1945) 357-358. A concept of renewal is implicit in *Bell. Civ.* 1.72-80; see Brisset 59. In Florus see 1 pr. 4-8, esp. 1 pr. 4: *Si quis ergo populum Romanum quasi unum hominem consideret totamque eius aetatem percenseat* .... Although the importance of the destruction of Carthage is not lost on Florus (1.31.1-6), he believes that the cause of the decline was more closely related to the conquest of Syria and its aftermath of increased luxury, which then corrupted Rome (1.47.7ff). Renewal of the cycle for Florus occurs under Trajan (1 pr. 8). A contemporary of the elder Seneca offers parallels. See Vell. Pat. 1.17.5-7; 2.3.4; 2.10.1; in his opinion the loss of *metus Punicus* played a vital role in the decline (2.1.1). Cf. Richard L. Anderson, *The Rise and Fall of Middle Class Loyalty to the Roman Empire: A Social Study of Velleius Paterculus and Ammianus Marcellinus* (diss., Berkeley 1962) 52-54. Tacitus also offers parallels for a cyclical-moralistic pattern of history in *Ann.* 3.55; cf. *Hist.* 1.16; but see also *Hist.* 3.34 and *Ann.* 3.34; also younger Seneca *Ben.* 1.10.1. Cf. Ammianus 14.6.4; Vopiscus *Vita Cari* 2.1-3.2. All of the preceding may possibly have been influenced directly or indirectly to some extent by the elder Seneca's *Histories*. See also Lucan *Bell. Civ.* 1.159-182. Here again there is a close correspondence to the Lact. fragment. See also Brisset 41ff. Lucan sees two causes for the fall of the Republic: (1) the decadence of the Roman state, and, more immediately, (2) the triumvirate.
[38] Convincingly argued and supported by Brisset 53-54; cf. Hahn "Appien" 203.
[39] Brisset 59.

4. Sources

Many histories of the period encompassing the civil wars appeared, and Seneca was familiar with the best of them. For example, in the sixth *Suasoria* ("Cicero deliberates whether to seek Antony's pardon"), he mentions or gives specimens from the works of Livy, Pollio, Aufidius Bassus, Cremutius Cordus, Bruttedius Niger, and Sallust. [40] History and epic were thought to be closely related (Quint. 10.1.31), therefore Seneca provides specimens from historical epics by the poets Albinovanus Pedo *(Suas.* 1.15), Cornelius Severus *(Suas.* 6.26-27), and Sextilius Ena *(Suas.* 6.27). Seneca knew many historians personally, and perhaps they influenced him to write his own version of the civil wars. [41] Nevertheless, his exact motivation is hard to determine; so many writers more talented than he had written on the subject.

Seneca's admiration for Sallust and a number of similarities in thought and expression between the two men suggest significant Sallustian influence upon the *Histories.* The great respect shown for the elder Cato (1 pr. 9) implies familiarity with the style and content of the *Origines*; perhaps the *Histories* began where Cato's work ended. [42]

Exactly how Seneca used his sources, primary and secondary, must remain a matter of speculation. A hint may exist, however, in the sixth *Suasoria*—admittedly a special case—where Seneca strives for completeness in the depiction of Cicero's character by presenting quotations from various historians which range from harshly negative to highly

---

[40] Seneca specifically discussed a good number of historians; Sallust, *Suas.* 6.21 (cf. 3 pr. 8; 9.1.13-14): Livy, *Suas.* 6.16-17, 22 (on the death of Cicero cf. 9.1.14; 9.2.26; 10 pr. 2; *Suas.* 6.21): Pollio, esp. *Suas.* 6.24-25: Aufidius Bassus, *Suas.* 6.18, 23: Cremutius Cordus, *Suas.* 6.19, 23: Bruttedius Niger, *Suas.* 6.20-21: Labienus, 10 pr. 5-8: Timagenes, 10.5.22. A check of the index to Winterbottom's edition of the elder Seneca reveals the names of several others who are better known for their efforts in different fields, yet who also wrote history: Messalla, Maecenas, Agrippa, Arruntius, Augustus, Dellius, the elder Cato, Sextilius Ena, and Julius Caesar.

[41] From some remarks it seems that he probably knew the following writers of historical works: Messalla (2.4.8, 10; *Suas.* 6.27; cf. 1.7; 2.20), Labienus (10 pr. 4-8; 4 pr. 2; 10.2.19, etc.), Pollio (4 pr. 2-6; *Suas.* 6.27, etc.), Augustus (2.4.12-13; 2.5.20; 4 pr. 5, 7; 10 pr. 14), Agrippa (2.4.12-13), and Maecenas (2.4.13; 9.3.14; *Suas.* 1.12; 2.20). He may well have also known Livy, Cremutius Cordus, and Aufidius Bassus.

[42] The *Origines* ended apparently with the praetorship of Servius Galba (151 BC), cf. Peter *HRR* I, CXXXXII. Thus the elder Seneca's *Histories* may well have had a brief reference to the third Punic War, the destruction of Carthage, and the ending of the *metus Punicus*, whose absence, to many Roman writers, contributed to the causes of the civil wars.

favorable assessments (*Suas.* 6.14-27). [43] Throughout this *suasoria*
Seneca reveals that he has obviously studied with great care all the
major sources on the death of Cicero, a man he greatly admired. He
nevertheless strives for impartiality. In the case of Pollio, one of
Cicero's greatest detractors, he points out the discrepancy between his
accusations against the orator and the weight of all the other authorities.
Seneca also noticed an inconsistency in two different works of Pollio;
in a speech he made several charges against Cicero which were so
outrageous that he declined to repeat them in his historical work.
However, Seneca reproduces the offending passage from the speech,
even though it contains untrue and unfavorable criticism (*Suas.*
6.15). [44]

For his balanced (and favorable) evaluation of Cicero, Seneca
praises Livy as "naturally the most fair-minded judge of all great
genius." [45] Although pro-Ciceronian himself, Seneca is fully prepared
to admit the man's good and bad qualities. Thus when he says regarding
the declaimers he will present in the anthologies, "... I shall be scrupu-
lous in giving every man his due," we can easily believe that he tried to
enforce the same standard of *sine ira et studio* in the *Histories*
as well. [46]

The elder Seneca's *Histories* are lost. Regrettable as that may be,
their value to scholarship would be much less than the recovery of
Livy for the period, or Asinius Pollio. Nevertheless, it would be very
useful to discover how Seneca handled the framework of a biological-
moralistic cycle of history, and to ascertain exactly what influence,
if any, he exercised on such writers as Lucan, Tacitus, Suetonius,

[43] The elder Seneca venerated Cicero, so it is not unusual that he familiarized
himself with the various traditions about his last days. Nevertheless, his approach
may be indicative of his general methods in the *Histories*. It could be that he was
working on the *Histories* at the same time he was collecting the *Suasoriae*
extracts, or at least doing his historical research.

[44] In *Suas.* 6.19 Seneca interrupts a quotation from Aufidius Bassus to notice
that both he and Cremutius Cordus preserve a tradition that Cicero had considered
seeking out either Brutus, Cassius, or Sextus Pompey, but decided finally against
it and to accept death. Here Seneca has reported an additional point where two
writers record information which others have not. It is plain that at least in regard
to the life of Cicero Seneca knew his sources very well.

[45] *Suas.* 6.22; Winterbottom transl.

[46] 1 pr. 11; Winterbottom transl. Cf. 10 pr. 16; *Suas.* 6.14. On this ideal of
historians, see B. L. Ullman, *"Sine Ira et Studio,"* *CJ* 38 (1943) 420-421. To
Ullman's enumeration of the influences on the memorable phrase from Tacitus
(*Ann.* 1.1), one could add: ... *statui res gestas populi Romani carpatim ...
perscribere; eo magis, quod mihi a spe, metu, partibus rei publicae animus liber
erat* (Sall. *Cat.* 4.2).

Florus, and Appian. Still more valuable would be the preservation of Seneca's opinions on the change from Republic to Principate, and on the very nature of the Principate itself. His was the viewpoint of a wealthy provincial equestrian, ambitious for his family's political advancement, yet sentimentally attached to the old Republican virtues. The thoughts of this important class are woefully underrepresented in our sources for the period.

CHAPTER SIX

THE ELDER SENECA: AFTERWARDS

The elder Seneca wrote only two works: the anthologies of declamation specimens (*Oratorum et Rhetorum Sententiae Divisiones Colores*) and the *Histories* of the Roman civil wars. [1] The present state of the texts, one fragmentary, the other lost, makes it difficult to gauge their effects on other writers.

In the chapter on the *Histories* the evidence there examined indicated eventual publication. The Suetonius and Lactantius fragments would attest to the work's significance and influence, but their definite ascription to the elder Seneca has yet to be established. And although some very distinguished scholars have argued elaborately that the *Histories* were a source for Lucan, Tacitus, Suetonius, Florus, and Appian, here too the fragmentary nature of the evidence leaves room for serious doubts. [2]

Thus, to trace the influence of Seneca we must turn mainly to the collection of declamation specimens, while remembering that his own words and thought form but a small proportion of the work. The importance of these anthologies is inextricably entwined with the dominant position of declamation in the educational system not only until the end of the Empire, but also, to a lesser extent, through the Renaissance. The prevalent emphasis in the schools upon rhetorical artifice left a deep imprint on Latin literary style. [3] For this reason alone, a study of Seneca's influence on declamation and the school system leads naturally into the more important consideration of his effect upon Latin and subsequent literatures.

1. *Influence upon the Roman Declamation Collections*

By design Seneca intended his anthologies to be a useful reference tool for subsequent generations of declaimers. Although they enjoyed

---

[1] The younger Seneca's *De Vita Patris* vaguely hints at the existence of other works not intended for publication.

[2] See above, 138, note 4.

[3] Cf. Norden *AK* I, 270-300; J. De Decker, *Juvenalis Declamans* (Ghent 1913) *passim*; Clarke 100-108, 130-157; J. F. E. Raby, *A History of Secular Latin Poetry in the Middle Ages* (2 vols., Oxford 1957) I, 25-42; Whitehorne 24-25. An especially thorough account of the effects of declamation on Roman literature is found in Bonner 149-167.

at least a measure of popularity, the extent of his influence upon the major surviving declamation collections is difficult to determine. Direct references to him are totally lacking. But even more frustrating is the inability to discriminate between Senecan influence and the cumulative effect of the long declamatory tradition of which he was only a part. The total evidence consists of inferences from identical themes and a number of parallel wordings. Any attempt to trace his influence upon the major surviving declamation collections therefore requires extreme caution. Calpurnius Flaccus, for example, preserves a number of *controversia* themes either similar or identical to those in the Senecan corpus and some very close parallel wordings. [4] A virtually identical situation prevails in the relationship of Seneca to the Greater and Lesser Declamations ascribed to Quintilian. [5]

2. Influence upon Roman Literary Criticism

Seneca's critical outlook was essentially Ciceronian, though sufficiently flexible to accommodate the saner developments of the emerging new Silver style. He is important therefore as the only major surviving proponent of Ciceronian standards until Quintilian and may in part have helped to pave the way for his neo-Ciceronianism. [6] Seneca was the first Roman critic to perceive a decline in Roman eloquence since the age of Cicero, and the first to theorize on the causes. He was thereby the first voice in an extensive literary debate which lasted for nearly a century. [7] As the numerous parallels in Chapter IV amply demonstrate, Seneca's critical theories frequently hearkened back to Cicero, and were themselves often reflected in the leading writers on the subject, including the younger Seneca, Persius, Petro-

[4] Flaccus is usually assigned to the second century AD; cf. Bornecque 31; Clarke 136. Some similar themes are: *Contr.* 9.6, Flaccus 12; 6.6 and 42. The many parallel wordings evident stem naturally from the similar situations and the limited number of ways to express recurring topics.

[5] Cf. *Contr.* 2.3, *Decl. Maj.* 349; 3.9, 380; 4.4, 369; 6.5, 386; 6.6, 354; 7.3, 17; 7.8, 309; 9.6, 381. Many of the laws are the same or similar, as one would expect; see Bonner 86-132 *passim.* Winterbottom in his notes also points to numerous parallels in text; e.g., *Contr.* 1.1.14, *Decl. Maj.* 417.4; 2.3.1, 375.14; 2.3.14, 374.6; 6.7, 291, 420.5; 7.8.1, 217.24ff; 7.8.2, 218.9; 7.8.3, 218.20; 7.8.4, 216.4ff; 7.8.5, 215.12; 7.8.7, 217.5, 218.2; 7.8.8, 217.18; 7.8.9, 218.27. Cf. Bornecque 30. Senecan influence may be present in the works of the later Greek rhetoricians; cf. below, 167 and note 73.

[6] Atkins 153; cf. Whitehorne 24.

[7] Gudeman's *Prolegomena* to the U.S. edition of Tacitus *Dialogus* (Boston 1894) has an extensive discussion of this literary question; cf. Sussman "Decline of Eloquence" *passim.*

nius, Juvenal, Quintilian, Tacitus, the younger Pliny, and "Longinus." [8]
The true extent of his direct influence on these writers is impossible
to determine; more significant is his very presence near the beginning
of a sound and productive branch of the Roman critical tradition.

Seneca sounded the first extant warning signal against the wilder
excesses of declamation. In matters of style he called attention to a
growing list of abuses such as the overuse of rhetorical figures, faulty
diction, and the subordination of sense to sound—all of which he
roundly denounced. He also questioned the ability of these exercises
to prepare students for the courts. In several of the prefaces (notably
to books 3, 7, 9) he presents scathing indictments of declamatory
education as it then existed and even questioned the sanity of the
leading rhetors. Seneca was therefore the first critic to articulate
the dangers of an educational system which centered upon these exercises. One of his chief goals was to restore a sense of perspective
and moderation about declamation, an attitude later adopted by others,
but to no avail.

3. *Influence upon Latin Literature*

Nearly five centuries ago, frustrated in his attempts to obtain
testimonia on Seneca, Faber threw up his hands and declared that an
altum silentium existed in the sources. [9] Fortunately the silence is
perhaps not quite as deep as he thought; there are, as we saw, a number
of literary references which quite possibly point to him and some
inferences can be drawn from elsewhere to assist in assessing his
influence on other Roman authors. [10] The picture however is sketchy
and must largely be reconstructed. A complication previously mentioned
also impedes the process: the difficulty of separating the influence of
Senecan influence from the effect of the long declamatory tradition.

Of one fact we can be sure: the *Controversiae* and *Suasoriae* were
published and were circulated, probably quite widely. Their great
usefulness in the schools alone insured broad dissemination. But the
works also boasted some literary polish and, especially in the prefaces,
they provided information that would prove interesting to all practitioners of declamation. The author's family name alone might have
been helpful: Lucius Annaeus Seneca, father of the politician-philos-

---

[8] Cf. Chapter IV *passim*; also Cousin I, 127 and note 128.
[9] Cf. above, 18 and note 2.
[10] *Ibid.*

opher, grandfather of a popular epic poet, and an intimate of the leading figures in literature, oratory, and government during the early Empire. The very survival of the works, and their later appearance in epitomized form confirm their popularity through a long period of time. Given this and the primacy of declamation in education, Seneca's anthologies must have been available, if not familiar, to most Roman writers.

An early testimonium to the influence of the *Controversiae* and *Suasoriae* may come from the mouth of the Emperor Gaius, as recorded by Suetonius, if we accept Grisart's interpretation of a passage usually considered to be a reference to the younger Seneca:

> As regards liberal studies, he [Gaius] gave little attention to literature but a great deal to oratory, and he was as ready of speech and eloquent as you please, especially if he had occasion to make a charge against anyone. For when he was angry, he had an abundant flow of words and thoughts, and his voice and delivery were such that for very excitement he could not stand still and he was clearly heard by those at a distance. When about to begin a harangue, he threatened to draw the sword of his nightly labours, and he had such scorn of a polished and elegant style that he used to say that Seneca, who was very popular just then, composed "mere school exercises," and that he was "sand without lime." He had the habit too of writing replies to the successful pleas of orators and composing accusations and defences of important personages who were brought to trial before the senate.... [11]

The *Controversiae* and *Suasoriae* were probably published by the early years of Gaius' reign. According to Grisart the phrase *Senecam tum maxime placentem* would therefore apply more aptly to the elder, especially since the younger Seneca was only then at the very beginning of his literary career—his period of great popularity lay some twenty or thirty years from this date. Gaius was not a literary man at all; he was more interested in oratory, the topic treated in this passage. The

---

[11] Suet. *Gaius* 53; translation from J. C. Rolfe's Loeb edition of Suetonius (2 vols., London 1913, rev. 1951) I, 485, 487. The Latin text: *Ex disciplinis liberalibus minimum eruditioni, eloquentiae plurimum attendit, quantumvis facundus et promptus, utique si perorandum in aliquem esset. Irato et verba et sententiae suppetebant, pronuntiatio quoque et vox, ut neque eodem loci prae ardore consisteret et exaudiretur a procul stantibus. Peroraturus stricturum se lucubrationis suae telum minabatur, lenius comptiusque scribendi genus adeo contemnens, ut Senecam tum maxime placentem commissiones meras componere et harenam sine calce diceret. Solebat etiam prosperis oratorum actionibus rescribere et magnorum in senatu reorum accusationes defensionesque meditari ....* Cf. Grisart 303-307; also above, 139 and note 6.

phrase *commissiones meras* here denotes declamations, and the phrase following, *harenam esse sine calce* ("sand without mortar"), well describes the nature of the elder Seneca's anthologies of declamation specimens. [12]

The younger Seneca acted as literary executor, publisher, and biographer of his father; he was certainly intimate with all the writings. Unfortunately the moral impression made by a stern father is all that survives; there is nothing directly from or about the elder Seneca's writings except for a brief description of the *Histories* and a cryptic mention of some other unnamed works in the *De Vita Patris*. However, the extent of the father's influence in such areas as style, vocabulary, and literary theory was great and several exhaustive studies have appeared on the subject. [13]

In the area of literary criticism the younger Seneca's great concern for the effect of innate character on a man's literary style closely parallels his father's. [14] Strong similarities also exist in their views on imitation theory; ultimately both are indebted to Cicero. [15] Both recognized that there were no infallible rules for attaining eloquence and that the poverty of the Latin language was a serious handicap for

---

[12] The description *commissiones meras* may be translated as "mere prize declamations"; cf. Suet. *Aug.* 89. Suetonius could also be referring to the speeches of the younger Seneca; the arguments of Grisart are attractive, but not necessarily the final word on the question. The tone of Gaius' remarks is insulting. A reason other than the one offered for his dislike of the elder Seneca's works (if we accept the Seneca in question as the elder) might stem from the moral outburst against the degenerate habits of contemporary youth in 1 pr. 7-10: the vices castigated are almost identical to those assigned to Gaius immediately before and after *Gaius* 53; cf. 51-52, 54-55. Seneca's words may have hit too close to home, rankling the Emperor and causing him to insult the author. Suetonius' memory of the Senecan text may have prompted his recollection of the matter.

[13] E. Rolland, *De l'influence de Sénèque le Père et des Rhéteurs sur Sénèque le Philosophe* (Gand 1906); he concludes that the influence of the father was especially great in style, thought, and intellect. Cf. C. Preisendanz, "De L. Annaei Senecae Rhetoris apud Philosophum Filium Auctoritate," *Philologus* 67 (1908) 68-112; *idem, De L. Annaei Senecae Patris Vestigiis in Senecae Philosophi Scriptis Deprehendendis* (Tübingen 1908); G. H. Müller, *Animadversiones ad L. Annaei Senecae Epistulas Quae Sunt De Oratore Spectantes* (Thüringen 1910). Cf. Bardon 101-102. Again, the question arises of whether the many parallels are due to direct influence or come from the younger Seneca's education, experiences, and, indeed, saturation with declamation. The large number of correspondences is overpowering, however, and must in some measure spring from direct influence; cf. Rolland, *op. cit.* 8, note 4.

[14] Cf. Rolland (above, note 13) 10; Kennedy *ARRW* 330. See also Seneca 1 pr. 6-10; younger Seneca *Ep.* 114; above, 99.

[15] Rolland (above, note 13) 17-18, 62; *Contr.* 1 pr. 6; cf. Cic. *De Or.* 3.215; Quint. 10.2.10-11.

Roman writers in challenging the Greeks. [16] Like his father, the younger Seneca was a very capable literary critic who reflected his father's penchant for retelling related anecdotes and good stories. [17] They expressed rather similar judgments, both literary and personal, on Sallust, Publilius Syrus, Fabianus, Julius Montanus, and Haterius. [18] In keeping with their shared highly moralistic attitudes, both Senecas looked upon the elder Cato as a semi-divine oracle. [19]

The son repeats certain historical errors made by his father and reproduces similar wording on Timagenes, Augustus, the humble birth of Agrippa, chastity, ugliness, the fragility of memory, the vigor resulting from relaxation, and the fatigue from prolonged attention to a subject. [20]

In style, they share a mutual fondness for *sententiae*, often exercise similar word choice, and exhibit a curious lack of logic in the ordering of comparisons. [21] Each tends to use the stronger demonstrative *ille* in place of the weaker *is*, and to pepper his writings with such exclamations as *quid ergo* or various circumlocutions, as *quis est qui*. [22] More specifically, Rolland concludes that the younger Seneca drew upon his father's works for numerous topics, commonplaces, historical exempla, descriptions, and *sententiae*. [23]

There were, however, sharp disagreements between the two men, most notably on the value of philosophy. [24] The younger Seneca in *Ep.* 97 refutes the idea of a continuous fall from virtue in Rome espoused by his father (1 pr. 7-10), and contrasts the sinfulness in the time of the younger Cato (*Ep.* 97.2ff) with the high moral standards of the youth in his own day (*Ep.* 97.9).

Close blood ties alone would probably argue for Lucan's familiarity with his grandfather's collection of declamation specimens. Indeed, he must have found them useful in his own studies, since he undoubtedly declaimed at school. Lucan continued to declaim even after he com-

---

[16] Rolland (above, note 13) 18; cf. Winterbottom note *ad loc.*, 7 pr. 3. See above, 124 and note 125.
[17] Rolland (above, note 13) 11-14; he also shared his father's good memory.
[18] *Ibid.* 16-17, 19-22.
[19] 1 pr. 9; younger Seneca *Ep.* 94.27-28; cf. *Ep.* 11.10; 25.6.
[20] Rolland (above, note 13) 22-25.
[21] *Ibid.* 26-27, 54-57; cf. Bardon 101-102.
[22] Cf. Rolland (above, note 13) 62. Some balance is required. Although there is, as documented, a discernible effect of the father's style upon his son's, nevertheless, in overall terms the two styles are quite dissimilar; cf. *ibid.* 9, note 1.
[23] *Ibid.* 29-60, with many examples.
[24] Cf. above, 27-28.

pleted his formal education and was greatly devoted to these practice exercises. In Vacca's life of the poet we learn that he preferred to declaim on real historical themes. [25] The effect of Lucan's declamatory training upon his poetry was profound as it was pervasive. [26] A verse *suasoria* actually appears: "Did Cato rightly give the hand of his wife Marcia in marriage to Hortensius?" [27] Although this theme does not appear in Seneca's extant collection, the argumentation in another poetic *suasoria* closely resembles the division of a Senecan declamation on an analogous situation. [28] Elsewhere, in describing a storm scene, Lucan exhibits the influence of a declaimer quoted by Seneca. [29] The elder Seneca's high praise for two lengthy quotations from historical epic poetry are significant (*Suas.* 1.15, 6.26). Both attest to a deep interest in this type of poetry, one which, in some way, may have passed down to his grandson. [30] Although he was unable to hear first-hand accounts from his grandfather, some of the material and the attitudes expressed on the subject of civil war in the *Controversiae* and *Suasoriae* may have been influential in Lucan's choice of a subject for his epic poem. Seneca speaks of the "frenzy of the civil

---

[25] One was the lurid court case of Octavius Sagitta in AD 58 concerning the murder of woman with whom he was conducting an adulterous affair; cf. Tac. *Ann.* 13.44; Bonner 36, 77. He also declaimed *de incendio urbis*; cf. Schanz-Hosius II, 494-495.

[26] René Pichon, *Les Sources de Lucain* (Paris 1912) 262-264.

[27] *Bell. Civ.* 2.338ff; cf. Bonner 8, note 3. He argues from Marcia's point of view.

[28] The speech of Vulteius, urging suicide, *Bell. Civ.* 4.476-520. He and his men are trapped at sea on a boat and must decide whether to commit suicide. The situation resembles *Suas.* 6, "Cicero deliberates whether to beg Antony's pardon." Cf. M. P. O. Morford, *The Poet Lucan: Studies in Rhetorical Epic* (Oxford 1967) 8; he points out the close similarities of Lucan's argumentation to *Suas.* 6.8, 10, 12.

[29] *Bell. Civ.* 5.560ff; cf. *Contr.* 8.6 and Morford (above, note 28) 33; also *Bell. Civ.* 5.546-550, and Fuscus, as quoted in *Suas.* 3.4, who, in turn, reveals the influence of Aratus *Phaen.* 778-818; Vergil *Georg.* 1.427-435. Cf. also the general effect of *Suas.* 1, especially Fabianus in 1.6; Morford (above, note 28) 35. He cautions (*ibid.* 36), referring to the storm scene in the younger Seneca's *Agamemnon*, that both "... owe their similarities, not so much to direct imitation, as to a sharing of a common literary training." Cf. also the description of the sea's stillness: *Suas.* 1.1; *Bell. Civ.* 5.443-444; also Curt. 9.4.18; Tac. *Agric.* 10.6; *Germ.* 45.1. See Winterbottom's note *ad loc.*, *Suas.* 1.1; also V. Tandoi, "Albinovano Pedone e la retorica giulio-claudio delle conquiste," *SIFC* 36 (1964) 129-168.

[30] Another noteworthy parallel between the two is the theme of the reversal of fate and retributive punishment; 10 pr. 6-7; cf. *Bell. Civ.* 10.21-34; also the remarks of Musa, 10 pr. 9, and *Bell. Civ.* 10.155ff. There is much material in Seneca on poisoning (*Contr.* 3.7, 6.4, 6.6, 7.3, 9.6) which one might have expected to reappear in Lucan, but does not; whatever similarities do occur, according to Morford (above, note 28) 68, are "more in the manner than in the matter."

wars" which detained him in Cordova, and a number of declamation themes, most notably *Suas.* 6 and 7, deal with this idea. [31] Even more influential would be Seneca's *Histories* which dealt with the same period. [32] Family pride, an attribute never lacking in the Annaei, would dictate familiarity with the contents of the grandfather's *magnum opus*. And even if it were not a direct source, the themes and contents of the work would be imprinted on his mind. [33] Lucan links moral decay with a cyclical progression in human affairs as both the backdrop and underlying cause for the civil wars. In this he immediately calls to mind the elder Seneca's conception in the *Histories*, insofar as it can be reconstructed through evidence in the *Controversiae, Suasoriae*, and *De Vita Patris.* [34]

Shortly before their deaths in the aftermath of the Pisonian conspiracy, the younger Seneca and Lucan befriended the Spanish poet Martial, who in two cryptic references points out three members of the clan as especially notable. At least one of these probably refers to the elder Seneca. [35] Martial may even have been familiar with the anthologies; a few very close parallels exist. [36] More striking are the parallels found in Martial's later contemporary, Juvenal, whose debt to declamation in both content and expression has been well attested. [37] The large number of these parallels argues for some acquaintance with the elder Seneca's works. [38]

---

[31] I pr. 11; other themes dealing with the civil wars are Contr. 4.8, 7.2, 10.3.

[32] See the discussion above, 145 and note 27; also Jacqueline Brisset, *Les Idées Politiques de Lucain* (Paris 1964) 146. She believes that his most profoundly expressed feeling was the fear and horror of civil war (cf. *Bell. Civ.* 4.189ff). Seneca was alive during some of the bitterest fighting in Spain; as an impressionable youth he unquestionably heard first-hand accounts from relatives and family friends. He would not have slighted the bloodiness of the wars, and might have transmitted, through the *Histories* and/or personally through his sons, this deep emotional picture to Lucan. Cf. E. M. Sanford, "Lucan and Civil War," *CP* 28 (1933) 127.

[33] See Brisset (above, note 32) 35. Cf. P. Wuilleumier and H. le Bonniec (eds.), *M. Annaeus Lucanus: Bellum Civile, Liber Primus* (Paris 1962) 4; also above, 138 and note 4.

[34] Cf. above, 146-149. They also share similar conceptions of *fortuna* and *fatum*; see Brisset (above, note 32) 54ff; cf. I pr. 7.

[35] The passages are treated above, 145 and notes 25, 26: *Duosque Senecas, unicumque Lucanum/facunda loquitur Corduba* (Mart. 1.61.7-8); cf. *Atria Pisonum stabant cum stemmate toto/et docti Senecae ter numeranda domus* (Mart. 4.40.1-2).

[36] See G. Friedrich, "Zu Seneca und Martial," *Hermes* 45 (1910) 591.

[37] De Decker (above, note 3) *passim.*

[38] Cf. the numerous ones cited *ibid. passim.* Winterbottom also remarks upon some important parallels; e.g., the description of a brothel (*Contr.* 1.2.7; cf. Juv. 6.121ff), the thinness of ships' hulls (*Contr.* 7.1.10; cf. Juv. 12.58, 14.289; also

Nowhere in his long and thorough work does Quintilian specifically mention the elder Seneca, but there are two quotations ascribed only to a Seneca which might with equal probability be from a lost portion of his or his son's works. 39 Although scholarship has divided on the issue, some evidence points to the elder Seneca as the man mentioned in 9.2.98. Shortly before this citation, Quintilian very briefly recounts, while omitting proper names, the incident in which Albucius lost a court case by introducing an inappropriate oath figure (7 pr. 7). The close verbal correspondences suggest strongly that Seneca was the source. 40 The appearance of the anecdote shortly before the problematical reference only to a Seneca could indicate that Quintilian, who just had the elder Seneca's account of the incident in mind, then reproduced from a lost part of the works one of his judgments on the proper use of oaths (9.2.98), a subject which greatly concerned both. 41

Elsewhere in Quintilian a series of parallels occurs which suggests a Senecan source. Without any ascription, Quintilian briefly retells the anecdote about Latro's embarrassment in a real court case held outside; the judge finally had to remove the session inside since Latro, unused to an open air (*caelum*) setting, became hopelessly confused (10.5.18). Shortly thereafter Quintilian compares the proper manner of preparing for court oratory with the training of gladiators (10.5.20). The incident concerning Latro appears in Seneca's long

---

younger Seneca *Ep.* 49.11). In the notes *ad loc.*, *Contr.* 2.1, Winterbottom lists an especially large number of parallels to Juvenal. Cf. *Contr.* 1.6.4 and Juv. 8.272-273 (also younger Seneca *Ep.* 14.1). However, the possibility of independent sources and Juvenal's overall debt to the general declamatory tradition cannot be discounted.

39 *Novi vero et praecipue declamatores audacius nec mehercle sine motu quodam imaginantur, ut et Seneca in controversia cuius summa est quod pater filium et novercam inducente altero filio in adulterio deprehensos occidit*: "*duc, sequor: accipe hanc senilem manum et quocumque vis inprime,*" *et post paulo*: "*Aspice*" *inquit* "*quod diu non credidisti. Ego vero non video: nox oboritur et crassa caligo* (Quint. 9.2.42). Also: *Nam et in totum iurare, nisi ubi necesse est, gravi viro parum convenit, et est a Seneca dictum eleganter, non patronorum hoc esse, sed testium* (Quint. 9.2.98). Another mention of a Seneca and some quotations (8.3.31; 9.2.91, 95) are less likely candidates for attribution to the elder; see the discussion of this problem above, 18 note 2.

40 *Iura per patris cineres* (7 pr. 7): *Iura per patris* [MSS *patroni*] *tui cineres* (Quint. 9.2.95). *Clamabat Albucius: non detuli condicionem; schema dixi .... Albucius clamabat: ista ratione schemata de rerum natura tolluntur* (7 pr. 7): *... clamante multum advocato schemata de rerum natura tolli* (Quint. 9.2.95). There is the possibility that Quintilian used an intermediary source or the same one used by Seneca; he says that the anecdote was famous (Quint. 9.2.95).

41 Cf. above, 120-123, for Seneca's criticism of figures in general.

quotation from Votienus Montanus (9 pr. 3), and thereupon follows a passage in which Montanus states that the open air setting (*caelum*) greatly disturbs those educated in the indoor declamation halls; the hardy manner of gladitorial training, he maintains, should be the pattern of preparation for the courts, not effete declamation exercises. [42] The closeness of the two parallels suggests a Senecan source. [43]

However, Quintilian failed to use the *Controversiae* as a source in at least one instance where we might have expected it. In alluding to virtually the same declamation theme as *Contr.* 2.3, Quintilian (9.2.90-91) reproduces a quotation from Latro which Seneca does not preserve in the section devoted to his friend. [44] A substantial number of other parallels to Seneca exist in Quintilian, but most are commonplaces or such well-known incidents that it would be foolish to posit an ultimately Senecan origin for most or even any of them. [45] However Bardon detects some debt on Quintilian's part to Seneca's vocabulary, especially his use of picturesque terms. [46] But, in general, each man is ultimately in the debt of Cicero for much of his critical terminology. Indeed, many parallels between Seneca and Quintilian merely reflect shared Ciceronian ideas, as in their devotion to the *vir bonus* definition of an orator. [47]

---

[42] 9 pr. 3; cf. Quint. 10.5.17, 19-20, also *Contr.* 3 pr. 17; 9 pr. 5.

[43] Seneca's source for the ninth preface could have been a written work of Montanus; Seneca himself mentions some (9.5.16; 9.6.18). Alternatively, Quintilian could have directly referred to one himself, if they were still available.

[44] On the other hand, Quintilian (9.2.91) does preserve a quotation from Gallio which appears in the Senecan declamation (*Contr.* 2.3.6); cf. Winterbottom's notes *ad loc.* Either Quintilian mixed his sources, used a totally different though parallel secondary tradition, or directly referred to the extant works of Gallio and Latro. A number of other declamation themes in Seneca's collection are mentioned by Quintilian: e.g., *Contr.* 1.3, cf. Quint. 7.8.3, 5-6; *Contr.* 3.7, alluded to in Quint. 8.2.20, 8.5.23; *Contr.* 4.4, cf. Quint. 5.10.36.

[45] E.g., Hortensius' memory feats, 1 pr. 19 (see Winterbottom note *ad loc.*); cf. Quint. 11.2.24; *Contr.* 1.7.18 (also Winterbottom notes *ad loc.*), cf. Quint. 8.3.22; judgments of Ovid, *Contr.* 2.2.12, cf. Quint. 10.1.98 (this may be a special case; see discussion below); the vagaries of memory, *Contr.* 1 pr. 4-5, cf. Quint. 11.2.6-7; the importance of historical knowledge for speakers, *Contr.* 1 pr. 18, cf. Quint. 3.8.66, 10.1.34; the *vir bonus* definition of an orator, *Contr.* 1 pr. 6, 9-10, cf. Quint. 1 pr. 9, 12.1.1. Both have similar ideas on the concealment of artifice, but both are part of a long critical tradition here; cf. Jean Cousin, *Études sur Quintilien* (2 vols., Paris 1935, 1936) I, 101 note 1. Augustus' remarks on Vinicius (*Contr.* 2.5.20) seem similar to Quint. 6.3.111. Both quote the same famed line from Publilius Syrus (628 Meyer): *Contr.* 7.3.8, cf. Quint. 8.5.6, 9.3.64.

[46] Bardon 102-104.

[47] See above, note 45, also 67 and note 113; cf. Michael Winterbottom, "Quintilian and the *Vir Bonus*," *JRS* 54 (1964) 90-97.

In not one single instance does the evidence collected conclusively prove that Quintilian ever really mentioned the elder Seneca, employed his works as a source, or displayed any Senecan influence. Nevertheless, Quintilian names and refers to works by numerous other writers, many less distinguished and more obscure than Seneca. How could so thorough a writer be unfamiliar (or relatively so) with the works of a fellow Spaniard, the patriarch of so distinguished a family, a fellow Ciceronian, and a critic sympathetic to many of his preferences? With ample justification Edward calls Quintilian's apparent silence on the elder Seneca "remarkable." [48] But a simple explanation exists: Quintilian harbored an incredibly deep antipathy towards the Annaei. In fact, a case can be made that Quintilian was indeed familiar with the elder Seneca, [49] but pointedly refrained from mentioning him by name.

The most notable object of Quintilian's dislike was the younger Seneca, to whom he devotes a famed critical passage (10.1.125-131). In his discussion of the various authors Quintilian says that he has saved Seneca for last in order to dispel once and for all the commonly held notion that he hated the man. Thereupon Quintilian delivers an ostensibly balanced critical portrait of the younger Seneca and his works, devoting about the same amount of space as he did to Homer and Cicero. But although the latter two men are mentioned and quoted many times in Quintilian, the younger Seneca merits only several brief and ambiguous references; clearly something is amiss and public opinion may well have been correct in diagnosing Quintilian's hatred. [50] W. H. Alexander has studied Quintilian's disclaimer of hatred and compels us to agree with his conclusion that the attempt at even-handedness is an obvious sham intended to cloak an ulterior purpose. [51]

---

[48] Edward xxiii.

[49] See above, 162 and note 43 (on Quint. 10.5.18-20; cf. *Contr.* 3 pr. 16; 9 pr. 3, 4).

[50] The younger Seneca is mentioned in Quint. 8.5.18, 9.2.9, 12.10.11, and is probably meant, rather than his father, in 8.3.31. As discussed above, he is less certainly meant in 9.2.48ff and 9.2.98.

[51] "The Professor's Deadly Vengeance," *Univ. of Toronto Quarterly* 4 (1935) 239-258. He refers to the passage's "studied malevolence" (242), and considers it "exceedingly unfair both in its matter and also the manner of its presentation" (257). The passages elsewhere in Quintilian about the younger Seneca are relatively innocuous except 8.5.18, where there is a quotation from a letter supposedly written by him for Nero. It was sent to the Senate after the death of Nero's mother, apparently in the hope of impressing the body that Nero was in critical danger. Thus Quintilian raises two serious charges against the younger Seneca: ghostwriting and moral complicity in matricide. See also Tacitus *Ann.* 14.10-11; cf. Paul Faider, *Études sur Sénèque* (Gand 1921) 40-41.

Quintilian does pay the younger Seneca one apparent compliment; he cites in a favorable context the "fluency of Seneca," *copiam Senecae* (12.10.11). But in the critical portrait he describes Seneca's fluency as occurring in excess (10.1.130-131). One epigrammatic utterance deserves repeating in this context (Quint. 10.1.130): "One could wish that he had spoken with his own native talent, but with another's judgment" (*Velles eum suo ingenio dixisse, alieno iudicio*). The total effect is very reminiscent of the elder Seneca on Haterius:

> Nec verborum illi (i.e., Haterius) tantum copia sed etiam rerum erat.... Regi autem ab ipso non poterat; alioqui libertum habebat cui pareret; sic ibat quomodo ille aut concitaverat eum aut refrenaverat. ... In sua potestate habebat ingenium, in aliena modum. [52]

In a fit of spiteful irony it seems that Quintilian may have turned the elder Seneca's criticism of Haterius against his son. Quintilian also tells us that the younger Seneca excessively loved anything he wrote (*si non omnia sua amasset*: 10.1.130). This echoes an earlier criticism made of Ovid, which, in turn, seems derived from the elder Seneca. [53] If both critical descriptions are not commonplaces, then Quintilian has adapted some well-known criticisms in the elder Seneca and applied them to his son, a crafty piece of malevolence which suggests that Quintilian was familiar with the elder, but refused to refer to him except obliquely, and in a manner embarrassing to his son.

Quintilian's antipathy to the Annaei extended to Lucan, although upon initial viewing the major reference to the epic poet seems to contain some praise:

> Lucan is fiery and passionate and remarkable for the grandeur of his general reflections [*sententiae*], but, to be frank, I consider that he is more suitable for imitation by the orator rather than the poet. [54]

This is Quintilian's only mention of Lucan, perhaps the most rhetorical of poets, one who is classed in a contemporary work with Vergil

---

[52] 4 pr. 7-8: "He was full of ideas as well as words .... But he couldn't do his own controlling. He had a freedman to look to, and used to proceed according as *he* excited or restrained him .... He had his talents under his own control—but the degree of their application he left to another's" (Winterbottom transl.).

[53] Quintilian also repeats the substance of this criticism on Ovid elsewhere: *nimium amator ingenii sui* (10.1.88). ... *si ingenio suo imperare quam indulgere maluisset* (10.1.98). Cf. Seneca on Ovid: *non ignoravit vitia sua, sed amavit* (2.2.12); *nam et Ovidius nescit quod bene cessit relinquere* (9.5.17).

[54] *Lucanus ardens et concitatus et sententiis clarissimus et, ut dicam quod sentio, magis oratoribus quam poetis imitandus* (Quint. 10.1.90; Butler transl.).

and Horace (Tac. *Dial.* 20). In the phrase *ut dicam quod sentio* ("but, to be frank") Quintilian seems to be displaying his opposition to current high opinion of Lucan. [55] Quintilian's deprecatory statement afterwards that he is more to be imitated by orators than poets, is an unveiled attack on Lucan's literary ability. In effect he has summarily dismissed Lucan as a poet; his only value is for orators. Yet Quintilian is not primarily interested in pure literary criticism at all. The objective of the long section on the Greek and Latin writers (10.1) is to provide orators with a reading list designed to be a guide to models for imitation, and Quintilian's following chapter (10.2), appropriately enough, is a technical discussion of imitation theory. [56] But more specifically, in passages bracketing the criticism of Lucan, Quintilian frankly admits that he is mainly concerned with models for oratory. [57] This contradiction plainly reveals that the statement on Lucan is a clever piece of spite.

The elder Seneca himself may be responsible for Quintilian's hostility to the Annaei. In the tenth preface Seneca says that he will not mention the names of undistinguished speakers; by way of example he mentions several of this class, among them one named Quintilianus senex (10 pr. 2). He later quotes a man identified only as Quintilianus (10.4.19), but because of the earlier promise and the lack of the *senex* epithet, the two are probably not the same. The author of the *Institutio Oratoria* was born *ca.* AD 40, so perhaps the man mentioned in 10.4.19 is Quintilian's father, who was a declaimer (cf. Quint. 9.3.73), and Quintilianus senex was his grandfather.

But an insult to his grandfather might not have rankled Quintilian as much as Seneca's negative attitudes towards the professional rhetors (or *scholastici*), many of whom appear in his works as foolish or even bordering upon the insane. [58] Seneca repeatedly questions the value of declamatory education as an effective preparation for real legal cases, and he displays a notable lack of tolerance for hair-splitting gram-

---

[55] Cf. W. Peterson (ed.), *Quintiliani Institutionis Oratoriae Liber X* (2nd ed., Oxford 1903) note *ad loc.*, *Lucanus*, Quint. 10.1.90.

[56] Cf. Quint. 10.1.1ff; 10.2.1ff.

[57] Cf. his remarks on Varro of Atax (10.1.87), and on Terentius Varro (10.1.95). Quintilian did not look down on the subject matter of Lucan's poem (as Eumolpus may have; Petr. *Sat.* 118): two other poets who wrote epics on nearly contemporary historical events receive at least faint praise from Quintilian; Albinovanus Pedo (10.1.90) and Cornelius Severus (10.1.89). The elder Seneca quotes both and praises their efforts more highly (*Suas.* 1.15; 6.25-27).

[58] Cf. above, 136 and note 169.

marians (*Suas.* 2.13). This explanation for Quintilian's dislike of the Annaei seems the more likely one. [59]

Tacitus, a great orator who himself evinced interest in rhetorical criticism, may also have been acquainted with the *Controversiae* and *Suasoriae*. [60] In particular, Seneca's discussion of the decline of eloquence and the citation of political changes as a possible cause would have recommended at least the first preface to Tacitus when writing the *Dialogus*. Marked similarities exist between the two men in the attitudes expressed on this issue, and perhaps in their politics. [61] Bardon, however, finds little Senecan influence on Tacitus' critical vocabulary. [62] The short account of Haterius' eloquence may ultimately stem from Seneca's fourth preface, and Tacitus' use of the phrase *monumenta ingeniorum* and *monimenta ingeni* has a suspiciously Senecan flavor. [63]

Suetonius has already entered our discussion of Seneca's influence in regard to the *Histories* and a possible early testimonium to the *Controversiae* and *Suasoriae*. [64] In addition, his Vergil biography, as preserved by Donatus, may contain a possible fragment from a lost section of Seneca concerning the poet Julius Montanus. [65] But while here and elsewhere it is tempting to identify material from Seneca in Suetonius, in virtually each instance minor additions or slightly varied facts make this both difficult and dangerous. Thus Suetonius preserves an account of L. Plotius Gallus which is reminiscent of, but fuller than the Senecan notice (*Rhet.* 2; cf. 2 pr. 5). Seneca merely mentions that

---

[59] The younger Seneca shared his father's views. Cf. Alexander (above, note 51) 240: "[the younger] Seneca, in his works, had laughed publicly at academic aims and academic ineffectiveness, and had even omitted to remain stylistically a Ciceronian in doing so ...." The younger Seneca's philosophical training undoubtedly influenced this relatively low estimate of the rhetorical educational system; for the elder Seneca it was common sense which led him to a similar view. Quintilian probably felt the need to defend the rhetorical domination of education against its detractors—after all, he was the Regius Professor of Rhetoric. It is conceivable, also, that party factions and rivalries in Spain may have influenced Quintilian's dislike of the Annaei, or jealousy of the family, or perhaps some other relatively minor slight to a fellow provincial family.
[60] He probably would also have known something about the *Histories*.
[61] Cf. Sussman "Decline of Eloquence" *passim*.
[62] Bardon 104-105.
[63] 4 pr. 7-11; cf. Tac. *Ann.* 4.61; also 10 pr. 6-7; cf. Tac. *Agr.* 2; *Ann.* 15.41.
[64] See above, 138-139; 156-157.
[65] *Et Seneca tradidit Iulium Montanum poetam solitum dicere involaturum se Vergilio quaedam, si et vocem posset et os et hypocrisin; eosdem enim versus ipso pronuntiante bene sonare, sine illo inanes esse mutosque* (Donat. *Vita Vergilii* 28; cf. Grisart *passim*).

Plotius taught when Cicero was a boy, while Suetonius preserves the letter in which the orator reminisces about his teacher. The account of Albucius (*Rhet.* 6) preserves a number of close parallels with Seneca's seventh preface on this man. [66] Here again the Suetonian version contains some material not found in Seneca, while other matters are recounted in less detail, as in the description of Albucius' style and the proceedings during the oath incident. But in the latter instance Suetonius provides more context for the court case. Here he may have been using Seneca as a supplemental source or another source entirely, which ultimately, in part, depended upon Seneca. [67] In his short history of declamation, Suetonius differs substantially from Seneca and obviously did not refer to him or purposely ignored his faulty account. [68]

We might have expected Suetonius to use Seneca for the lost sketch of Latro's life, but even the small amount preserved in Jerome provides more information than the Senecan parallel. [69] The early church writer does, however, repeat Augustus' judgment of Haterius quoted in Seneca, and so he may possibly have been acquainted with the rhetorical works. [70]

Elsewhere, Dio repeats the Senecan anecdote about Antony and Father Liber (48.39.2; cf. *Suas.* 1.6), while Lucian displays an uncanny number of parallels with *Contr.* 4.5. [71] Macrobius preserves an account of the incident concerning Caesar and Laberius similar to the one found in Seneca, but it is difficult to establish the *Controversiae* as his source. [72] Seneca's works appear to have circulated in the Greek speaking world; several close parallels exist between *Contr.* 1.5.6 and the later Greek rhetoricians. [73]

---

[66] Both say that he declaimed while seated unless passion made him rise (7 pr. 1), and agree on his polish, use of vulgar vocabulary in order not to seem a *scholasticus* (7 pr. 4), and the outcome of the oath figure incident (7 pr. 6-7; cf. Quint. 9.2.95). See W.-D. Lebek, "Zur Vita des Albucius Silus bei Sueton," *Hermes* 94 (1966) 360-372.

[67] *Ibid.* 361, note 2.

[68] 1 pr. 12; cf. Suet. *Rhet.* 1. See the discussion in Chapter I, above; also Rodney P. Robinson (ed.), *C. Suetoni Tranquilli: De Grammaticis et Rhetoribus* (Paris 1925) notes *ad loc.* (pp. 35ff; esp. *ad loc., Olim autem eas ...,* pp. 41-43); also Bonner, Chap. I *passim.*

[69] 1 pr. 13; cf. Jerome *ad Ol.* CXCIIII, I (a. 750-754).

[70] Jerome *PL* 23.365; cf. 4 pr. 7.

[71] Cf. Winterbottom notes *ad loc.*

[72] *Contr.* 7.3.9; cf. Macrob. *Sat.* 2.3.10, 7.3.8; also 2.7.6.

[73] E.g., Marcellinus and some anonymous figures; see Walz, *Rhet. Graeci* IV 270,21ff; VII 653,12ff; cf. Bornecque 32, also Winterbottom note *ad loc.* 1.5.6.

168 THE ELDER SENECA: AFTERWARDS

4. *Influence in the Late Classical Period through the Middle Ages and Renaissance*

A trace of a Senecan declamation appears in *Apollonius, Prince of Tyre*, a Latin romance of the fourth, fifth or sixth century AD which was especially popular in the medieval and early modern periods. The author includes the tale of a young woman who remained a virgin while working in a brothel, a situation analogous to *Contr.* 1.2, and he seems to have been quite familiar with this declamation theme. [74]

During the fourth century an anonymous scholar condensed all ten books of the *Controversiae*, to which he added the complete prefaces of books 1, 2, 3, 4, 7, 10. [75] The omission of the preface to book nine, the most outspoken attack on declamation contained in the work (presented in the words of Votienus Montanus), was no accident; the excerptor was unquestionably a rhetor himself, and the version was intended for school use. [76] The very existence of the *Excerpta* and the large number of manuscripts testify to the great influence of Seneca's works in the late classical and medieval periods. [77] The popularity of his works reflected the continued importance of declamation in the educational system of Western Europe after the fall of Rome and until well into the Renaissance. Even Christian converts such as Tertullian and St. Augustine turned their rhetorical training,

---

[74] See Ben E. Perry, *The Ancient Romances* (Berkeley 1967) 294, 314. Perhaps the declamation themes formed inspiration for the stage, and through this medium may also have influenced the anonymous author; cf. *ibid.* 314. The Latin text of Apollonius may well be a translation of a Greek original dating from the second or third century A.D.

[75] On the date, cf. Schanz-Hosius II, 339.

[76] On the relationship between the *Excerpta* and the original text see Winterbottom I, xix. He makes the following observations: the *sententiae* sections occupied most of the excerptor's attention, individual attributions are omitted; correspondingly, divisions and colors are virtually unrepresented, occasional anecdotes appear, the full text (where preserved) is adapted, occasionally new epigrams are composed mistakenly from the "flotsam of the old," subjects and objects not in the original are added to make the new version clearer, and prose rhythm is improved. *Clausulae* appear only in scattered instances in the original text; cf. the study of relative clausulation in the two texts by H. Hagendahl, *Apophoreta Gotoburgensia Vilelmo Lundström Oblata* (Göteborg 1936) 299ff.

[77] Cf. Bornecque 32; Schanz-Hosius II, 339. About 90 MSS of the *Excerpta* exist; approximately 30 MSS contain medieval commentaries on the *Excerpta*; cf. H. D. L. Vervliet, "De Gedrukte Overlevering van Seneca Pater," *De Gulden Passer* 35 (1957) 179-222. One commentary was written as late as the thirteenth century by the monk Nicolaus de Treveth; cf. the Bursian ed. of the elder Seneca, VIII; also Schanz-Hosius II, 340.

gained in pagan schools, to the defense and propagation of the Faith. [78]
Ennodius, the bishop of Pavia (511-521) was also a devotee of rhetoric;
he composed fictitious speeches for mythological figures and *controversiae*. [79]

The ninth century marked a revival of interest in the classics when
many of the old works were recopied and read again. During this
approximate period the major manuscripts of Seneca were recopied
and distributed. [80] Fabricated practice lawsuits similar to *controversiae*
(some in verse) soon became popular, as did the analogues to *suasoriae*
known as *dissuasiones*. [81] More specific influence of Seneca appears
in the widely circulated medieval *florilegia* which contain quotations
from the *Controversiae* side-by-side with selections from the works of
Tibullus, Publilius Syrus, the younger Seneca, and others. [82]

The *Controversiae* provided themes for one of the most significant
works of the Middle Ages, the *Gesta Romanorum*, a widely circulated
collection of romantic tales. [83] At least eleven of the tales are taken
directly from the declamation themes contained in the *Controversiae*. [84]
The *Gesta Romanorum* considerably influenced later European literature, although the Senecan inspired tales seem to have been less important than the others. [85] However, Mlle. de Scudéry's romance,

---

[78] On St. Augustine in particular, and the effect of rhetoric in general on
Christianity, see Clarke 148-157.

[79] One of the latter, *Dict.* 21, employs a theme from *Decl. Maj.* 363. In his
collection the familiar stock figures of tyrants, stepmothers, *et al.* appear: "Thus
the old tradition of declamation survived almost without change from Augustus
to the Ostrogothic kingdom" says Clarke (156), who also finds evidence of
declamation in fifth century Gaul; *ibid.* 198, note 54.

[80] In both the full text (A, B, V) and *Excerpta* (M) traditions; cf. Whitehorne 25, who also points out that during this period the poet Walafrid Strabo
might have been the first to distinguish between the elder and younger Senecas.

[81] W. R. Trask (transl.), E. R. Curtius, *European Literature and the Later
Middle Ages* (New York 1953) 154-155.

[82] Cf. B. L. Ullman, "Tibullus in the Medieval Florilegia," *CP* 23 (1928)
128-174, esp. 130-131; Curtius (above, note 81) 51.

[83] Their popularity is attested to by the great number of MSS; cf. Ella
Bourne, "Classical Elements in the Gesta Romanorum," in Christabel Forsyth
Fiske (ed.), *Vassar Medieval Studies* (New Haven 1923) 345; see also Schanz-
Hosius II, 339; Curtius (above, note 81) 155; Edward xxxvi.

[84] Cf. A. B. Gough (transl.), L. Friedländer, *Roman Life and Manners under
the Early Empire* (4 vols., London 1913) IV, 297 (= *Sittengeschichte Roms*,
7th enlarged and revised ed.). As a source, Seneca was about as important as
Valerius Maximus, Pliny the elder, and Herodotus; see also Whitehorne 25,
27 note 17. Cf. Bornecque 32; Bourne (above, note 83) 349, 351.

[85] *Ibid.* 345, 349.

Ibrahim ou l'illustre Bassa (1641) is based upon the theme of *Contr.* 1.6 or *GR* 5. [86]

More recently Falconi has traced the influence of Seneca on the humanist Leonardo Bruni's novella, *Antioco e Stratonica* and on Boccaccio's *Decameron.* [87] Other important scholars and humanists throughout Western Europe from the Middle Ages on were also acquainted with the elder Seneca, or at least had his works in their libraries. Among them are, for example, Gerbert of Aurillac (950-1003), Gilbert de la Porrée (*ca.* 1075-1154), John of Salisbury (1115-1180), and the Marquis de Santillane (or Don Iñigo Lopez de Mendoza, 1398-1458). [88]

But for English speaking peoples, the most unusual manifestation of Seneca's influence appears in the *Discoveries* of Ben Jonson. Although long thought to be original, the work is actually an assortment of quotations translated into English from Latin writers, predominantly of the Silver Age. In it Jonson makes notable use of Seneca, especially the prefaces. [89] The most striking borrowing is contained in the well-known appreciation of Shakespeare, which reproduces very closely Seneca's critical remarks on Haterius in the fourth preface. Jonson criticizes Shakespeare's tendency towards verbosity and volubility: this playwright "needed the brake," but had

> ... brave notions and gentle expressions; wherein hee flowed with that facility, that sometime it was necessary he should be stop'd. ... His wit was in his owne power; would that the rule of it had beene so too. Many times he fell into those things could [sic] not escape laughter. ... But hee redeemed his vices, with his vertues. There was ever more in him to be praysed then to be pardoned.

---

[86] Cf. Curtius (above, note 81) 155; also C. S. Rayment, "Medieval Recasting of an Ancient Declamation," *CB* 34 (1958) 61-62.

[87] R. Falconi, "Il motivo del malato d'amore in un argumentum di Seneca Padre," *GIF* 13 (1960) 327-336; cf. Whitehorne 26. *Contr.* 6.7 treats the theme of a young man who falls in love with his stepmother; the story reappears in Val. Max. 5.7 *ext.* 1, and then in Bruni. The influence on Boccaccio is less direct, but apparently some of the characters and arguments of the declaimers affected his writing; cf. R. Falconi, "Valori di poesia negli argumenta e deformazione retorica negli sviluppi di alcune Controversiae di Senecae," *GIF* 14 (1961) 214-229.

[88] Cf. Whitehorne 25, 27 note 15; also M. Manitius, *Geschichte der Lateinischen Literatur des Mittelalters* (3 vols., Munich; vol. II, 1923; vol. III, 1931) II, 731; III, 213; Curtius (above, note 81) 51; Marie Schiff, *La Bibliotheque du Marquis de Santillane* (Amsterdam 1970) 103. See also U. Kindermann, "Die fünf Reden des Laurentius von Durham," *Mittellateinisches Jahrbuch* 8 (1973) 108-141.

[89] Cf. Atkins 154.

Compare this with a modern translation of the parallel passages from the fourth preface:

> He (Haterius) was full of ideas as well as words. ... He could be controlled—but not exhausted. ... His speed of delivery was such as to become a fault.... He had his talents under his own control—but the degree of their application he left to another's.... he often fell into expressions that could not escape derision.... There was much you could reprove—but much to admire.... But he made up for his faults by his virtues, and provided more to praise than to forgive.... [90]

Jonson's appreciation of Bacon also follows Seneca closely, in this case, the portrait of Cassius Severus. [91] In what has been termed "the most vivid passage of autobiography in the *Discoveries*," where Jonson describes the effect of the aging process on memory, we may also point to a direct Senecan source in the first preface. [92]

Also testifying to the popularity and influence of Seneca is the publication history of his works which began shortly after the invention of printing. Surprisingly, the *Excerpta* were published first (1475), while the first full edition appeared in 1490 (Venice), followed by reprintings in 1492 and 1503. [93] More scholarly editions appeared with some degree of regularity; notably those of Erasmus (1515), N. Faber (1587), A. Schott (1603), and J. F. Gronovius (1649). In 1672 the widely circulated Elzevir edition was published, with prefaces and notes from the editions of the latter named three men

---

[90] Ben Jonson, *Discoveries*, ed. M. Castelain (Paris 1906) sec. 64, and Winterbottom's translation of selections from 4 pr. 7-11. The corresponding Latin text: *Tanta erat illi velocitas orationis ut vitium fieret. ... Nec verborum illi tantum copia sed etiam rerum erat ... ita ut regi posset nec consumi* (4 pr. 7). ... *In sua potestate habebat ingenium, in aliena modum* (4 pr. 8). ... *saepe incidebat in ea quae derisum effugere non possent* (4 pr. 10). ... *Multa erant quae reprehenderes, multa quae suspiceres. ... Redimebat tamen vitia virtutibus et plus habebat quod laudares quam cui ignosceres ...* (4 pr. 11). Cf. Atkins 154; Marchette Chute, *Ben Jonson of Westminster* (New York 1953) 340.

[91] *Discoveries* sec. 71; cf. 3 pr. 2, 4; Atkins 154-155.

[92] *Discoveries* sec. 56; cf. 1 pr. 2, 5; C. H. Herford and Percy Simpson (eds.), *Ben Jonson: The Man and His Work* (11 vols., Oxford 1925, repr. 1954) II, 442-443. For other Senecan borrowings, see Wesley Trimpi, *Ben Jonson's Poems: A Study of the Plain Style* (Stanford 1962, repr. 1969) 24, 84, 262 note 21. Castelain (above, note 90) under the English text conveniently provides the Latin source; he provides these correspondences: *D.* 49/4 pr. 1; *D.* 54/3 pr. 11-14; *D.* 63/3 pr. 15; *D.* 64/4 pr. 7, 8, 10, 11; *D.* 68/1 pr. 13-15, 21, 23, 24; *D.* 69/3 pr. 8, 9; *D.* 70/3 pr. 1, 3-6; *D.* 71/1 pr. 6, 3 pr. 2; *D.* 72/1 pr. 6, 7, 11; *D.* 120/*Suas.* 1.11-12.

[93] On the 1475 *Excerpta* edition, see Müller XXXVI.

plus additional material from J. Schulting. No real improvement on the text occurred until the latter half of the nineteenth century, when three editions were produced in the relatively remarkable span of thirty years: Bursian (1857), Kiessling (1872), and Müller (1887). [94]

On the other hand, very few translations of Seneca have been attempted. Presumably, readers who would find the work of any interest would know Latin in the first place, besides which, by its very nature the work is very difficult to translate. Over one hundred different people are quoted in a wide variety of styles and often out of context. Then, too, Seneca himself uses or quotes a substantial number of technical literary terms which are very difficult to render accurately into English. The only full English translation is Michael Winterbottom's fine Loeb edition. [95]

While the elder Seneca could never become a widely known author in the usual sense of the word, his works are finally beginning to receive overdue attention from the world of classical scholarship. Certainly a thorough and systematic investigation of the Medieval and Renaissance periods would uncover more significant traces of his influence. But by far his greatest interest to scholarship lies in his activities as a literary critic and his unique position in the tradition of ancient literary criticism.

---

[94] On the various early printed editions of Seneca and their distribution in Europe, see Vervliet (above, note 77).

[95] *The Elder Seneca: Declamations* (2 vols., London 1974). The first translation was into French by Mathieu de Chaluet (Paris 1604); upon it two successive ones were largely dependent; Lesfargues (1663) and Damien (1889, containing only the prefaces and *Suas.* 6). An excellent French translation and improved Latin text (based largely on Müller) was done by Henri Bornecque (Paris 1902; 2nd ed. 1932). W. A. Edward rendered the *Suasoriae* into English and provided extensive notes in *The Suasoriae of Seneca the Elder* (Cambridge 1928), while Lewis A. Sussman translated the prefaces only, "Early Imperial Declamation: A Translation of the Elder Seneca's Prefaces," *Speech Monographs* 37 (1970) 135-151. A. D. Leeman, *Orationis Ratio: The Stylistic Theories and Practice of the Roman Orators, Historians, and Philosophers* (2 vols., Amsterdam 1963) translates a number of key passages, especially from the prefaces, relating to theoretical matters.

BIBLIOGRAPHICAL NOTE

J. E. G. Whitehorne provides a very useful critical bibliography on the elder Seneca in *Prudentia* 1 (1969) 14-27, under the following headings: (1) texts, translations, and commentaries, (2) manuscript tradition, (3) Seneca as a literary critic, (4) rhetoricians mentioned, (5) rhetorical terminology and grammatical studies, (6) Seneca as a historian, (7) declamations and the law, (8) declamations and education, and (9) Seneca's influence. S. F. Bonner in *Roman Declamation in the Late Republic and Early Empire* (Liverpool 1949, repr. 1969) 169-177 supplements, corrects, and brings up to date (i.e., 1949) the bibliographies of Henri Bornecque, *Les Déclamations et les Déclamateurs d'après Sénèque le Père* (Lille 1902, repr. Hildesheim 1967) 3-6, and William A. Edward (ed. and transl.), *The Suasoriae of Seneca the Elder* (Cambridge 1928) xlv-xlvi. All these are broader in scope than Whitehorne, who is primarily concerned with Seneca himself. More current work can be found in *L'Année Philologique*, which in recent years has been listing unpublished dissertations. Several useful articles on declamation and Seneca are found in Pauly-Wissowa, *Real-Encyclopaedie der classischen Altertumswissenschaft* (Stuttgart 1894—): W. Kroll, "Melete," vol. XV, cols. 496-500; *idem*, "Rhetorik," Supplementband VII, cols. 1039-1138; and O. Rossbach, "Lucius Annaeus Seneca" (Annaeus no. 16), vol. I, cols. 2237-2240, and Supplementband I, col. 85. A number of important emendations to the text of Seneca which appeared after Winterbottom's Loeb are found in Lennart Håkanson, "Some Critical Notes on Seneca the Elder," *AJP* 97 (1976) 121-129. The most basic works on the subject of Seneca and declamation are found in the list of frequently cited works at the beginning of this book.

GENERAL INDEX

accusatio (part of argument), 115
(L. Aelius) Sejanus, 63&n, 92-93
Mamercus (Aemilius) Scaurus, 50, 66n,
78n, 79&n, 92, 93, 110&n, 123,
(Scauri, 23&n)
aequitas (equity), 39, 40, 41n, 103
Aeschines (a Greek declaimer) 2, 7n
Agrippa, *see* Vipsanius
Albinovanus Pedo, 62n, 72, 150, 165n
Albius Tibullus, 16, 169
C. Albucius Silus, 16, 18n, 41, 49&n,
50, 58n, 65&n, 66n, 78n, 79-80, 82n,
91n, 96n, 97-99, 108-109, 114n, 117,
121, 122, 124, 125, 129, 161, 167&n
Alexander the Great, 2, 112&n, 130-1
Alexander, W. H., 163&n
alliteration, 122&n
altercatio, 104, 110
Ammianus Marcellinus, 140n, 142, 149n
anecdote, 60, 61&n, 62&n, 63&n, 74,
83, 89, 96, 98, 112, 122, 132, 158,
168n
Annaei (Seneca family collectively), x,
19, 21, 22, 26, 29, 30, 31, 33, 74n, 91,
160, 163, 164, 165, 166&n
L. Annaeus Florus, 138&n, 140n, 142,
149&n, 152, 153
(Annaeus) Mela (youngest son of
elder Seneca), 23n, 24, 25, 31n, 46, 48,
56, 84
(Annaeus) Novatus (eldest son of
elder Seneca; later adopted by Junius
Gallio and known by adoptive name
Junius Gallio Annaeanus), 21n, 22,
24, 31n
L. Annaeus Seneca (second son of
elder Seneca, referred to as the
younger Seneca), xi, 19n, 21&n, 22,
23, 24, 25, 26&n, 28, 29&n, 30, 31&n,
32n, 48, 92, 138, 139, 141, 148, 149&n,
154, 155, 156, 160, 163-4, 166n, 169;
possible source for a supposed fragment of elder Seneca's *Histories,*
139-41; influence of elder Seneca on,
141, 157-8; source for father's biography, 18, 138&n; biography of father, *De Vita Patris,* 18, 23, 92&n,
137-8&nn, 139, 141, 142, 143n, 144&n,
148, 157, 160

(Annaeus) Mela, (Annaeus) Novatus,
and L. Annaeus Seneca (i.e., all the
sons, collectively), 18, 22, 23, 26n, 27,
33, 48, 52, 53, 54, 58, 64, 66, 67, 70,
71, 72, 74, 83, 84, 85&n, 89
L. Annaeus Seneca (the father of
Mela, Novatus, and the younger Seneca; author of the *Controversiae,
Suasoriae,* and the *Histories*; see
also individual entries on his works
following; also Criticism, rhetorical),
e.g., ix, x, 1, 4, 13, 17, etc.; account
of beginnings of *controversiae,* 6-10;
first to use term *suasoria,* 11; sources for biography, 18ff; name,
19&n, 20, 141&n, 155; birthplace,
19; birthdate, 20&n; life, career,
and death, 20-26 141&n, 160n; not
a *rhetor,* 25, 26, 135; character, philosophy, and politics, 26-33, 144, 146,
157, 166; respect for Cicero, 32&n;
memory capability, *see* Memory;
autobiographical data, 56-57
———, Rhetorical works collectively
(*Controversiae* and *Suasoriae*), e.g.
153, 155, 156, 157, 159, 160, 166;
title of collection, 19&n; objectives
and reasons for composition, 38, 46,
47, 54, 55, 63, 64, 83-91; structural
unity, 45ff, 63-4; sources, 75-83;
accuracy of quotations, 79ff; intended audience, 84-5; publication, 91-
92, 155, 157; date of composition,
92-93; as works of literary criticism, 134; referred to by son elliptically, 137; later publication and
translation, 171-2; MS tradition,
34-5, 168&n, 169&n; influence of,
general, 153; on younger Seneca,
141, 157-8; on Roman declamation
collections, 153-4; on Roman literary
criticism, 154-5; on Roman literature
(generally), 155-167, (specifically) on
Lucan, 158-160; Martial, 160; Juvenal, 160; Quintilian, 161-6; Tacitus,
166; Suetonius, 166-7; influence in
late classical period, Middle Ages,
and Renaissance, 168-172.
———, Prefaces to the rhetorical works

Bassus, *see* Julius or Aufidius

Blandus, *see* Rubellius

Boccaccio, 170&n

Bonner, S. F., x, 3, 15

book burning, (*see* also, Speech, freedom of), 23-4, 29, 32, 33, 46-7, 50, 56, 87&nn, 92, 93, 110&n, 143

Bornecque, Henri, xi

brevity, 128&n, 129

Bruni, Leonardo, 170&n

Bruttedius Niger, 73n, 150&n

Brutus, *see* Junius

Bursian, C. 172

Caecilius (of Calacte; 1st C. BC critic of rhetoric), 99

Caesar Augustus, 1, 7, 12, 15&n, 22, 24, 26, 30, 31, 32, 33, 61n, 66, 90, 100n, 114, 133, 143, 149, 150n, 158, 167 (also referred to as Octavian, 14, 29, 32)

Gaius Julius Caesar Germanicus (commonly, Gaius or Caligula; emp. AD 37-41), 24, 92, 105, 126n, 137, 139, 142, 143, 156-7

Nero Claudius Caesar (commonly, Nero; emp. AD 54-68), 24

Tiberius Julius Caesar Augustus (commonly, Tiberius; emp. AD 14-37), 15n, 23, 24, 26, 30, 31, 33, 90, 93, 105, 143

Caligula, *see* Caesar

Calpurnius Flaccus, 7, 154&n

Calvus, *see* Licinius

Capito, 58n, 66n, 78n

Carthage, 140, 142, 149 (*metus Punicus*, 148, 149n, 150n)

C. Cassius Longinus (assassin of Julius Caesar), 151n

Cassius Severus, 9n, 23, 26, 33, 46, 48&n, 49, 50, 65&n, 78n, 79n, 82n, 88n, 92, 97, 99n, 109n-10n, 117, 124, 129, 133&n-4, 171&n

causa, 6, 7, 10n

Celsus, *see* Cornelius.

L. Cestius Pius, 32n, 48&n, 58n, 61&n, 78n, 79&n, 86n, 112-3, 116n, 121, 124, 129, 130

chriae (type of *progymnasmata,* q.v.), 3&n

Churchill, Winston, 13

Cineas, 132

circles, literary, 14

clarity (of style), 118, 119-20

(Tiberius) Claudius Nero Germanicus (commonly, Claudius; emp. AD 41-54), 143&n

clausulae, see Prose rhythm

Clodius Turrinus (pater), 21, 23, 26, 29n, 58n, 110n, 129

Clodius Turrinus (pater et filius), 31, 50, 57, 65, 66n, 91n

colloquial language, *see* Diction

-colon; isocolon, 123; tricolon, 123; tetracolon, 123

colors (or *colores*), 23, 35, 36, 41-3, 44, 45, 46, 58, 59-61, 62&n, 66, 80, 84, 95, 97, 113&nn-4&nn, 118, 127, 134, 168n

comedy, 37, 94, 129 (*see* also, Laberius, and Publilius Syrus)

commentarii, 81&n, 82, 131

commonplace, 3, 38&n, 39, 41, 43&n, 44, 57, 60, 87, 100n, 107, 108, 110, 111, 114&n, 115, 116, 131, 158, 164

composition (aspect of style; *see* also Prose rhythm and *Sententiae*), 120, 126-9; periodic sentences, 126&n

concealment of artifice (*see* also *Subtilitas),* 98, 115, 121, 131, 134, 162n

conclusions (part of elder Seneca's *Suasoriae*), 62, 69, 116

Controversiae (collection of extracts from declamation exercises of same name by elder Seneca; *see* under L. Annaeus Seneca, Rhetorical works of, collectively, Prefaces, *Controversiae, Excerpta*)

controversiae (declamation exercise; *see* also Declamation), e.g., ix, xi, etc., 110, 118, 134, 135, 169; origins of, 1-10; theatricality in, 9&n, 113, 133&n; practiced after *suasoriae* 11; themes, 39, 45, 58; colors in, 41-3; relationship to real court cases, 8, 45, 47, 48, 49-50, 59, 74, 86, 87, 99, 109n-10n, 111, 112&n, 114n, 116&n, 120, 131, 155, 162, 165

Cordova, 19&n, 20, 21, 23, 28&n, 29&n, 30&nn, 53, 145, 160

Corinth, 142

Cornelius Celsus, 17

Cornelius Severus, 72, 73n, 119, 150, 165n

Cornelius Tacitus (historian), 9n, 11, 24n, 31n, 33, 54n, 55n, 57, 109, 117, 134n, 138&n, 141n, 142n, 146n, 149n, 151&n, 153, 155, 165; as source for

Rolland, E., 158
Romulus, 140
(Rubellius) Blandus, 4, 48n
P. Rutilius Lupus, 81n

Sabinus, *see* Asilius
Saenianus, 128&n
(C.) Sallustius Crispus (Sallust, the
  historian), 61, 83, 128, 140n, 142&n,
  146, 148&n, 150&n, 158
sanity (of style and expression; also
  the opposite quality), 100n, 102, 129,
  136&n; of rhetors, 155, 165
Santillane, Marquis de (or Don Iñigo
  Lopez de Mendoza), 170
Scaevola, *see* Mucius
Scaurus, *see* Aemilius
scholastica, 6
scholastici, 72n, 73, 96, 98, 114n, 125,
  127, 165, 167n
Schott, A., 171
Schulting, J., 172
Scudéry, Mlle. de, 169-70
Sejanus, *see* Aelius
Tib. & C. Sempronius Gracchus, 142,
  146, 149
Seneca, *see* Annaeus
Seneca Grandio, (62n), 110n
sententiae, 35-8, 43, 44, 45, 58, 59,
  60&n, 61, 62, 63, 65, 66, 69, 80, 83,
  84, 88, 90, 102, 103&n, 104, 114n, 117,
  118, 120, 127-9, 134, 146, 158, 168n;
  Seneca's crit. of, 127-9 (*see* also,
  Composition, Prose rhythm); as a
  tool of criticism, 96, 134, 164
Sextilius Ena, 150&n
Q. Sextius, 48n
Shakespeare, William, 108n, 170-1
simile, 99-100, (102), 105n, 135
Simonides (lyric poet and deviser of a
  memory system; *ca.* 556-468BC),
  77&n, 132
Sochatoff, A. Fred, 66&n
Spain, 19, 21, 23, 31, 56, 91
Sparsus, *see* Fulvius
Spartans, three hundred (theme of
  Suas. 2), 119&n
speech, freedom of (*see* also Book
  burning), 13, 32-3, 87&n, 92, 112-3
stasis (or *status*), 40&n, 111, 112
Stoicism, 28, 48&n, 110, 148, 149
Strabo, 28n
style (*see* also Ornamention), 1, 12,
  17, 35, 45, 60, 62n, 64, 70, 71, 74, 75,

79, 82, 86, 87, 88, 90, 95, 96, 97, 98,
  109, 110n, 117, 130, 134, 135, 148,
  154, 155, 156, 158, 167; ornateness
  in declamation, 11, 71&n; periodic,
  38, 45; one of five parts of rhetoric,
  43; of *narratio*, 115; of *epilogus*,
  117; four virtues of as basis for
  Seneca's criticism, 118-31 (*see* also,
  Criticism, rhetorical)
suasiones, 11
suasoriae (declamation exercise, *see*
  also, Declamation), e.g., ix, xi, 1, 2,
  3, 4, 11, 37, 61-2, 70&n, 69-74, 109,
  116, 159-60; practiced before *controversiae*, 11; historical accuracy in,
  11n; no *colores* in, 41, 61; *ethos* and
  pathos in, 113&n
Suasoriae (collection of extracts from
  declamation exercises of same name
  by elder Seneca; *see* under L. Annaeus Seneca, Rhetorical works of,
  collectively, *Suasoriae*, Prefaces)
subtilitas (*see* also Concealment of
  artifice), x, 97, 109, 112&n, 121
C. Suetonius Tranquillus, 4, 5, 7, 8,
  10, 14&n, 15&nn, 18n, 23, 24n, 126n,
  138&n, 139&n, 140, 151, 153, 156&n;
  putative fragments of Seneca in,
  18n, 139&nn, 140, 166-7
P. Sulpicius Rufus (figure in Cic. *De
  Or.*), 99
syncresis (σύγκρισις), 99

Tacitus, *see* Cornelius
Tarquinius Superbus (Tarquin, the last
  king of Rome), 140
P. Terentius Varro Atacinus, 61
Tertullian (Q. Septimius Florens Ter-
  tullianus), 168
Theophrastus, 118
theses, 3, 4, 5, 6, 11, 14&n
Thucydides, 61, 128&n, 146
Tiberius, *see* Caesar
Tibullus, *see* Albius
Timagenes, 61n, 150n, 158
tractatio (in division), 39-40&n, 103&n
tropes, *see* figures
M. Tullius Cicero (orator, cos. 63BC),
  4, 5, 6, 7, 8&nn, 9, 11, 13, 14&n,
  15&n, 16&n, 20, 21, 32&n, 36, 42&nn,
  47, 48n, 52n, 53, 54n, 62n, 63, 67, 70,
  72, 73, 78, 82n, 83&n, 85, 86, 88, 90-
  1, 95, 97, 99, 100, 101, 102, 103, 104,
  105&n, 106, 108, 110n, 111&n, 116n,

123, 125, 127, 132&nn, 134n, 135, 146, 147, 150-1&n, 154, 162, 163, 166n, 167; detractors of, 32&n, 48n, 49n, 73, 74, 151
M. Tullius Cicero (son of the orator), 23n, 62n, 74
tyrants, 13, 14-5

Vacca, 159
M. Valerius Martialis (Martial), 19n, 145&n, 147&n, 148, 160&n
M. Valerius Messalla Corvinus (Messalla), 1, 12, 15n, 26, 61n, 83, 118, 150n
Vallius Syriacus, 61n
Varro, *see* Terentius
vegetarianism, 27&n
Velleius Paterculus, 31n, 142, 149n
P. Vergilius Maro (Vergil), 16, 61, 62nn, 83, 88, 92n, 117n, 122&n, 134n, 139n, 159n, 166
veritas, 142, 143n, 146-8
Vibius Gallus, 61n
C. Vibius Pansa, 14, 20
(C. Marius) Victorinus, 142
Vinicii, 31&n

L. Vinicius, 31n, 61n
M. Vinicius, 31n
P. Vinicius, 31n
M. Vipsanius Agrippa, 1, 12, 15n, 22, 61n, 114, 150n, 158
vir bonus (see also, Criticism, rhetorical, psychological), (32), 47, 52, 56, 67&n, 68, 85&n, 86, 94, 107&n, 162&n
virtus, 146
Vitruvius (cognomen uncertain), 17
voice (*vox*; aspect of delivery), 5, 8, 9, 71n, 97, 104, 132-3&n, 156, 166n
(Volcacius) Moschus, 66n, 121, 129
Vopiscus, 140n, 149n
Votienus Montanus, 9n, 46, 50, 61n, 65n, 66n, 78n, 79&n, 82n, 83, 88n, 110n, 112, 119, 123, 162, 168; *Montanianus* (adjective coined from his name), 101

Weinrib, E. J., 21
Whitehorne, J. E. G., x, 21
Winterbottom, Michael, x, xi, 172
word coinage, 125-6&nn

Xenophon, 78

INDEX OF MAJOR PASSAGES CITED IN SENECA

CONTROVERSIAE

SUASORIAE